Sabine Adler

UKRAINE AND ITS WESTERN ALLIES

Germany's Failure and the Necessary Lessons for the Future

With a foreword by Andreas Umland

Bibliografische Information der Deutschen Nationalbibliothek
Die Deutsche Nationalbibliothek verzeichnet diese Publikation in der Deutschen Nationalbibliografie; detaillierte bibliografische Daten sind im Internet über http://dnb.d-nb.de abrufbar.

Bibliographic information published by the Deutsche Nationalbibliothek
Die Deutsche Nationalbibliothek lists this publication in the Deutsche Nationalbibliografie; detailed bibliographic data are available in the Internet at http://dnb.d-nb.de.

Cover picture: The gas leak at Nord Stream 2 seen from the Danish F-16 interceptor on Bornholm.
Source: Forsvaret / Danish Defence

Translation from the original German version, published in 2022 by Ch. Links Verlag. Original German title: *Die Ukraine und wir. Deutschlands Versagen und die Lehren für die Zukunft.* © Aufbau Verlage GmbH & Co. KG, Berlin 2022 (Published by Ch. Links; »Ch. Links« is a trademark of Aufbau Verlage GmbH & Co. KG)

ISBN-13: 978-3-8382-1832-8
© *ibidem*-Verlag, Stuttgart 2023
Alle Rechte vorbehalten

Das Werk einschließlich aller seiner Teile ist urheberrechtlich geschützt. Jede Verwertung außerhalb der engen Grenzen des Urheberrechtsgesetzes ist ohne Zustimmung des Verlages unzulässig und strafbar. Dies gilt insbesondere für Vervielfältigungen, Übersetzungen, Mikroverfilmungen und elektronische Speicherformen sowie die Einspeicherung und Verarbeitung in elektronischen Systemen.

All rights reserved. No part of this publication may be reproduced, stored in or introduced into a retrieval system, or transmitted, in any form, or by any means (electronical, mechanical, photocopying, recording or otherwise) without the prior written permission of the publisher. Any person who does any unauthorized act in relation to this publication may be liable to criminal prosecution and civil claims for damages.

Printed in the EU

Sabine Adler

Ukraine and Its Western Allies
Germany's Failure and the Necessary Lessons for the Future

With a foreword by Andreas Umland

Table of Contents

Foreword 7

Introduction to the English edition 11

The tragedy 13

Chechnya as a blueprint for Ukraine 19

Putin, Schröder, Warnig — pretty clever friends 27

Merkel's no to Kyiv's NATO membership 33

Ukraine — a jewel in Putin's tsarist crown 49

The Crimean "referendum" — a vote under Russian occupation .. 65

Sanctions as threatening as cotton balls 71

Fascists, patriots, and pacifists 77

Bahr, Eppler, Schmidt, and Schröder — the quartet of
vain old men 89

German business in the interests of the Kremlin 99

Russia Day and climate foundation 105

Dangerous amateur historian — Putin declares the unity of
Russians and Ukrainians 113

Blank spaces — Stalin's terror and the unknown holocaust 119

One-sided consideration due to selective memory 135

More than just art theft — the Nazi foray through Ukraine 141

Merkel's cold farewell, Chancellor Scholz's tough start, and a
scuttled joker 153

The *Zeitenwende* (turn of the times) speech 163

And in the future? 179

Sources 195

Acknowledgements 209

Foreword

by Andreas Umland

When the German version of this book, under the original title "Ukraine and Us" (i.e. the Germans), was published in autumn 2022 by Ch. Links Press in Berlin, this was an event by itself in Germany. Sabine Adler's critical review of Berlin's Ukraine policy represented then and still represents today a landmark in German political publicism. These are some reviews of the book's German edition in a number of influential German media:

- "A dramatically revealing book" — Christian Thomas for *Frankfurter Rundschau*;
- "An authoritative contribution to enlighten [the readership about German-Ukrainian relations]" — Natascha Freundel for *RBB Kulturradio*;
- "Adler evaluates [Germany's relationship to Ukraine] with wisdom and the sharpness of a razor" — Viola Schenz for *Süddeutsche Zeitung*;
- "Adler manages with her book to hold a mirror up to us. She points out the errors in [our] thinking." — Paul Toetzke for *Liberale Moderne*;
- "This book explains a lot. You will be wiser afterwards." — Jörg Thadeusz for *WDR 2*;
- "This [book] might be unique at the [current] moment, with its degree of depth and sharpness." — Bernd Schekauski for *MDR Kultur*.[1]

Adler's study was in 2022 and remains in 2023 one of the most consequential contributions to the currently ongoing German rethinking of the so-called *Ostpolitik* (literally: Eastern Policy) after the end of the Cold War. The German attitude towards Eastern Europe, in turn, has been one of the most significant international relations in

---

1 Source: "Die Ukraine und wir: Deutschlands Versagen und die Lehren für die Zukunft Gebundene Ausgabe–16. August 2022 von Sabine Adler," *Amazon.de*, https://www.amazon.de/Die-Ukraine-wir-Deutschlands-Versagen/dp/3962891803/.

Europe as a whole–in the past and until today. It will co-determine much of Europe's future. It thus made sense to provide a wider public outside Germany with an English translation of Adler's seminal study.

Like myself, Adler is an East and not West German with considerable life experience in the former Soviet bloc (we both studied, in different periods, at the Journalism Section of the then Karl Marx University of Leipzig). With her background in the GDR, Adler brings to the table a somewhat, in comparison to West Germans, different background and viewpoint on Russia, Ukraine, and Germany's role in Eastern Europe. In her particularly long and strong skepticism towards Putin, as well as her explicit sympathy for Ukraine and other former Soviet republics, Adler joins a number of further influential German analysts of Eastern Europe with a biography in East Germany.2 They include, among several others, the late Werner Schulz who was a long-term member of both the German and European parliaments for the German Green party, Stefan Meister of the German Council on Foreign Relations (DGAP), Jörg Forbrig of the German Marshall Fund (GMFUS), and Andre Härtel of the German Institute for International and Security Affairs (SWP). Like these analysts, Adler has, for more than two decades now, been among those German experts on Eastern Europe who have, with their written publications and oral interventions, prepared the recent radical turn in Berlin's attitude to Russia and Ukraine.

Readers should keep in mind that Adler's book was originally written not for a foreign, but for a German-reading audience. It addressed especially readers among the political and intellectual elites of the Federal Republic, and, in particular, those living or working in Berlin. It is also not the only such recent German book which critically reviews German policies towards Russia and East Central Europe. Several important new studies by various journalists have come out after the start of the famous *Zeitenwende* (change

---

2   See, for instance: Jörg Thadeusz, "Sabine Adler - Journalistin und Expertin für Osteuropa," *WDR 2*, 30 Jamuary 2023. https://www1.wdr.de/mediathek/audio/wdr2/joerg-thadeusz/audio-sabine-adler---journalistin-und-expertin-fuer-osteuropa-100.html.

of times) in February 2022. Among the most important and deep additional such studies are, in chronological order of their appearance:

- Thomas Urban, *Verstellter Blick: Die deutsche Ostpolitik* [Biased View: The German Eastern Policy]. Berlin: Tapeta, 2022;
- Michael Thumann, *Revanche: Wie Putin das bedrohlichste Regime der Welt geschaffen hat* [Revanche: How Putin Created the Most Dangerous Regime of the World]. München: C.H. Beck, 2023;
- Reinhard Bingener and Markus Wehner, *Die Moskau-Connection: Das Schröder-Netzwerk und Deutschlands Weg in die Abhängigkeit* [The Moscow Connection: The Schroeder Network and Germany's Path to Dependence]. München: C.H. Beck, 2023;
- Winfried Schneider-Deters, *Russlands Ukrainekrieg und die Bundesrepublik: Deutsche Debatten um Frieden, Faschismus und Kriegsverbrechen, 2022-2023* [Russia's Ukraine War and the Federal Republic: German Debates on Peace, Fascism and War Crimes, 2022-23]. Stuttgart: *ibidem*-Verlag, 2023 (forthcoming).

Yet, Adler's study represents, as of June 2023 when this foreword was written, still the only such German book specifically focusing on Ukrainian-German relations within *Ostpolitik*. Moreover, she has written not an academic study, but a book for a broader audience. Her investigation should thus be of interest also to a non-German and wider readership interested in the evolution of Berlin's position vis-à-vis Kyiv and Moscow. It constitutes a vivid illustration, documentation, and interpretation of recent German debates, concepts and policies regarding the Ukrainian state, security in Eastern Europe, and the Russian threat. Whoever wants to understand the past, current, and future German relationship with Ukraine needs to read Adler's book.

Stockholm, 11 June 2023

Introduction to the English edition

When Europeans woke up on February 24, 2022, a war raged in Europe. Many think the first war since 1945, having forgotten the Balkan wars of the early 1990s and the war in eastern Ukraine that has been going on since 2014. Now Putin's troops are attacking Ukraine from many directions; towns everywhere are being shelled with rockets, and tanks are moving in. A full-scale invasion is underway. Western military experts have long observed that more and more Russian troops are stationed on the Ukraine border. The US had warned the public in detail months in advance. The German government, the European Union, and the United States did their best to dissuade Vladimir Putin from his increasingly aggressive course toward Ukraine and NATO. But in response to Ukraine's immediate need and request for help, Germany was late and persistently hesitant.

How could this escalation have happened? What have we overlooked? What mistakes were made in Germany and the European Union? These questions have been hotly debated in public since the beginning of the war and are the focus of this book. To answer them, looking only at the current situation is not enough. For that, it is also necessary to look back into history. Not only to 2014, when Putin occupied Crimea and fueled the war in eastern Ukraine, not only to 2013, when Ukraine refused to sign the EU Association Agreement, or till 2008 when Ukraine and Georgia were denied accession to NATO. And even beyond 2005, the year in which Chancellor Gerhard Schröder launched the first Nord Stream project with Vladimir Putin. It is necessary to look back even further: to the Chechen wars, to the collapse of the Soviet Union, of which not only Russia remained, but 14 successor states of the USSR, and of course, to the Second World War, from which Germany's responsibility for Ukraine arises in a very special way. It has not been fully recognized until today.

I have observed the developments of the past 25 years as a correspondent from Russia, Ukraine, and Berlin. This regular change of perspective between Germany and Eastern Europe has shaped my perception of our relationship with troubled Ukraine. This book will also discuss this issue.

Berlin, May 2023

The tragedy

... begins with a joke that makes you laugh your head off. The world will witness a gigantic Russian troop deployment along the Ukrainian border for almost a year. In January 2022, there will be at least 130,000 soldiers armed to the teeth. In the face of this threat, the Ukrainians' request for German weapons is becoming louder and more urgent. On January 19, the government in Kyiv asks again and becomes precise: Can Germany help with helmets and protective vests? Later, Ukrainian Ambassador to Berlin Andrij Melnyk added warships and air defense systems. The capital turns a deaf ear.

They have neglected Ukraine since 2014. Only a few, very few, are hearing the cries for help. Robert Habeck is open about it. In May 2021 — before the German election campaign — he was on the front lines in eastern Ukraine. Habeck is one of the two Green Party leaders. There, he not only has a close look at the war that has not wanted to end for seven years but also listens to the hardships of the Ukrainian population on the demarcation line to the separatist areas. While still on the trip, he makes a strong case for the people asking for support to defend themselves against the pro-Russian occupiers. "Weapons for defense, for self-defense, I think it's hard to deny Ukraine," he told Deutschlandfunk Radio. "Ukraine feels left alone in terms of security policy, and it is left alone."

In Germany, he is received with shame and disgrace. The CDU-led federal government at the time pointed to the principle of not supplying weapons to crisis regions. This is a political line also taken by Habeck's co-chair of the Green Party, Annalena Baerbock. Unlike former party leader Jürgen Trittin, Baerbock does not distance herself from Habeck openly, but she does so audibly enough: "That's also in our program, and that's how we both see it as party leaders." Habeck relents for the sake of Baerbock, the candidate for chancellor.

Unlike the Greens, the then SPD parliamentary group vice-chairman Sören Bartol is not plagued by doubts. Unlike Habeck, he has never visited Ukraine, nor have most members of the Bundestag, not before or after the annexation of Crimea, not during the fighting in the east, not since Russia's invasion. With Habeck, he said, you can see where such a trip leads: "Habeck visits Ukraine and already he's denouncing the consensus. That's naive." Germany would be well advised to rely on diplomacy.

Berlin's former mayor, Michael Müller of the SPD, also warns against traveling to Ukraine in the *Berliner Zeitung* on April 21, 2022. Not because there is a war there and it is too dangerous, but because Anton Hofreiter (Bündnis 90/Die Grünen), Marie-Agnes Strack-Zimmermann (FDP), and Michael Roth (SPD) have come back full of emotion and with demands on the federal government, which is really not helpful. Strack-Zimmermann, who is considered to be a far more capable defense minister than Müller's party friend Christine Lambrecht, then spoke plainly in the *Tagesspiegel*: "I would be happy to offer the new security expert Michael Müller to develop emotions in order to understand that a brutal war of aggression by Russia against Ukraine is not something that can leave us cold."

The Left Party Member of Parliament Sevim Dagdelen outrages Habeck's empathy with the Ukrainians, who for seven years have been trying, if not to oust the occupants in the east of their country, at least to prevent them from advancing further. "Anyone blinded by hatred of Russia who ignores the ultra-right militias in Ukraine and claims that the country is defending Europe's security and therefore needs to be armed is a real danger to security in Germany and Europe." For Die Linke, the real security threat comes not from Russia but from Habeck, Strack-Zimmermann, Roth, and Hofreiter, and those who want to help Ukraine defend itself against the aggressor. Dagdelen is not the only one who would like to see the Ukrainians sacrifice themselves to Putin, hoping his appetite would be satisfied. They sell this as a peace solution, pointing to Germany's historical responsibility. Daria Kaleniuk cannot hear it anymore. The young Ukrainian, who heads the Kyiv Anti-Corruption Action Center, gets upset that Germany is holding back on military cooperation because of its role as a perpetrator in World War II, saying it is "one of the stupidest statements ever made." On Twitter, she asks as early as January 2022, "Germany's history has already killed millions of Ukrainians once, and now more should die because of Germany's history?"

Meanwhile, Kyiv's list of required weapons, helmets, and protective vests is on display at the Foreign Office, but the ministry remains silent. Finally, the defense minister sets a "very clear signal." Christine Lambrecht announced on January 26 that Ukraine will receive 5000 helmets. President Zelenskyy cannot believe his ears and struggles to keep his composure. Vitali Klitschko rumbles: "An absolute joke! The mayor of the Ukrainian capital voices what is thought not only in Kyiv: 'What does Germany want to send next for support? Pillows?' "

While Germany continues discussing weapons assistance, more armed Russian soldiers appear on the Ukrainian border. Meanwhile, the country is threatened from three sides. From the east, where Russian troops have never really withdrawn after maneuvers despite repeated announcements. From the south, where the Crimean peninsula has been upgraded to a military base since the Russian annexation in 2014. And even in the north, there is Russian military in a foreign country, Belarus. There, the election fraudster Alexander Lukashenko is only holding on to power with the help of Vladimir Putin, to whom he has, in return, laid his country at his feet as a deployment area. The 200 kilometers to Kyiv are a stone's throw. The engines are already running, initially for a Belarusian-Russian maneuver. In parallel, the Winter Olympics will begin in Beijing on February 4. Putin promises Xi Jingping not to overshadow them with war. At the 2014 Sochi Games, too, he sent his "green men " — special forces of the Russian armed forces in uniforms without insignia — to Crimea only one day after the closing ceremony. The countdown is on.

Poland, Latvia, Lithuania, and Estonia have long supplied weapons to the threatened country. Tallinn may have started supplying them in December 2021. The Baltic states wanted to give Ukraine nine howitzers. But because they came from stocks of the National People's Army of the German Democratic Republic, the Estonians first had to ask Berlin for permission because German arms legislation requires a declaration of end-use. Anyone who buys weapons in Germany and then passes them on must state to whom and wait for approval. Berlin's officials are taking their time. In mid-February 2022, when the three Baltic heads of government visited the new chancellor Olaf Scholz in Berlin, the Estonian colleague Kaja Kallas still received no answer as to whether she could use the old GDR weapons.

The German government has not decided whether or not it will be allowed to send these simply constructed guns to Kyiv. The Federal Republic of Germany sold 218 of them to Finland in 1992, and 42 howitzers were taken over by the Estonians in 2009, who now want to pass on exactly nine of them as quickly as possible. The new German government is putting on the brakes and acting like the old one in the coronavirus crisis: primarily bureaucratic. There is no trace of leadership.

Germany becomes an international laughing stock, first the helmets, then the howitzers. The Ukrainian house threatens to go up in flames, but Germany hands out the water bottle instead of calling the fire department. The traffic light coalition makes itself known to the world with a disastrous false start, to which Annalena Baerbock initially also contributes. On February 7, the foreign minister once again declared during her visit to Kyiv that there would be no arms deliveries from Germany. In doing so, she once again distanced herself from Robert Habeck. The Russian side would interpret Berlin's massive armament of Ukraine as a provocation and make war more likely. Military aid could also damage Germany's role as a mediator. However, this is impossible now because its reputation has already been permanently tattered on the world stage. Germany's loss of authority means far more than just an image problem. The appearance as an international mediator, which Berlin would like to have, not least because of its supposedly good relations with Moscow, ended before it had even begun. Later—the war in Ukraine has already lasted almost two months—things worsen.

Frank-Walter Steinmeier is disinvited when he spontaneously wants to join a trip by his Polish counterpart Andrzej Duda from Warsaw to the Ukrainian capital in mid-April. The German head of state is an unwelcome guest in Kyiv now.

A scandal, an affront.

After Russia's invasion, the German president sided with Ukraine and later admitted that he had made mistakes in his policy toward Russia. He seems to be getting away with it among Germans. However, German presidents have had to vacate Bellevue Palace for more trivial reasons. The Ukrainians do not make it so easy for Steinmeier. For them, he is the face of the German appeasement policy with Moscow par excellence. Moreover, no politician has so permanently and unswervingly championed energy dependence on Russia against all warnings. Steinmeier is now down for the count.

Meanwhile, Volodymyr Zelenskyy is waiting for Chancellor Olaf Scholz. Out of sheer consideration for those in his party who understand Russia, the so-called Russia-understanders, however, the Social Democrat wastes valuable time that Ukraine does not have. Scholz will first try his hand at crisis diplomacy and travel to Moscow to Putin's white table in mid-February. Across the six-meter-long marble slab, he can only communicate with the Russian president via a headset. Since the coronavirus pandemic, Vladimir Putin has been extremely reluctant to go among people; when he does, he keeps an exaggerated distance.

For this reason, the Russian youth calls him "grandpa in the bunker." Neither French President Emmanuel Macron, who was in the Kremlin before Scholz, nor Israeli Prime Minister Naftali Bennet, who will come after him, can get through to Putin. The German cannot because he does not mouth three words in Moscow: Nord Stream 2. A timely stop to the second gas pipeline from Russia to Germany might have made the ruler in the Kremlin sit up and take notice. But it did not come. Not after the annexation of Crimea, not at the beginning of the war in eastern Ukraine, not after the shooting down of passenger plane MH 17, not after the Novichok poisoning of Alexei Navalny. No offense, no matter how egregious, was significant to German Chancellor Angela Merkel. She had reason enough to pull the ripcord, and her successor has stuck to this course so far.

Putin's antennas, therefore, remain switched to transmit instead of receive. He follows only one agenda, namely his own. He shares with his rapidly changing interlocutors his insights from a multitude of history books about tsarist Russia and the communist Soviet Union, which he read during the coronavirus lockdown. He not only mourns both empires, which no longer exist in either extension, but he has also wanted to restore Russia according to their models for quite some time. This is impossible without Ukraine. The neighboring country became Putin's obsession, especially when he lost his most important man in Kyiv in 2013: Viktor Yanukovych, the president loyal to Moscow.

For years, Germany overlooked Ukraine, despite being the second-largest country in Europe. Only when the war approaches the EU border, when millions of Ukrainian women and children flee to Poland, Germany, and other EU countries while their men defend their homeland, is Ukraine finally noticed. Unlike politicians, citizens in Germany immediately understand that they must help. They become active with an enormous willingness to help. Many pick up war refugees directly at the Ukrainian-Polish border, take them in their cars to shelters or help at train stations to support the arrivals in finding their way. People are donating more money than ever before. Rarely have the electorate and politicians reacted so differently to a new challenge. Some do what they can, and others can do more.

Chechnya as a blueprint for Ukraine

If there were a world championship of Putinunderstanders, the winners would often come from Germany. Sometimes the race might be closer because Victor Orbán from Hungary, Aleksandar Vucic from Serbia, or Recep Tayyip Erdoğan from Turkey have caught up. But in 2001 and several times after that, the winner would have been Gerhard Schröder at the top of the podium. Schröder was and is unchallenged because no other foreign head of government can call Vladimir Putin his friend. However, such a friendship has to be worked for.

In 2001, Schröder did not simply invite the Russian president to Berlin as he had done the year before; this time, the guest from Moscow was to speak in the Bundestag. When Putin stepped up to the podium on September 25, he was 48 years old and had spent the longest period of his life in the KGB. He looks different from today, much slimmer, almost lanky. Two weeks before his trip to Berlin, Islamist terrorists attacked the US, sending passenger planes into the two towers of New York's World Trade Center and the Pentagon in Washington and probably crashing a fourth over Pennsylvania. Putin was the first foreign head of state to telephone his US counterpart George Bush and offer him cooperation in the fight against terrorism. It was an impressive gesture not lost on Russian-American relations, which appear to be turning a corner. Putin is now on the front line with the US, alongside President Bush, to fight together against terrorism. A front that, according to his account, has long since run through the North Caucasus, through Chechnya, where Russia is waging war against Islamists with all its might. After the declaration of solidarity with the United States, criticism from Western capitals of Russia's numerous human rights violations in this struggle fell silent.

The Russian begins his speech in the Bundestag in his mother tongue but immediately switches to German. Now everyone can hear how well he speaks the language of the country where he has lived for years. He speaks of the end of the Cold War, for which he receives a standing ovation. Only CDU chair Angela Merkel murmurs to her seatmate in the Bundestag: "We have the Stasi to thank for the fact that he knows German."

While Berlin politicians enthusiastically applaud Putin, his troops are fighting against the population in Chechnya. The speaker mentioned the war: It was the answer to the attempt to establish a caliphate in the Caucasus. But the methods to stop the Islamists have been extremely questionable for two years. Moscow's soldiers commit crimes against the civilian population. Men with their hands tied with barbed wire are found in Chechen mass graves, as in Bucha near Kyiv in 2022. In 1999, a maternity clinic in Grozny is shelled, killing 27 mothers and newborns, and a similar attack is repeated in Mariupol in 2022. Anyone still in the Chechen capital in October 1999 is considered a terrorist. Twenty years later, Ukrainians are called neo-Nazis or fascists by Putin. To sell the Chechen war in 2001 as a fight against international terrorism is Putin's very own truth. He manages to make the crimes against the civilian population disappear from the politics of the day.

Chechnya could be a blueprint for Ukraine: first, a region is reduced to rubble, then the civilian population is further decimated and massively intimidated by massacres, and finally, it is forced under Moscow's thumb by force. After the small Caucasus Republic, Putin has now set himself a much more ambitious goal with Ukraine, but the man in the Kremlin has long since lost touch with reality. He will not voluntarily return to the negotiating table, but only if defeat threatens and his calculations do not add up.

For German Chancellor Gerhard Schröder, who criticized Russia for the violence in Chechnya in 1999, it ceased to be an issue in 2001. Six months before September 11, he initiated the Petersburg Dialogue with Vladimir Putin. The two are close, have the same macho posturing, and have a similar background from a low-income family. The supposedly civil society forum is linked to the German-Russian government consultations. The organizers see the presence of the chancellor and the Russian president as a maximum dialogue enhancement. But the media interferes with this right from the start. At the founding event in April 2001 at the University of St. Petersburg, Peter Boenisch, ex-government spokesman for

Helmut Kohl and now chairman of the steering committee, was telling German journalists that they were not needed here. Reporting with their negative headlines about the war in the Caucasus would only spoil the mood. A declaration of war from the highest—German!—place. From now on, reporters and non-governmental organizations (NGOs) that receive a similarly brusque reception are considered troublemakers.

The business representatives regard the Petersburg Dialogue more as a club of dignitaries than a platform for civil society exchange, which is how the committee should be sold to the public. Those who do not allow their interest in Russia to be paid for with sponsorship money, who are interested in an open exchange of opinions, have not understood the actual purpose in the eyes of these people and are out of place here. Since the German economy partly finances the association, it belongs to it. This is, to put it casually, the motto. A business card as a member of the Petersburg Dialogue opens many doors for Moscow companies. And, of course, no one wants to be seen forgetting about democracy and freedom when contacts can be made. Human rights activists and the media are in the way. They are treated with corresponding hostility. The Russian side makes it even easier by inviting almost no Kremlin critics at first and, later, none at all.

At that time, Vladimir Putin had been president of the Russian Federation for just under a year. Before that, he had been prime minister for a few months; a post President Boris Yeltsin offered him in August 1999 because no one else wanted to lead the ailing Russian state. Yeltsin went on to fight the first Chechen war from 1994 to 1996. The second war in the Caucasus Republic is added to Putin's new post gratis. Despite his past as head of the Security Council and director of the domestic intelligence service FSB, he is completely unknown in his own country. Russia is in a ruble crisis; the oil price is so low that extracting it is proving more expensive than selling the fuel. There is still no peace in the Caucasus, despite the first war. Quite the contrary. There is fighting again. This time, foreign Islamists want to establish an Islamic state with Chechens and Dagestanis. All the politicians had only waved them off when Yeltsin offered them the post. Putin jumped at the chance. He is the right man for the outgoing president because he is prepared, without much ado, to grant Yeltsin lifelong immunity from prosecution.

"Who is Mr. Putin?" everyone asks in 1999. But soon, the answer is known. In early September, apartment buildings explode in Moscow, Buinaksk, and Volgodonsk. These are attacks in which more than 300 people die, and the Russian security authorities attribute them to Chechen terrorists. An accusation that is never proven in court. Rumors persist that Russian intelligence blew up the houses to provide a new pretext for another Chechen war. Duma deputies and journalists pursuing this lead are killed. The ex-agent Putin puts himself in the spotlight. Russians are supposed to understand that he is the antithesis of the incumbent head of state with his heart and alcohol problems. To demonstrate strength and determination, Putin issues a threat in a televised address to the nation on September 23, 1999: "We will follow the terrorists everywhere. Whether we get hold of them in airports or—excuse me—in toilets. Then that's where we'll kill them!" Many viewers will never forget the ice-cold look on the prime minister's face, distorted with rage, and will recognize it in the later hate speeches against Ukraine.

The Ukrainians are currently experiencing the same mercilessness of Putin as the Chechens before them, who are also citizens of his own country. The czars had already cut their teeth on Chechnya. The ex-KGB spy used force to bring the small rebellious people in the Caucasus to their knees. It was only after ten years that the "Anti-terrorist operation" ended. Alexander Dvornikov leads it. Putin later relied on this general in Syria and Ukraine, who was known for his brutality. Much is repeated in terms of warfare. The Chechen capital Grozny is completely bombed, as is Aleppo in Syria in 2015 and Mariupol in 2022, where Chechen special forces are deployed.

They are "Kadyrovtsy," troops of Ramzan Kadyrov, to whom Putin has entrusted control of the punished rebel republic. Kadyrov enjoys a fool's license in the Kremlin; he is Putin's man for the rough stuff. He has journalists and politicians shot, such as Anna Politkovskaya in 2006, Natalya Estemirova in 2009, and Boris Nemtsov in 2015. Renegade Chechens are executed in Austria and also in Germany. Zelimkhan Khangoshvili is shot dead in the so-called Tiergarten murder in Berlin in 2019. Investigations at home and abroad lead directly or indirectly to Chechnya and thus to the head of the Russian constituent republic, as in the case of the murder of the Russian opposition politician Boris Nemtsov, the two female journalists and other colleagues of the independent newspaper *Novaya Gazeta,* or the victim in Berlin's Tiergarten.

However, the president is also guilty of several other law violations. But no matter what Kadyrov is guilty of, Russia's criminal authorities, who take the toughest possible action against the free press or the opposition, look the other way in the governor's case, born in 1976 in Zentoroi, Chechnya. Corruption, rightly deplored in Ukraine, is blooming wildly in Chechnya. A palace on a plot the size of two soccer fields in the center of Grozny, costing more than four million Euros, belongs to Fatima Khasuyeva. The 30-year-old owns other apartments in other cities. Her official salary in the presidential administration, where she works, is less than 900 euros. How the office worker owns a palace, Maria Sholobova has found out. She is a journalist in the Russian investigative research group "Project" and uncovered a major real estate and corruption scandal involving Kadyrov in 2021, with the result that her Internet portal was closed and she had to flee abroad.

Maria Sholobova's research team did what would have been the duty of the tax authorities and the Land Registry office: to determine whether everything was correct with this palace. The journalist made inquiries and found out: Kadyrov has a second wife, Fatima Khasuyeva, in addition to his first, and lives with her quite openly. Russian laws also apply to the constituent republic of Chechnya; polygamy is forbidden. Ramzan Kadyrov does not care. Rather, he lectures on how several wives must be treated simultaneously: equally well dressed, with equally valuable houses, and given furs, and cars. The devout Muslim Kadyrov has introduced a strict traditional regime in Chechnya; the laws of blood feud apply, and women have to wear headscarves. Medni Kadyrova, whom he first married, obeys him. According to Kadyrova, her religion allows her husband to marry three more women. If that is what he wants, she agrees. Medni Kadyrova also owns several valuable properties. Since the marriages with the second, third, or fourth wives are only concluded in front of the imam, but not in the registry office, everything is supposedly legally in order. Almost, because with the help of the two wives, whether in registered marriage or not, Kadyrov is allegedly concealing part of his wealth. Real estate alone amounts to 800 million rubles, or just under nine million Euros. The head of the 1.5-million-strong republic earned around four million Euros in 2020. The year before, he earned only 1.6 million Euros, and in 2018, as little as 80,000 Euros.

The citizens do not find out how these large fluctuations occur. According to him, the car fanatic does not own a vehicle as he often presents himself. Not a single car in his impressive fleet, including sports cars from the most expensive brands such as Bugatti, Ferrari, and Mercedes-Benz since the beginning of his political career, is his own. The Russian news portal *lenta.ru* added up the horsepower gathered there and came up with over 3800 hp, although allegedly only the luxury models were counted for this. Similarly, the more than 100 horses of his racing team do not appear in the official data of his ownership. They win almost a million Euros in prize money from 2014 to 2018 in the United Arab Emirates and Russia. The secretary general of Transparency Russia, Ilya Shumanov, was careful to point out in this context that it is possible to earn money in horse racing, but it must be controlled.

Ramzan Kadyrov becomes prime minister at 29, then president of Chechnya at 30. He succeeds his father, Akhmed, in office. Akhmed is killed in an assassination attempt. The son feels himself to be the unrestricted ruler of his empire and beyond. He likes to brag about his possessions, which should be of interest to tax inspectors, and at the same time, raise questions about their finances. Kremlin spokesman Dmitry Peskov summarily dismisses the discrepancy between Kadyrov's income and his wealth, as the report by the research group "Project" proves: "Research is one thing, declarations are another. All the heads of the regions fill out declarations, which are then checked. The data checked by state anti-corruption units are much more reliable than that of the media."

Independent journalists like Maria Sholobova of "Project" live dangerously in Russia, so many work from abroad. The award-winning author took a big risk with her research on Kadyrov. Russian authorities are often not interested in those who violate the law but in those who expose it. This has never been as obvious as in the case of the anti-corruption activist Alexei Navalny. For Kadyrov, such publications have so far remained inconsequential. He is untouchable. If secret torture prisons and extrajudicial killings do not resonate with law enforcement agencies, his illegal enrichment certainly does not.

The Chechen government orchestrates mass arrests, abductions, and mistreatment of people because of their sexual orientation. Veronika Lapina of the LGBT network has tried to initiate investigations. "But Russia either doesn't have the capacity or the will to deal with it," she states. Since 2017, 235 persons have been arbitrarily arrested, imprisoned, and tortured by Chechen security forces, or at least that is how many have contacted the St. Petersburg-based network. Most affected are homosexual or bisexual men whose way of life does not fit with Ramzan Kadyrov's understanding of gender. Russian law enforcement agencies do not deal with these crimes. The reason for this is an agreement, the human rights lawyer from St. Petersburg is convinced: Kadyrov ensures that terrorist and separatist activities are stifled, and in return, he receives full freedom of action in Chechnya. President Putin spreads his hands protectively over Ramzan Kadyrov.

Russia could wage war in eastern Ukraine, Syria, Georgia, or Chechnya—for the Germans, everything was far away, too special, and not important enough for a continuous and intensive occupation. Those who pointed out the crimes and demanded consequences were only annoying. Russia was just different, too big, and incapable of democracy, were the explanations of those who understood Russia, who did not notice how much arrogance was in their words. But above all, it is about business.

Not supplying Ukraine with weapons would not mean ending the deaths faster, as some pacifists are convinced, but it would mean that Putin can establish another terror regime—on Ukrainian territory.

Putin, Schröder, Warnig
— pretty clever friends

Despite the start of the second Chechen war in 1999, German Chancellor Gerhard Schröder does not keep his distance from the Kremlin but gets closer and closer to it. Ten days before the 2005 federal election, whose outcome is expected to be close, Schröder and his now longtime friend Vladimir Putin strike a deal. They wrap up a deal in case the Social Democrats lose the election. On September 8, in Schröder's and Putin's presence, representatives of Russia's Gazprom, BASF's German subsidiary Wintershall and E.ON sign a contract to lay a gas pipeline on the seabed of the Baltic Sea from Vyborg to Lubmin. The German-Russian agreement seals the creation of the operating company Nord Stream. Matthias Warnig becomes managing director. The idea for such a 1224-kilometer pipeline originated in 1997 from the Russian gas producer Gazprom and the Finnish oil and gas company Neste. Now Putin wants to turn it into reality.

On December 9, 2005, the former chancellor receives a call on his cell phone from the Kremlin. At a late hour, Putin offers him the Nord Stream shareholders' committee chairmanship. Schröder finds this premature, less than three weeks after leaving politics. But since he has never kept a secret that he mainly wants to earn money in his new life, Schröder agrees. Criticism is not long in coming because it is one thing to stand up for his country's energy security as a politician but quite another to profit personally from an investment project worth billions that he has just pushed as chancellor. But nothing blows Schröder away that quickly. He has always been proud of his friendship with the Russian president, whose closest allies for the new pipeline are now two Germans. For Putin, the SchröderWarnig duo represents the ideal appointment. The Social Democrat has had an ardent career as prime minister of Lower Saxony and chancellor of Germany and has left politics at just the right time for Putin's taste. And he has the necessary temerity. A few days before his resignation, the outgoing chancellor secured a loan guarantee of over one billion Euros from the German government for Nord Stream. This was completely overlooked in Berlin's political scene amid coalition talks. The bombshell only explodes six months later when the finance ministry informs the Bundestag's economic committee in writing. The SPD comrades, who had entered into a grand coalition with the two CDU/CSU parties, were mortified by the billion-euro guarantee. But the former chancellor is long gone by then. Frank-Walter Steinmeier has to prove himself for the first time as Schröder's most important man in the new federal government and sweep up the pieces as quietly as possible. But after twelve years at Schröder's side, the chief diplomat has had practice at this.

The ex-chancellor needs a new sense of achievement. The consulting contract for the Swiss publishing house Ringier, which he signed just a few days after leaving office as head of government, is a nice start, but he needs more. At 61, he is still bursting with energy and has excellent contacts with the EU heads of state and government. He wants to keep them on the ball. When he calls, he does not have to introduce himself. Ideal conditions for Nord Stream. Above all, the countries bordering the Baltic Sea are needed now because they are supposed to approve the gas pipes on their section of the seabed. Since Poland, Lithuania, Latvia, and Estonia are likely to give up on a project initiated by Russia, the route for the pipeline has been defined differently. Finland, Sweden, and Denmark have to be asked. Fortunately, their heads of government come from the international social democratic party family. For Schröder, this is a manageable task.

Matthias Warnig, who signed on as Nord Stream's future CEO on September 8, is already a heavyweight in the Russian economy. The extent to which he enjoys the president's confidence can be seen from his supervisory board seats: at Rusal, the world's largest aluminum producer, and the Rossiya and VTB banks. He sits on the board of Transneft, the world's largest oil pipeline company, and Rosneft, the oil producer. He is also chairman of the board of Gazprom Switzerland. In many companies, Schröder, the comrade of bosses, as he was called in his active days as a politician, will follow Warnig.

Putin has known the East German much longer than the man from Lower Saxony, most likely since his time in Dresden from 1985 to January 1990. The Stasi district administration was only a stone's throw away from the KGB villa. Warnig had signed up as a full-time employee for state security at 18. In 1975, he was trained as an agent in the foreign espionage department Hauptverwaltung A and later, under the code name "Arthur," was an officer in the special assignment in Düsseldorf. One of his main tasks was the so-called economic reconnaissance. On October 7, 1989, the last day of the Republic in the GDR, Stasi chief Erich Mielke awarded him the "Medal for Faithful Service in the National People's Army" in gold. One object of his surveillance is said to have been the Dresdner Bank. It was one of his later employers in St. Petersburg, where Putin and Warnig's paths crossed again. Astonishingly, Warnig is charged with building up the representative office of Dresdner Bank in the city of the Neva. Many former GDR citizens had to undergo a background check for activities in the Ministry for State Security to enter the civil service or top economic positions. In the case of Warnig, those involved, including Dresdner Bank, apparently looked the other way. Gerhard Schröder did not fear contact with the former Stasi agent, just as he was not bothered by Putin's KGB past. Perhaps the two long-serving spies even concocted the plan to wrap Schröder up for their own purposes together.

In 2005, despite all the criticism, the trio began its collegial collaboration. Schröder has always been able to withstand headwinds, even though they have never been as strong as they have been since the start of the Russian war against Ukraine. He is still not bothered by the fact that he has not only ruined his reputation and gambled away his political legacy but is also perceived as a tragic figure in a disastrous pact with the devil. Although he left the supervisory board of the Russian oil company Rosneft on May 20, 2022, when the European Parliament threatened him with sanctions, he still did not utter a critical word about the warmonger Putin personally. His attempt at mediation in Moscow in mid-March 2022 should show the world how useful this friendship, unspeakable for many, is, even if he was unsuccessful in his first attempt. Schröder is convinced that he is still needed. If he cannot bring himself to apologize, he would do his comrades the greatest favor to at least get out of the Russian embrace. He is a burden for the SPD and the personification of its Ostpolitik, which ultimately ignored the interests of all Eastern European partners except Russia.

As little picky as Schröder is with his friends, he is even less squeamish with his business partners. The new job at Nord Stream required him to work hand in hand with Matthias Warnig from 2005. The man is described as warm and sociable. Like the ex-politician, he has invaluable contacts, admittedly of a completely different kind, which may come in handy when the willingness to cooperate needs a little help. Schröder and Warnig set to work. The Swede Göran Persson, the Finn Paavo Lipponen, and the Dane Poul Nyrup Rasmussen must be brought on board. Persson, the prime minister in Stockholm, has made a name for himself internationally as a convinced climate protector. Accordingly, he thinks nothing of an additional gas pipeline, at least as long as he is prime minister. After losing the election, Schröder asks him to lunch on May 7, 2007, and is very convincing. One day later, Persson introduces himself as a lobbyist for Nord Stream's major customer E.ON. In July 2008, Schröder invites the Finn Paavo Lipponen to a meeting in Berlin. The two of them dine together with Warnig. Finland is more his construction site. The GDR maintained an unusually large embassy in the country of five million inhabitants. Like their Soviet colleagues, who were also represented in large numbers, the East German diplomats had to find as many spies in Finnish politics as possible.

The top politicians who cooperated with the Stasi at that time can be read today in the so-called Tiitinen list, which, however, not everyone gets to see. After the fall of the Berlin Wall and the opening of the Stasi archives, it fell into the hands of the BND, which handed it over again to the Finnish secret service. Its chief Seppo Tiitinen, hence the name, knows the 18 people on this Stasi payroll. Only two names leaked out: Prime Ministers Kalevi Sorsa and Paavo Lipponen. The rumors about Lipponen's Stasi activity persist, especially since he reported a recruitment attempt in 1970. But it has not been proven until today because the Finnish secret service does not want to publish the list. Lipponen, who is said to speak so slowly that one could insert commercials between his sentences during interviews, is exceptionally one of the fastest at the interview in Berlin. He immediately accepts the WarnigSchröder offer to become a Nord Stream lobbyist. His office in Helsinki is strategically located in the fancy parliament building. But because he is supposed to be writing his political biography there and not convincing parliament members to support a private company's plans, the Finnish ex-prime minister has to vacate the office.

Schröder also has access to rooms in the Bundestag, regardless of whether he works for Nord Stream, Gazprom, Rosneft, TNK BP, or Rothschild Bank or is preparing a lecture for which he receives a princely fee thanks to the New York agent Harry Walker. Until May 2022, most members of the Bundestag tolerate his office use, even though he has long since ceased to work for the country as its former chancellor. He rakes in a lot of money as a business lobbyist, and the four-person office team, including personal security and a driver, is also used for this purpose and has met with increased criticism—abundantly late—only since the beginning of Russia's war against Ukraine. However, his office team abandoned him when he called the war a mistake but did not distance himself from Vladimir Putin. He explains to the *New York Times* why he cannot: otherwise, he would lose the trust of the only man who can end the war, Putin's trust.

"I have always served German interests. I do what I can do. At least one side trusts me." In this country, Schröder can hardly show his face anywhere. Not because his commitment to Russian gas would be universally criticized—he has provided the economy and consumers with cheap energy for too long, but because his standing shoulder to shoulder with the warlord permanently damages Germany's image worldwide. And so something unprecedented happens: at the end of April 2022, the Bundestag calls for cross-party sanctions against the former chancellor.

As the new chancellor, Angela Merkel had every opportunity in 2005 to challenge the declaration of intent to build Nord Stream, especially since Poland, Lithuania, Latvia, and Estonia have accused her of working with Russia to divide the European Union and ignore the interests of its neighbors. Polish Foreign Minister Radosław Sikorski even compares the German-Russian treaty to the Hitler-Stalin Pact. Schröder's successor, nevertheless, does not give up on the project, not even when it became known that the former chancellor was to become head of the supervisory board of the operating company on December 9, 2005, less than three months after losing his election.

"A flawless nepotism," commented Reinhard Bütikofer, then co-chairman of the Green Party, on the career move of the former coalition partner. An allusion to the "flawless democrat" that Schröder indirectly described Vladimir Putin as in a television interview a year earlier.

While SPD board member Hermann Scheer thinks Schröder should have refrained from doing so, Matthias Platzeck comes to the Lower Saxon's defense: "I consider Gerhard Schröder to be a man of complete integrity." He says that this was a purely private initiative that asked Schröder, a private citizen, for his cooperation. This is a position that Angela Merkel has also retreated to in case of doubt and has done so for many years.

Merkel's no to Kyiv's NATO membership

It took three years before the German Chancellor paid her first state visit to Ukraine in 2008. This is rather late for the second-largest country in Europe, especially since it has just been punished by Russia for the Orange Revolution in 2004 and even more so for its desire to join NATO. Cooperation between Ukraine and the Western military alliance has been in the NATO-Ukraine Action Plan since 2002, but joining is complicated because of Russia's Black Sea Fleet stationed in Crimea. However, President Viktor Yushchenko, who emerged from the Orange Revolution, remains committed to NATO accession. This goal was rejected by the majority of the population in 2005. Parliament, therefore, decides that a referendum must be held to join NATO.

The Russian president is enraged by the idea of the parliamentarians wanting to lead Ukraine into NATO. He wants to teach Kyiv a lesson: Ukraine should pay market prices for Russian gas, unlike in the past. This contradicts an agreed price fixing until 2009, but at the same time, it is obvious that the Russian subsidization of the gas price will have to end sooner or later. After all, Ukraine gets gas much cheaper than customers in Russia itself. As a result, it sells gas to Russian customers at a dumping price, and therefore the Siberian producers are overreached. This grievance urgently needs to be discussed, but it escalates before it can happen. The result is a gas dispute in January 2006, which triggers worries in Europe that the parlors could remain cold for the first time because Moscow and Kyiv do not agree.

This dispute is by no means only about money for Putin. Ukraine must also be presented to the public as an insecure cantonist that no longer guarantees reliable transit. For this reason, a supply route independent of Ukraine is recommended, for example, Nord Stream. Several spin doctors have been working for years on a powerful campaign. Even Ukrainians are getting involved. Igor Volobuyev, for example. He was born near the Russian border in 1973, studied at the State University of Oil and Gas in Moscow, still the Soviet capital at the time, from 1989 onward, and works first for Gazprom and then for Gazprombank. He observes at close quarters that the prices for natural gas are not set in the company but in the presidential administration and confirms that Russian gas is used as a political weapon. For example, while Poland will have to pay $850 for 1000 cubic meters of gas in 2021, Belarus will have to pay only $30.

In 2005 and 2006, when Yushchenko's rapprochement with the West became known, Ukraine was supposed to bleed, and then again in 2008, when it makes a second push toward membership at the NATO summit in Bucharest. The Ukrainian Gazprom insider explains how Ukraine is to be discredited: "My job was to assure Europe that the Ukrainian system is failing, that the pipes are rotten and that it is too expensive to rebuild the system and that it is easier to abandon it. I have developed the idea that Ukraine has no money and is stealing from us. We have an image of Ukraine as a scrupulous country.

We have managed to discredit Ukraine as a reliable supplier in the eyes of the world. Gazprom has made a great contribution to this. For this reason, it was decided to build gas pipelines bypassing Ukraine: Nord Stream 1, TurkStream, and Nord Stream 2. Ukraine was deprived of the status of a transit country." According to Volobuyev, Gazprom CEO Alexei Miller received the instructions for this ongoing smear campaign from Alexei Gromov, who was then the deputy head of the presidential administration and still heads Gazprom's information policy as a gray eminence.

In his interview with the Polish daily *Gazeta Wyborcza in* May 2022, Volobuyev regretted betraying his country. The Russian denigration of the demonstrators on the Kyiv Maidan in 2013 had already annoyed him, and the war in eastern Ukraine had robbed him of any illusions about Russia, but he had not reacted. He said that Russia's war against Ukraine made him rethink. The images from his bombed-out hometown of Ochtyrka, destroyed in the first days of the war: "I felt disgusted. (...) These are not shots of journalists or politicians, but of my family, so it did not occur to me to question this content. And many wrote to me directly that they were ashamed of me, that they felt repulsed by me. In one message I read that if I don't do something, I will no longer have the right to say that I am Ukrainian, and that my hometown is not Moscow, but Ochtyrka. (...) It took me a few days, but I decided to go to my homeland. On March 2, I packed my bags."

Because President Viktor Yushchenko and Prime Minister Yulia Tymoshenko are constantly at loggerheads and simply cannot settle their power squabbles, they do not make it easy for their potential partners to enter into talks with them. Since the rigged elections of 2004, which forced a rerun and were won by the Orange Revolution team headed by Yushchenko, the country is still very much preoccupied with itself. There is much to discuss with Germany, such as the NATO accession or an EU association agreement. Angela Merkel is decidedly skeptical on one issue and on the other. The country, which is still dominated by oligarchs and corruption in the background, seems to her to be far too little democratically consolidated.

US President George W. Bush has far fewer concerns. He holds out the prospect of Ukraine and Georgia joining the transatlantic alliance in 2008, much to the delight of Viktor Yushchenko and Mikheil Saakashvili, who emerged as president from the Georgian Rose Revolution. Bush wants to get the two countries a quick commitment at the NATO summit in Bucharest in early April — with the justification in Russia's direction: "The Cold War is over." Putin angrily counters, "We consider the arrival of a military bloc on our borders, whose membership obligations include Article 5, a direct threat to our country's security."

NATO has long since reached out to the Russian Federation, as Latvia and Estonia became members in 2004 during the alliance's eastward enlargement. The Kremlin propagandists regard sharing a common border as a threat only in the case of Ukraine. Moscow has not been fighting for its Baltic neighbors for a long time; they have been considered lost since their independence after the end of the Soviet Union. Instead of resisting such a view, the German chancellor and the French president took Putin's objections seriously and relented. In doing so, they stab George W. Bush in the back and leave Yushchenko and Saakashvili to starve on the outstretched arm. The people in the two former Soviet republics are being put off until "maybe later" without a date ever being given.

Merkel does not want to irritate Moscow and thinks the two candidate countries are unprepared for NATO because of their internal conflicts. Yushchenko and Saakashvili are deeply disappointed.

In 2008, then US ambassador to Moscow, William Burns, warned the Bush administration against admitting Ukraine to NATO for a more explosive reason. This could prepare fertile ground for Russian intervention in Crimea and eastern Ukraine. Some six years later, that is exactly what is happening—albeit without Ukraine joining NATO. Burns is now CIA director under US President Joe Biden.

For now, the Bucharest summit is one of Putin's last official acts as Russian president. He faces a four-year sabbatical until 2012. After that, he will return to the state's highest office for at least six years. But for now, he has to take a back seat. The presidential election has already occurred, and the pompous power transfer to his replacement, Dmitri Anatolyevich Medvedev, will be celebrated in May. The US Embassy in Moscow learns from Russian opposition members why Putin chose Medvedev in particular. Because he can be sure, even a few centimeters shorter and 13 years younger, the St. Petersburg resident would never allow investigations into Putin's illegal income and secret assets. This information became known via Wikileaks in 2010.

First of all, Georgia must pay for its—in Putin's eyes—insubordinate desire to join NATO. Unlike in its republics of Chechnya, Ingushetia, and Dagestan, whose struggle for independence Moscow rejects outright, Russia has supported the separatists in South Ossetia and Abkhazia for some time. They want to break away from Georgia and defect to Russia, which the Kremlin encourages by issuing Russian passports. Moreover, the Duma has already recognized Abkhazia and South Ossetia as separate states. Starting in May, Medvedev sends his troops to Georgia to train South Ossetian militias. Because Medvedev has expressed himself much more liberally than Putin in the past, one can be sure that the new guy in the Kremlin is not the one who will now determine foreign policy, president, or not. It is much more likely that Putin is pulling the strings in the background and that Russia is vigorously fomenting unrest in Georgia, presumably to prevent its NATO membership in the long term. NATO has formulated as an exclusion criterion that no country engaged in a security conflict can be admitted to the defense alliance. Putin is beating NATO at its own game.

In July, Russian maneuvers begin in Georgia's immediate vicinity, which Tbilisi responds to with its own exercises with the United States, Azerbaijan, Armenia, and Ukraine. Following the exercises, Russia orchestrates an escalation leading to an early August war that claims 850 lives.

The scenario is partly repeated in 2014 and 2022 in Ukraine. And yet the narrative of Russia's threat from NATO's eastward expansion and its encirclement remains an integral part of the public discussion when explaining Russia's invasion of Ukraine. How NATO is supposed to encircle the largest territorial country on earth remains a mystery. Only the shortest part of the border, the European section, is occupied by NATO countries; the longer borders Russia shares with Caucasian, Central, and East Asian states.

Moreover, one argument has almost become a mantra concerning attempts to explain Russia's aggressive policy: the broken commitment. Behind it lies the false claim that NATO has never committed to expanding eastward.

As late as December 2021, Vladimir Putin insists on his list of demands that NATO withdraws behind the borders of 1997. In addition, all NATO troops are to be withdrawn from the Eastern European accession states, and all NATO military activities there are to be discontinued. It also demands a contractual renunciation of any further NATO membership and an end to "nuclear sharing," i.e., the stationing of short and medium-range nuclear missiles by the United States in Europe.

Moscow believes it can dictate a new political and military order and has absolutely nothing to offer in return. Putin is not interested in disarmament talks or confidence-building measures, which the NATO countries want to discuss with the Kremlin. Thirty years after the fall of the Iron Curtain, the record of the alleged renunciation of NATO's eastward expansion is being replayed repeatedly. Archives are searched, and new papers are unearthed to support the thesis of the broken pledge. According to one version, in January 1990, West German Foreign Minister Hans-Dietrich

Genscher and his US counterpart James Baker thoughtfully worked out a special military status for the soon-to-be-defunct GDR. However, this idea did not come to fruition. Genscher described the deliberations afterward as a feeling-out process before starting negotiations. German, Russian, and American historians still recapitulate the talks based on the parties' meeting minutes. The search for a compromise at the beginning of 1990 is complicated and anything but straightforward; instead, the parties involved perform remarkable multifaceted maneuvers.

After Baker met Soviet Secretary General Mikhail Gorbachev, the American noted in January, the "Result: united Germany anchored in a changed (political) NATO—whose area of responsibility would not move east!" After Baker's memo, the White House is alarmed and immediately recaptures this position. Baker's non-extension of NATO jurisdiction and NATO forces is not embraced by the White House, which instead calls for finding a special military status for the territory of the GDR but leaves open what kind that should be.

When Secretary General Gorbachev meets Chancellor Helmut Kohl on February 10, 1990, the Russian assures the German: "As far as the main point of departure is concerned, there is an agreement between us that the Germans must make their own choice." Gorbachev thus declares his agreement in principle to German reunification without specifying any further conditions, nor does he insist that the statements of Baker, Genscher, and Kohl be set down in writing.

Kohl also made this clear at a press conference on the same day: "General Secretary Gorbachev gave me an unequivocal assurance that the Soviet Union would respect the Germans' decision to live in one state, and that it was up to the Germans themselves to determine the time and the path to unification." On February 24, Kohl becomes the first chancellor to travel to Camp David, the US presidential retreat, and utters the sentence Bush had hoped for: "A united Germany will be a member of NATO." Bush immediately informs Gorbachev and tells him on the phone that special military status was now being sought for the territory of the GDR. Historians see this as evidence that the Soviet Union had been informed of the change of position. From the West's point of view, the "no tariff to the East" proposal was thus off the table. Whether Gorbachev and Shevardnadze were aware at the time, however, that the formula of the special military status of the GDR territory could also include the potential expansion of NATO remains unclear. The fact is that neither Gorbachev nor his foreign minister attempted to remove this ambiguity in new negotiations. With the fall of the Berlin Wall, events in Europe came to a head. Czechoslovakia demands the withdrawal of Soviet soldiers, and Hungary follows a few days later. Poland declares its interest in NATO membership, and the Hungarian prime minister advocates the dissolution of the Warsaw Pact.

In the Soviet Union, Gorbachev, the perestroika inventor, radically restructures the country. He entrusts the hitherto ineffectual government institutions with tasks previously performed by the Communist Party. Its power, which had forced the Union of Soviet States together, eroded in a flash. The country is disintegrating. The Soviet Union now has tons of construction sites that demand its full attention. Lithuania leaves the Union first, then Estonia and Latvia follow. Gorbachev makes another push to help determine the future of NATO and proposes the Soviet Union's membership in NATO. But his idea was not taken up; the negotiating partner was already acting from a position of weakness.

The May 31, 1990, Soviet-American summit achieves a breakthrough for all-German NATO membership. The minutes record Gorbachev's words: "Sovereign Germany can decide for itself which military political status it will choose—membership in NATO, neutrality, or something else." Gorbachev may have blessed Germany's freedom of alliance, but he is far from satisfied. Especially as the Soviet Union continues to go downhill. Only when Kohl offers him the five billion DM loan does his face brighten somewhat. He calls the German guarantee for the loan a great move because the sum repairs his reputation in the Soviet Union at least a little. The NATO Declaration, adopted at the July 1990 summit, is also a help to Gorbachev in getting his negotiating outcome better accepted at home. According to this declaration, the Atlantic Alliance wants to turn to the countries of the East, "which were our adversaries in the Cold War, and extend to them the hand of friendship."

The Warsaw Pact pledged to end thinking in terms of spheres of influence. At one of its last meetings in Moscow in the summer of 1990, the heads of government of the member countries agreed to "begin its transformation into a pact of sovereign states with equal rights on a democratic basis." The Soviet Union's claim to leadership was thus obsolete, and each country could henceforth decide whether it wanted to join an alliance and which one — an unheard-of change in policy.

On September 12, 1990, the four victorious powers, France, Great Britain, the Soviet Union, and the United States, plus the Federal Republic of Germany and the German Democratic Republic, sign the Two-Plus-Four Treaty, an international agreement marking the final peace settlement with Germany after World War II. It replaced the Potsdam Agreement of 1945 and enabled the reunification of Germany in the same year. In the treaty, the four victorious powers renounced all their rights in Germany, and the two German states became the sole and sovereign subjects of the reunified Germany. The treaty stipulates, among other things, that a united Germany will belong to NATO. In November 1990, the Conference on Security and Cooperation in Europe (CSCE) adopts the Charter of Paris. It is approved in December 1990 and once again guarantees all signatory states, including the Soviet Union, full sovereignty and free choice of alliances.

If an eastward expansion of NATO were to be ruled out once and for all, a new treaty binding under international law would have been necessary. However, neither side initiated such a treaty; it was never negotiated. This is because eastward enlargement was not seen as a problem then. In the summer of 1993, the US government still rejects Poland's desire to join NATO. The US State Department turns down the government in Warsaw. There can be no question of a US master plan for NATO's eastward expansion.

On the one hand, the West is firmly willing to take Russia into account; on the other hand, it also takes it for granted that the Western order will now extend to Eastern Europe and across the globe. For a while, the signs point to rapprochement. In 1994, the Russian

Federation becomes a Partnership for Peace program member. James Goldgeier, professor of international relations at the American University in Washington, later described the dilemma thus: "The problem was that neither the West nor Russia found a place for Russia in the new Europe."

In 1997, two years before the first NATO enlargement with the accession of Poland, the Czech Republic, and Hungary, the NATO-Russia Founding Act is agreed upon. It is intended as a mutual assurance not to threaten or use force against each other. For its part, NATO wants to refrain from stationing substantial troops in the new member states if there is no significant change in the current and foreseeable security situation. Substantial troops are understood to be those that could threaten Russia. For its part, Moscow promises restraint in stationing conventional forces in Europe. Russia is vastly superior to its European neighbors in military terms and thus cannot seriously speak of a threat posed by them. 2002 the NATO-Russia Council was established as a consultation and cooperation body. In addition, a permanent representation for Russia is opened at the headquarters in Brussels, a confidence-building measure in the run-up to NATO's enlargement to Estonia, Latvia, Lithuania, Slovakia, Romania, Bulgaria, and Slovenia in 2004.

But after the war in Georgia, the annexation of Crimea, and the war in eastern Ukraine, the NATO-Russia Council is only a shell. In February 2022, Russia will withdraw from it altogether.

Since 1998, NATO has significantly reduced its military capabilities in Europe. This has only changed since the Russian invasion of Ukraine. Conversely, Russia has continuously upgraded and modernized its armed forces since Vladimir Putin took office. It conducts large-scale military exercises much more frequently, according to experts, three times as often as NATO. Russia does not invite observers and, at best, only partially withdraws its troops after the exercises.

The maneuvers are followed by repeated wartime deployments, such as against Georgia, during the annexation of Crimea, in the Donbas, in Syria, and during the invasion of Ukraine. Moscow repeatedly violates its pledge to refrain from using force and threats against the other states of the Organization for Security and Cooperation in Europe (OSCE).

NATO is not preparing for an offensive against Russia anytime because the member countries would not support it. The alleged threat to Russia by the West is an assertion that does not become more true the more it is repeated. It serves only Putin's propaganda. The fact that German and European politicians have not consistently defended themselves against this has meant that they did not take the smoldering threat of war in Ukraine seriously or take decisive action against it. Instead, they continued to maneuver as before.

Putin's hubris, however, also tempts him to make more and more mistakes. With his war against his peaceful Ukrainian neighbor, he has ensured that Russia now has 1 a NATO border 1,300 kilometers longer than before because Finland has already become a NATO member after decades of being neutral. And Sweden has applied for membership as well. The people in both countries, who until now have been able to live well with their freedom of alliance, would now feel better if they could find shelter under the common roof because Russian expansionism has frightened them for a long time. Putin once again answered their request with a threat. In this case, he would have to strengthen the defenses in the region by stationing nuclear weapons.

Ukraine is knocking on NATO's door again in March 2022. However, President Zelenskyy knows the war is a bad moment to apply for membership. His country would probably never have experienced the Russian invasion had the 2008 decision been different. But for Chancellor Merkel, there was too much to argue against agreeing to admit Ukraine and Georgia at the time. At the Bucharest summit, the issue of NATO enlargement was by no means the only one on the agenda. On the horizon loomed the world financial crisis triggered by the bankruptcy of the investment bank Lehman Brothers in March.

Moreover, the US president had not necessarily made a name for himself as a wise geopolitician. George W. Bush, together with the UK prime minister Tony Blair and the "coalition of the willing," was still involved in the war in Iraq, which had begun with a big lie: Saddam Hussein's biological weapons of mass destruction, the existence of which US Secretary of State Colin Powell had informed the UN Security Council about in 2003 and which Iraq would allegedly use in the event of an attack on the USA, were practically nonexistent. But a withdrawal of the US Army from Iraq was still not in sight in 2008, and US forces had discredited themselves morally. In 2004 and 2006, it became known that American guards had tortured Iraqi prisoners in Abu Ghraib, sometimes to death. The Iraq war was a disaster for the US and Ukraine, and Georgia did not have the most respected advocate for their cause in Bush. Against this backdrop, it was easier for the public to reject his advance on NATO expansion than to give in to him, especially since Putin was threatening on the other side. Thus Merkel and Sarkozy turned their backs on him.

Was this an appeasement policy? At the very least, the West missed the opportunity to strengthen its alliance. This allowed Medvedev and Putin to continue with their course of aggression, as the subsequent war in Georgia showed.

Although the Kremlin relies on confrontation rather than rapprochement, many Germans are steadfastly on Putin's side. They believe his propaganda myth of the threatening West, which wants to destroy Russia and its traditional values. Against their better judgment, some East Germans, perhaps also out of general frustration with the Western system, in which they still do not feel quite at home.

At the same time, Putin is cutting more and more ties with European society because a democratic understanding of power could threaten his rule. After the rigged parliamentary and presidential elections in 2011 and 2012, when hundreds of thousands of Russians protested for weeks, he experienced how easily his position of power could be shaken. More election observers than ever before documented the violations throughout the country. For their professional approach, an army of activists had been trained by "Golos," an NGO for election monitoring. The falsifications and manipulations in the vote are known and proven thanks to them, permanently damaging the Putin system. The system reacts as it so often does: with an attack. The Kremlin has the Duma deputies under its control pass the law on foreign agents. "Golos" is one of the first organizations to be put on the list. From then on, election observers must mark every publication with the stigmatizing label of a foreign agent. Shortly after that, the organization is banned altogether. Its European partner, the European Platform for Democratic Elections (EPDE), is later declared an undesirable organization. Its chair, Stefanie Schiffer, has since been banned from entering Russia.

The Euromaidan movement, which began in Ukraine in November 2013, must be stopped at all costs by Putin. Thanks to massive propaganda, he manages to ensure that it is not he, the revanchist and imperialist, who is denounced, but those who do not want to give in to him. The German foreign minister is intimidated and, in 2014, ready to give in to Russia for the sake of dear peace when Ukraine dares to make a new push toward NATO. Steinmeier would rather leave President Petro Poroshenko out in the cold than poke the Russian bear. The Ukrainian leader is nonetheless fighting for admission to the military alliance, although he knows that his country does not yet meet the requirements. Still, he wants to formulate membership as a goal and "do everything so that the country, the income level of its citizens, its gross domestic product, investments in defense, and the armed forces meet the criteria that apply today to countries aiming for NATO membership." Only in NATO does Poroshenko see a future for his country. At the end of 2014, the Verkhovna Rada voted to remove the non-alignment clause from the constitution, thereby removing an important obstacle on the road to NATO. The old constitution of 2010 is obsolete. In it, President Viktor Yanukovych, loyal to Moscow, enshrined the neutrality status.

Even without German backing, the Ukrainian parliament will amend the constitution again in 2019 and now formulates membership in NATO and the EU as the country's declared goal.

President Putin has railed against NATO's eastward enlargement for years, but his policies drive it forward more than anything else. The annexation of Crimea has shown the Ukrainians that the Budapest Memorandum of 1994 was not worth the paper it was written on. It was supposed to guarantee sovereignty and inviolability of borders for those successor states of the USSR that surrendered their nuclear warheads. In addition to Russia and Ukraine, Belarus and Kazakhstan also had nuclear weapons. Moscow took over these in addition to its own, and the three former nuclear powers received security assurances in return. The fact that these did not take effect when needed most is a devastating signal for global nuclear disarmament. It is at an end. All the more so after Putin's statement on February 24, 2022, that he would use nuclear bombs against those who help Ukraine defend itself.

Putin's worst of all threats does not miss its effect, and he scares NATO with it enormously. That is why each country first organizes its arms deliveries individually—with more or less conviction, as seen in Germany. NATO wants to avoid becoming a war party in Ukraine for several reasons. The most important one is the fear of a third world war. The alliance cannot risk such an escalation, and Kyiv equally little. Moreover, intervening as NATO would motivate the Russians. After all, seeing NATO as the enemy makes more sense to even the youngest recruits than shooting at their Ukrainian brethren.

Ukraine is serious about NATO, and membership might have saved the country from invasion. But Angela Merkel is still sticking to her decision of 2008. When the crimes against the civilian population of Bucha become known, a desperate Volodymyr Zelenskyy calls on the former head of government and Nicolas Sarkozy via a nightly video message on April 4, 2022, to come to the completely destroyed Kyiv suburb to see " where the policy of concessions to Russia has led in 14 years. You will see the tortured Ukrainians with your own eyes". Merkel is tracked down on the same day while on vacation in Italy. Her spokeswoman has her declare: "Former Federal Chancellor Dr. Angela Merkel stands by her decisions in connection with the NATO summit in Bucharest in 2008. (...) In view of the atrocities becoming visible in Butcha and other places in Ukraine, all efforts of the German government and the international community to stand by Ukraine and end Russia's barbarism and war against Ukraine have the full support of the former Federal Chancellor."

The Ukrainian Ambassador to Germany, Andrij Melnyk, is not letting up. The former chancellor should explain herself because she could have prevented Putin's war if Germany, the most powerful European country, had reacted earlier to Russia's imperial ambitions. Some political observers interpret the former German head of government's prolonged silence as a sign that she is ducking or hiding in the face of the dramatic developments in Eastern Europe. But Angela Merkel determines the time at which she declares herself. She does so exactly one day before her sabbatical comes to an end. She announced at the time of her departure at the end of 2021 that she wanted to take a six-month break and withdraw completely from the public eye. Anyone who sees her perform at the Berliner Ensemble on June 7, 2022, will believe that she is by no means hiding but rather wants to communicate and get involved. She offensively defends her decision in Bucharest in 2008, which Ukrainians resent so much today. She had thought about it for a long time, as she does about every decision she makes. She had wanted to prevent worse for the country, she said, because Putin had made it clear that Ukraine joining NATO would not be without consequences. "When you admit a country to NATO — and the Membership Action Plan is the clear precursor to that — you have to know that we are also prepared to actually defend such a country if there is an attack." She said she has been very sure " Putin will not just let that happen." For him, Ukraine joining NATO would have been a declaration of war. "That he sees the whole West as his enemy, that he finds that he has been permanently humiliated, I don't share all that at all. But I knew that he thought that and that he sees it the same way."

The fact that Angela Merkel often wrestles with herself for a long time, never deciding lightly or without thinking, was frequently observed during her 16 years as chancellor. One of the problematic aspects of her leadership style was that she did not explain her motives at all or only afterward, making it impossible for the public to understand her actions for a while. In any case, this explanation comes 14 years too late.

Whether it's the Rose Revolution or the Orange Revolution, election protests in Belarus, or the Arab Spring—the fact that peoples are turning their governments into cases and forcing presidents to resign does not feature in Vladimir Putin's understanding of "power vertical." Convinced of his steadfastness, he sides with Bashar al-Assad, Alexander Lukashenko, and Viktor Yanukovych. He is demonstrating solidarity with the Syrian dictator while expanding Russia's zone of influence in a region from which the United States has almost completely withdrawn. In Belarus and Ukraine, the issue is *Russkiy Mir*, the Russian world. It sees itself as an anti-Western, anti-liberal, and neo-imperial Russian nationalist cosmos. Putin wants to create this Moscow-led space of the East Slavic peoples of Russians, Ukrainians, and Belarusians, characterized by Russian linguistic culture, and does not question the Soviet myth of the common "victory over fascism" in the "Great Patriotic War."

Ukraine
— a jewel in Putin's tsarist crown

When Ukrainian President Viktor Yanukovych arrives in Vilnius on November 28, 2013, he is undecided. The clumsy giant wrestles with himself, not knowing what to do. He would not have traveled to the Lithuanian capital if it were up to Moscow. Now he is faced with the question: Should he sign? Or rather not? His compatriots are demanding that he put his name to the association treaty with the European Union and thus lead the country toward the West. They have been demanding this for years, ever more impatiently. This is another reason why Yanukovych is now in Vilnius. He wants to keep at least one back door to the EU open. At this very moment, he could walk in through the main entrance; the red carpet has been rolled out. In the round of heads of state and government, his counterparts notice his fear and indecisiveness. For months, Putin has been harassing him, threatening him with trade sanctions while at the same time enticing him with billions in loans and a gas price that has been cut almost in half. The German chancellor is annoyed. And meanwhile, against the agreement with Kyiv, Angela Merkel distrusts the political class in Ukraine and suspects it lacks the will and discipline to abide by strict Brussels dictates. Yanukovych stands like Buridan's donkey in front of the manger: on the right, Moscow with the Customs Union in the CIS, the Commonwealth of Independent States; on the left, the EU with a market twice as large, but one in which the rules would be transparent, putting an end to oligarchy and corruption.

Chandeliers costing eight million Euros, like the one in the president's residence in Meshigorje outside Kyiv, are no longer possible. Unfortunately, simultaneously, good relations with Europe and Moscow are not available. Vladimir Putin sees any flirtation with the West as a betrayal of Russia, which he sees as a giant empire and holds together with internal and external pressure. Ukraine, the largest country in Europe after Russia, with 44 million inhabitants, a granary, and a weapons factory, is the diamond in the Kremlin's ruler's tsar crown. No one should try to break it out. For the EU, the former Soviet Republic would be a heavy weight that would impressively demonstrate the appeal of democratic values. This is quite a pound with which the West could gain weight. But it could also choke on it. The balance of power in the Union would have to be completely realigned.

Yanukovych is not someone who can take so much pressure. He has only been in politics for a few years; he comes from a humble background and grew up in Yenakiieve near Donetsk in eastern Ukraine. He would like to disappear under the table at the festive dinner with his Lithuanian hostess. Instead of using the opportunity to promote his country as an enrichment of the European Union, he prefers to keep his feet still. After all, Putin is breathing down his neck too much, so he does not put his name to the association agreement.

The resolute president of Lithuania, Dalia Grybauskaite, has long since seen through him and says to his face: "Only those who lack the political will to withstand pressure can be blackmailed. For those who are not intimidated by this, the decision is clear. Either—or." The unhappy big man ducks away from her words.

After the Vilnius summit, the days are numbered for the skilled gas fitter and fleet manager, who served several terms in prison for theft and violent offenses before beginning his political career.

In Kyiv, a handful of students find themselves on the Maidan on November 30, 2013. Independence Square is anything but inviting on this day. The weather is cold and wet. But the young people hardly notice the sleet; they are outraged because their president has just squandered a historic opportunity. Under the hashtag Euromaidan, they have called for protests on social media. The police beat the small group apart with brutal force. In doing so, they are fueling the citizens' anger even more. With each passing day, there are new and larger rallies; a good week later, nearly a million protest against the corrupt government on the Maidan, against the privileges of the politicians and oligarchs who have installed an inscrutable system of dependencies.

Criminal entrepreneurs pay millions for a single mandate in parliament. The quasi-bought deputy must then vote in their favor. The voters are fed up with this fraud. The falsifications of the 2004 presidential election, which was already seen as a decision of direction between Moscow and the West, led to the Orange Revolution, against which the Russian president spewed venom and bile. Almost ten years later, the whole thing is repeating itself because nothing has changed since then. Officials hold out their hand whenever someone has to deal with state institutions. At the doctor's office, in the hospital, in government offices, in the police, in schools, and universities. The people understand that corruption will only be eradicated if verifiable rules govern the economy and society.

Many highly trained young lawyers have studied abroad and have long drafted laws for many areas of society. But there are hardly any members of parliament who are open to them. NGOs and think tanks, nevertheless, never tire of pointing out where the finger needs to be put. So far, everything has fallen flat.

The activists are serious. No longer willing to be pushed off the Maidan, they set up tent camps and took up residence in the trade union center, which provided dormitories and discussion rooms. The entire area around Independence Square is in a state of emergency. The streets up to the Presidential Palace, to the Verkhovna Rada, i.e., parliament, and over to St. Mary's Palace, down Hrushevsky Street to Khreschatyk, the magnificent boulevard—everything is in the hands of the activists, whom this time do not want to turn back halfway, unlike in 2004. Later, they will also spread out in City Hall. At first, there is a cheerful atmosphere. Young and old from all over Ukraine come to the capital on the weekend; in many places throughout the country, they have set up their own Euromaidan Square. Out of ten people who join, nine want to fight corruption. EU membership comes second, but they all know that the first goal cannot be achieved without the second. People assure each other that it can be done this time. The people are cheerful, affectionate, and almost in the mood of a folk festival until fear mixes into the euphoric atmosphere. Suddenly, the first reports start circulating that Titushki, young, strong guys in tracksuits, are beating up individuals or small groups in quiet side streets. No one knows on whose behalf they are terrorizing the demonstrators. Are they from Yanukovych's security apparatus? Are they acting on behalf of Moscow? The TV reporter, Olga Snitchuk of Channel Five and photographer Vladislav Sodel, met the Titushki thugs once before, on May 18, 2013. At the time, the two journalists were covering two rallies simultaneously in Kyiv that day. The opposition held one on St. Sophia Square under the slogan "Stand up, Ukraine!" and the other by the Party of Regions, to which the president belongs. On his behalf, the Titushki then moved to the opposition elites and instigated a brawl in which the two reporters were injured. Now the violent provocateurs have been hired again. Any path away from the protest camp is now no longer safe.

Correspondents only move around the city in groups of several. German colleagues report a veritable flood of e-mails. For days, their inboxes have been overflowing, something many have never experienced. The tone in the e-mails is different than usual: upset, aggressive, and hateful. Instead of wellfounded objections or criticism concerning specific programs and articles, journalists are called "NATO warmongers" or "agents of imperialism". In addition, they experience personal hostility. Again and again, journalists are called upon to report on the fascists on the Maidan finally. The hundreds of thousands on Independence Square are supposed to be neo-Nazis? Certainly, in the sea of blue and yellow Ukrainian and European flags, some also wave the red and black flags of the Right Sector. On the Maidan, the Right Sector acts as a kind of militia, engaging in increasingly fierce confrontations with the police. The demonstrators generally do not want to see or hear politicians on the Maidan because party representatives have not covered themselves with glory after the Orange Revolution. Even Yulia Tymoshenko, the former icon and presidential candidate with a blonde hair crown, is not well-liked. She is in prison for alleged abuse of office as head of government. Her deputy Arseni Yatsenyuk, like Vitali Klitschko of the UDAR (Blow) party, keeps to the background. The same applies to Petro Poroshenko, who fell out with President Yanukovych a year earlier and resigned as economy minister. The demonstrators on Independence Square have a problem with Poroshenko in particular. Not only because the ex-economy minister has also been foreign minister and head of the central bank, but above all because he is very rich. In 2013, the business magazine *Forbes* listed him as the wealthiest Ukrainian with a fortune of $1.6 billion. Poroshenko owns companies in the automotive, shipbuilding, and defense industries. The people know about all his confectionery factories. He is the "chocolate king" and owner of the popular TV station *Kanal 5*.

It is this intertwining of business and politics to which people attribute the shameless enrichment of a few oligarchs and which they hold mainly responsible for the all-present corruption in the country. But Poroshenko manages to use his opposition to Yanukovych and his experience in government to put himself on the map as an alternative to the hated president. When Yatsenyuk, Klitschko, and Poroshenko appear on the huge Maidan stage, which they do late and reticently at first, they always appear together, often with Oleh Tyahnybok. The head of Svoboda (Freedom) is an extreme rightwinger. His party made it into the Verkhovna Rada in 2012 with 10 percent. But Tyahnybok is by no means leading the protest movement. Nor does Dmytro Yarosh and his Right Sector, which unites the right-wing nationalist organizations. For them, the goal of Euromaidan, an association with the EU, is necessary. They want to overthrow the current regime as a "regime of internal occupation." But at first, nothing is heard from the Right Sector. Yarosh does not appear politically; he sees his task primarily as protecting the tent city.

Jewish friends from Germany also ask what the Nazis on the Maidan are all about. The narrative seems to be spreading at breakneck speed. What is true about it, and what is not? In contrast to Germany, the question is strangely of no interest to anyone in Ukraine. There is an opportunity to ask questions at the Right Sector Organizing Office. Two orderlies go ahead to the commander on duty. Neither the two companions nor the commander take off their balaclavas nor give their names. But they get right to the point. "We are not racists. We don't think the white race is the better race. However, we are against the mixing of blood. Multiculturalism does not exist with us. Ukrainian nationalism is not racism, but love for our country. Not anti-Semitism, not chauvinism." The commander refers to hundreds of Jewish activists with whom they would cooperate.

Ernesto, a 27-year-old business student from Ghana, spends time daily in the protest tent city, participates in discussions, and attends concerts. He is not afraid that violence could be done to him because of his skin color. Why should he? He looks astonished and irritated. "This is a freedom movement. They have chosen how they want to live. That impresses me." Arkady Monastirskiy of the Jewish Forum of Ukraine would probably have known if Jewish families were planning to leave the country in droves, according to the rumor mill. He does not know of a single case. Nor does he know of any danger from right-wing extremists on the Maidan, even if there is much talk about them. These are marginal groups, however, based on the nationalist and Nazi collaborator Stepan Bandera. Josef Zissels of the Euro-Asian Jewish Congress has observed over a quarter of a century of anti-Semites and neo-Nazis in the post-Soviet space.

Ukraine is by no means a problem, especially compared to Russia. More than 20 fascist groups are active in Russia and far more aggressive than their counterparts in Ukraine. Zissels' father's entire family died in the Chişinău ghetto, and his maternal grandparents were also killed in World War II. A physicist and mathematician by training, he joined the Ukrainian Helsinki Group as a dissident in 1978. He was twice sentenced to three years in a penal colony with a strict regime. He had investigated the use of psychiatry for political purposes during the Soviet period, distributed samizdat literature, and was involved in the Jewish national movement. The courts considered all activities defamatory to the Soviet state and social order. He declined an amnesty in 1987 because he did not want to commit himself to abstaining from political activities in the future. Zissels knows which way the wind blows when there is talk of fascists on the Maidan: from Moscow. The protest movement is to be vilified. What works best in the West is the accusation of anti-Semitism and fascism. Josef Zissels is a suspicious man who has not let the Right Sector out of his sight since its foundation. His conclusion so far: the Right Sector has not attracted attention with a single anti-Semitic statement. Of the total of 20,000 permanent Maidan activists, 200 belonged to this association. The alleged fascist infiltration of the protest movement is a propaganda trick from Soviet times, he explains, and it sounds a bit like: How often do you in the West actually fall for that? Nevertheless, he takes the trouble to give a tutorial:

> From Soviet times, we know that anyone who opposes Russia, who advocates national independence, is made a fascist. This is not new. More than two million people demonstrated on the Kyiv Maidan and throughout Ukraine. Are they all supposed to be fascists? I hardly think there are so many fascists in Ukraine.

He points out that the word fascist has a much more general meaning in this context. Just as in Germany, children played robber and gendarme; in the USSR, they played partisan and fascist. Anyone could be called a fascist: a road hog, a burglar, someone you cannot stand.

A group of Eastern European scholars explained why Russian propaganda focuses on the extreme right. Among them, besides Zissels, are Timothy Snyder and Yevhen Sakharov. As early as February 2014, the experts state:

> We even suspect that in some reports, especially those of mass media close to the Kremlin, the excessive emphasis on radical right-wing elements in the Kyiv Euromaidan is not based on anti-fascist motives. On the contrary, such reporting is possibly itself an expression of imperialist nationalism, in this case of its Russian variation. By deliberately discrediting one of the largest mass movements of civil disobedience in the history of Europe, Russian media reports provide a pretext for Moscow's political interference, and possibly even for a future Russian military intervention in Ukraine similar to the one in Georgia in 2008. (...) Reports that provide rhetorical ammunition for Moscow's fight against Ukrainian independence may unwittingly support a political force that poses a far greater threat to social justice, minority rights, and political equality than all Ukrainian ethno-nationalists combined.

From today's perspective, this warning has an almost prophetic character. Unfortunately, it did not have the hoped-for effect then, especially not among politicians on the far left and right. They extensively cultivate their skepticism toward the demonstrators on the Maidan and often use phrases from Russian propaganda programs in their argumentation.

The mood in Kyiv is heating up. Security officials do not like that the capital has been under siege for weeks, at least in the center. The police start eviction attempts, against which the tent dwellers resist with all means. Higher and higher barricades are erected, and tires burn. Thick clouds of smoke rise. Residents, who look more like well-behaved employees than militant demonstrators, stuff gasoline-soaked rags into bottles to push back the eviction squads with Molotov cocktails if necessary. Many now wear crash or bicycle helmets, shields, and masks to cover their faces. Kyiv's Khreshchatyk, which leads to Independence Square, has long since been closed to traffic, and the tent city has expanded across several intersections. On the night of February 18–19, 2014, 13 people are unexpectedly shot dead, and on February 20, the city center turns into a melee zone. Anyone out and about now has to take cover from gunfire. In front of a fast-food restaurant, eight corpses lie beside each other, covered with makeshift tablecloths. Frightened passers-by cross themselves and nod to the priests who guard the dead until paramedics take them away. Forty-nine deaths are counted this Wednesday. Many had tried to protect themselves with wooden shields, but the snipers' bullets penetrated them. No one knows on whose orders the snipers fired. At least 100 people die in a few days, and the crowd is horrified.

For Dmytro Yarosh, the many victims are a turning point. He spoke his mind when he met President Viktor Yanukovych on February 20. A truce with the head of state is no longer an option, only his resignation. The agreement reached by the parliamentary opposition leaders on February 20 and the agreement signed by President Yanukovych on February 21 is not enough for Yarosh's people from the Right Sector. They are calling for a much tougher approach. Either Yanukovych disappears, or they storm the presidential administration and parliament. Yarosh has also noticed that the future of the first man in the state is not regulated in the opposition's paper. No mention of impeachment, nothing about dissolving parliament, nothing about punishing the security forces who took the lives of some 100 protesters on their conscience. Yarosh also calls for the Party of Regions, dominated by the eastern Ukrainian oligarchs and to which Yanukovych belongs, to be banned, as well as the Communist Party of Ukraine.

The presidential palace is increasingly cordoned off. Amid this civil war-like atmosphere, a trio of European mediators arrives, hoping to prevent further escalation through their mere presence. Foreign Minister Frank-Walter Steinmeier, his Polish colleague Radosław Sikorski and the chief French diplomat Laurent Fabius want to convince the Ukrainian president to enter into a dialogue with the demonstrators. But at first, Yanukovych seems to have disappeared from the scene. Eventually, he does show up and receives the delegation, knowing that the European Union had imposed sanctions on him and his government the day before. He and his family are no longer allowed to enter the EU, and their foreign accounts are frozen. For weeks, EU member states postpone a decision. After the deaths on the Maidan, they finally got their way. Resolute moral support for rewards to the demonstrators, who are increasingly speaking out in favor of the European alliance, would have been different, according to those protesting in Kyiv for weeks.

Even during the talks with the president, violence occurs again on the Maidan. The three Maidan emissaries, Klitschko, Tyahnybok, and Yatsenyuk, listen to the mediation proposal at the EU headquarters. They, too, demand tougher action against Yanukovych: the withdrawal of his enabling laws and new elections. But after a few hours, the negotiations fail, and Yanukovych disappears. During the night of February 21-22, he seeks refuge in Russia. Moscow has long been in the picture and takes in the loyal vassal.

Five years later, on January 24, 2019, Kyiv's Obolonsky District Court sentenced former Ukrainian President Viktor Yanukovych in absentia to 13 years in prison for treason. In addition, the prosecution proves that Yanukovych supported Russia in waging a war of aggression against Ukraine. In February 2022, Yanukovych calls on his successor, Volodymyr Zelenskyy, to surrender. But unlike his 71-year-old predecessor, Zelenskyy did not abandon his homeland.

Let us go back to February 22, 2014, a memorable day in many respects. Parliament decides that Yanukovych, who ran away head over heels, can no longer call himself president. Most of the elected representatives depose him and appoint an interim president and a transitional government, so there can be no question of a coup. However, there are quite a few voices that suggest exactly that. A few days after Yanukovych's escape, Alexander Rahr said in a Panorama report on ARD:

> From my point of view, the right-wing sector was decisive for the *overthrow*. Because it is an organization that was also prepared to engage in combat with the police, with the security forces. They were well organized, they also always had a plan of how to attack, how to defend themselves, so they had a big part in the success of the Maidan

Until 2012, Rahr was a sought-after expert on Eastern Europe at the German Council on Foreign Relations (DGAP). Then he switched to business and has since been one of the Putin explainers. He has been independently soliciting empathy for Putin's allegedly wounded soul. Compassion for the victims of Putin's policies is something one waits for elsewhere. Putin alone is the focus. The ex-spy is fed up with the West's know-it-all attitude and does not need lessons in human rights. This argument underestimates that the EU and the USA were asked for help after the collapse of the Soviet Union and provided it financially and economically in transforming state structures into a democratic society. As long as Moscow wanted it, no one complained about alleged schoolmastery. Alexander Rahr is a member of the Petersburg Dialogue, but not only that, the historian made a name for himself because of his close ties to President Vladimir Putin and gained admission to the even more select Waldai Club. The club has held direct discussions with the Russian president once a year since 2004. The currency in which Rahr pays: Germany-bashing on Russian television. In 2014, the Waldai roundtable discussed: "World order: new rules or a game without rules?" The meeting took place at the end of the year. By then, the Maiden movement was history, and Putin had done his best to discredit it as fascist. Rahr echoed. Like Putin, he never tired of classifying it as a coup. The script of how Ukraine was to be destabilized in 2014 was written in the Kremlin. On that Saturday, February 22, 2014, events in Kyiv came to a head. It is important to take advantage of this. While the Verkhovna Rada formally deposed the runaway Ukrainian President Yanukovych, Putin announced that Russia was preparing to take back Crimea to allow the inhabitants to decide their fate. Translated, this means that Putin wants to grab the peninsula for himself. This is a clear violation of international law and territorial integrity. Ukraine is to bleed for its so-called color revolutions. The first one in 2004 got stuck on its own, and Putin wants to prevent the success of the second attempt with all his might. It must not come to that that the Ukrainian people get rid of their corrupt leadership.

But in Kyiv, the politicians are too busy with themselves. A new majority in parliament must be organized so that Yanukovych can be stripped of the presidential title. Then a new parliamentary president had to be elected and a transitional government installed. All within a very short time. Putin's dangerous announcement goes completely unnoticed. No one has any nerve for Crimea at this moment, either.

On Monday, Simferopol, the capital of the Autonomous Republic of Crimea, becomes the scene. An angry crowd, mostly Crimean Tatars, prevent pro-Russian deputies from entering parliament. They want to vote on whether or not Crimea should remain part of Ukraine. There are clashes with pro-Russian demonstrators who are supposed to secure the election for Moscow. The government is still busy sorting out its domestic politics in distant Kyiv.

Meanwhile, Russia is starting a hybrid war, which means creating confusion, violating the rules, then creating facts, denying everything immediately or later, then admitting some things, but in any case, continuing to lie. And then everything starts all over again. On February 27, a Thursday, Russian troops stationed in Crimea occupied strategically important buildings and facilities. Residents of the peninsula have been watching new deliveries of military equipment for days and posting their video footage online. They report Russian-speaking soldiers without sovereignty markings. But Russia denies any involvement. Then Moscow launches the euphemism of the friendly little green men, which is supposed to conceal the fact that the Russian Army is currently occupying Crimea.

The West cannot deal with these brazen lies. Instead of noting what is happening, it allows itself to be fooled. NATO reconnaissance has long had satellite images documenting the deployment. But the military would rather continue to guard their knowledge like a treasure, assuming that revealing their findings will also reveal their sources. Instead of supporting with additional evidence what is obviously happening in front of the eyes of the Crimeans, this knowledge is kept secret. Defense politicians in Brussels and Berlin refer to it at best in background discussions instead of making it public, thus exposing Moscow's lies. While Russia continues its troop deployment, Moscow's soldiers take one barrack after another. Ukrainian units desperately await orders from Kyiv, not knowing whether to defend their military airfields, naval bases, and other military facilities in Crimea or leave them to the occupiers.

A good week later, on March 6, the Crimean parliament decides to annex the country to the Russian Federation. Nevertheless, a referendum is to be held on March 16. Vladimir Konstantinov, the speaker of the parliament, makes a far from sovereign impression at the announcement.

He admits the referendum is "not a project with a long political strategy" but "an attempt to react to the situation. And the Russian Federation should decide by the time of the referendum whether to accept us or not, so that people don't feel like idiots." He does not say that he is acting under pressure from Moscow. The Crimean Tatars, from painful historical experience, are much quicker to understand what is happening. Their spokesman, Refat Chubarov, is asking the UN for peacekeepers and calling for an election boycott. The referendum is a humiliation for the Crimean people and absurd, especially since the decision to join Russia has already been made. Chubarov predicts a referendum in complete anarchy, with armed forces in the streets. It would only contribute to the further destabilization of Crimea. Moscow is neither interested in this nor the referendum's lack of legal basis. No region can vote alone on its affiliation with Ukraine; citizens nationwide must decide. But the regional government, which is already pro-Russian, has decreed that Crimea is Russian territory with immediate effect and that the Ukrainian armed forces are regarded as occupiers. The only currency is the ruble, no longer the hryvnia. The referendum is a farce.

Arseniy Yatsenyuk, prime minister of the interim government in Kyiv, declares on the same day that the date for the Crimean referendum is set that Ukraine does not accept the secession of Crimea.

In the next few days, some 50 OSCE observers plan to inspect Crimea to find out with what personnel and equipment the Russian armed forces are occupying the territory. The numbers of the Ukrainian Ministry of Defense and the Border Guard vary between 18,000 and 30,000 Russian soldiers. The arriving observers are prevented from entering Crimea with gunfire.

Poland has withdrawn its consular staff from Crimea, the USA warns against traveling to Ukraine, and the German Foreign Office warns to exercise caution in Crimea and eastern Ukraine.

Wood is being delivered to the protesters' tent city on the Maidan. Night temperatures are still around freezing. The activists continue to hold out, some considering leaving for Crimea. Some are quivering with rage. The bad news piles up. Russian soldiers occupy an air base and other facilities of the Ukrainian armed forces. From there, Ukrainians no longer monitor the skies over Crimea but Russians. Independent television stations have been shut down; only the programming of the Tatar minority can still be received for the time being.

A protest against the occupation of Crimea takes place on the Maidan in Kyiv as resentment grows that the Russian occupiers are not being resisted. Prime Minister Arseniy Yatsenyuk, the right-hand man of Yulia Tymoshenko, who has since been freed, has a bad hand with the demonstrators because he is sticking to his stance of wanting to resolve the conflict diplomatically and politically. Nevertheless, he does not want to give up an inch of "our country," as he declared in parliament. A weak reaction, many in Independence Square think. After all, the country's territorial integrity is in acute danger.

The Ukrainian painter and poet Taras Shevchenko was never as close to his compatriots as he was in the spring of 2014. How would he have reacted? Many are asking themselves this on March 9, 2014. Shevchenko was born the son of Ukrainian serfs 200 years ago to the day and was considered an indomitable fighter. In his honor, protesters on the Maidan erected a self-carved monument. The country boy was lucky that his parents could read and write. But at the age of 14, he became an orphan. His landowner took him to St. Petersburg, where the young Taras became acquainted with Russian culture and art and began to paint. He was so successful that he was able to buy his way out of his indenture with his paintings and began to write. Shevchenko's poetry struck a chord with Russian and Ukrainian readers alike. He never forgot where he came from and how unfree his homeland was, which he visited repeatedly. When he was in Kyiv, he always lived near the Maidan. He was a romantic and a rebel, much to the displeasure of Tsar Nicholas I, who sensed the explosive power of Shevchenko's Ukrainian poetry. After all, it is only a small step from one's language to one's nation. The tsar locked him up, first in prison, then in solitary confinement, where he could not paint or write. Because he did not care about either ban, he created many paintings and several literary works sold or published under pseudonyms. After his imprisonment, he was not permitted to travel to Ukraine, but he did so anyway. At the age of only 47, he died in St. Petersburg, where he was buried in the presence of Fyodor Dostoevsky. Shevchenko lived the tug-of-war between his Ukrainian homeland and the all-dominant tsarist Russia, which the revolutionary freedom poet defied throughout his life. Would Shevchenko have given Crimea up? Never, says interim President Turchinov. The politician was born in Dnipropetrovsk and grew up with Russian as his family language. He has been in office since February 22, 2014. On this cold March day, he shouts to the crowd that Shevchenko was Ukrainian at heart and stood up for his homeland. "His word of fighting is our slogan, our weapon, and our victory." Simultaneously, clashes with pro-Russian forces occur in Sevastopol, Crimea, where a Shevchenko memorial service is also taking place. Russian soldiers occupy another border guard post. It is the eleventh checkpoint now in their hands. Moreover, the western entrance to the peninsula is sealed off by the Russian military, which still does not identify itself as such.

At the Museum of Western and Eastern Art, not far from Shevchenko University in Kyiv, Olena Zhivkova considers whether she should have the two buildings evacuated. If Putin robs Crimea, he may send his "green men" to Kyiv. Now the team could still use the time to pack up paintings, busts, furniture, and Asian ceramics and transport them to an underground depot.

Although the interim government has been installed, political rallies continue to occur. The protest movement is vigilant after its defeat in 2004. Ukrainian stars and international personalities appear at short intervals on the largest stage of the Maidan. They always support the freedom movement. German politicians Marieluise Beck, Viola von Cramon, and Rebecca Harms of the Green Party have been regular guests from the beginning. The members of the Bundestag and the European Parliament are welcomed like friends. They have long felt connected to Ukraine, have close ties to liberal MEPs interested in Europe, and help with contacts and political know-how. Russian guests are only exceptionally allowed on the Maidan. Mikhail Khodorkovsky gets permission to speak because Putin's enemies are friends here. He was Russia's number one prisoner for ten years, just like Alexei Navalny today. The crowd gives him a reserved reception. After all, before his imprisonment, he was one of the oligarchs with whom the protesters had mostly bad experiences in their country. Khodorkovsky is not a big speaker, but he still hits a nerve when he talks about the lies of Russian propaganda and the dead on the Maidan.

> There are no more fascists and nationalists here than in Moscow or Saint Petersburg. What the Yanukovych government has done here, more than 100 dead, and 5000 injured, it has done in collusion with Moscow. I saw the wooden shields with which the demonstrators tried to protect themselves from the bullets. Tears came to my eyes. This is not my Russia. There is another one. People who take to the streets of Moscow despite the prison sentences they face, who care more about the friendship between Ukraine and Russia.

Spassiba, thank you, shouts the crowd. The Russian guest adds that he believes in a European future for Russia and Ukraine.

Phase two of the hybrid war in eastern Ukraine continues unabated: creating facts.

The Crimean "referendum"
— a vote under Russian occupation

March 16, 2014, the day of the Crimean referendum, is a Sunday. The Ukrainian peninsula has been occupied for almost three weeks by so-called green men. These Russian security forces in uniforms without national emblems initiated the occupation of parliament on February 24 and the scheduling of the vote on Crimea's affiliation with Russia. The OSCE declined to observe the unconstitutional vote. Instead, right-wing and left-wing extremists from Europe are now taking over. The Saxon AfD member of the Bundestag Ulrich Oehme comes from Germany; the second time, within a few weeks he pays a visit to the peninsula and their new masters from Moscow. A year later, he will sit on the federal executive committee of the Alternative for Germany and belong to the right-wing nationalist association "Der Flügel." Oehme also offers his services as an unofficial election observer in Crimea for the 2018 Russian presidential election, again intending to give the clearly illegal vote a legal veneer. Election observers from Mecklenburg-Western Pomerania come from the opposite fringe. They are the two members of the state parliament, Torsten Koplin and Hikmat Al-Sabty. Crimea is still a vacation paradise popular with locals and Russians alike, who have been welcome guests since Ukraine's independence. The Russian Black Sea Fleet base, anchored in Sevastopol since the 17th century and the reign of Tsar Peter I, will soon grow into a military base that will spread across the entire peninsula. The election observers do what they came to do: approve an election that is not an election but one forced under pressure from foreign occupiers. They have traveled from Schwerin and belong to the parliamentary group of the Left Party. Al-Sabty comes from Iraq; Torsten Koplin grew up in the GDR and was a soldier in the MfS guard regiment "Feliks Dzierzynski", a former member of the Stasi. He is a founding member of the Anti-Capitalist Left, classified as a left-wing extremist group. In 2008, he drew attention to himself with the statement that there had been injustice in the GDR but that the GDR had not been an unjust state. On this point, he agrees with Manuela Schwesig, then the federal family minister from the SPD. Like Koplin, she is at home in Mecklenburg-Western Pomerania. She, too, rejects the term *unrechtsstaat* [unjust state] for the GDR because it "comes across as if all of life was unjust." In 2011, more than 20 years after reunification, Koplin praised the construction of the Berlin Wall and the Iron Curtain, which stood for "a period of peaceful coexistence in Europe."

The AfD man and the two leftists overlook the small group of courageous people waving blue and yellow flags outside a polling station in Simferopol. Some have stuck a plaster on their mouths. As Ukrainians, they no longer have anything to say in Crimea. They do not see themselves as part of the population supposedly striving to join the Russian Federation. Moscow simply brushed aside the fact that the vote contradicts the Ukrainian constitution as an objection. An elderly woman cannot control herself; her hand with the paper flag is trembling with anger: "I want to vote, that these so-called liberators disappear. I don't want to live in Russia." Tears of anger come to her eyes. "Russia simply sets the rules, the currency. But is everything really okay in Russia? Above all, I want there to be no war."

For the past two weeks, Ukrainians have been looking at Crimea with disbelief and helplessness. In the meantime, fears of losing the peninsula give way increasingly to worries about war. German OSCE military expert Heiko von Rosenzweig puts the Russian troop deployment at 80,000 soldiers and up to 300 battle tanks. The Ukrainian interim president Oleksander Turchinov expects a Russian invasion at any moment. The Verkhovna Rada decides to establish a National Guard of 60,000 men. Defense Minister Ihor Tenyukh appeals to the oligarchs, the country's filthy-rich entrepreneurs, to help finance the army. What is needed now is pragmatism. For years, money has been stolen from the Ukrainian Army and police. Objections that the oligarchs might expect a quid pro quo for their billions in donations when awarding contracts for arms deliveries are hardly heard in public. Many know that a new cycle of corruption could start, but now it is a question of further areas that could be torn away from Ukraine.

Sergei Aksyonov, the so-called prime minister of the Autonomous Republic of Crimea, which is part of Ukraine under international law, is the man who is partly responsible for the unconstitutional referendum in Crimea. He was elected by the deputies of the Crimean parliament, who let the armed Russian occupiers into the session hall "to deal with the fascists in Crimea," as Aksyonov is reported to have said. And so the justification sounds more like a call for help pre-formulated by Moscow. So far, there have been no signs of fascists far and wide. Are they supposed to pose such a threat that Moscow must protect Crimea? Aksyonov is a bad actor. His learned phrases sound wooden and unconvincing: "We are told that fascism must not be allowed here. The armed fascists who have seized power in Kyiv, we must fight." Crimea's parliament also reportedly asked the Russian Duma to incorporate the peninsula into the Russian Federation even before the ballot. No one asks why the Kremlin should save and help so much. The result of the Crimean referendum reads almost like a Volkskammer election in the GDR: almost 97 percent voted in favor of Crimea's accession to the Russian Federation at a voter turnout of over 83 percent.

Less than two days later, a big celebration occurs in the Kremlin. The occasion is the incorporation of Crimea and the city of Sevastopol into the Russian Federation as the 84th and 85th subjects, respectively. Russian imperialism in the 21st century. Putin's speech in the Kremlin's St. George's Hall, where the signing ceremony of the treaty on affiliation to the Russian Federation is taking place, contains lies, distortions, and doom-laden announcements, especially when he addresses the sufferers, the Ukrainians:

> Nationalists, neo-Nazis, Russophists and anti-Semites carried out this coup [in Kyiv]. They still set the tone in Ukraine today. Those who opposed the coup were immediately threatened with repression. Of course, Crimea, the Russian-speaking Crimea, was the first in line. In view of this, the inhabitants of Crimea and Sevastopol turned to Russia for help defending their rights and their lives. (...) Of course, we could not let this request go unheard; we could not abandon Crimea and its inhabitants in their plight. That would have been a betrayal on our part

In the speech, which will be broadcast on Russian television, he addresses the Europeans, and especially the Germans, many of whom he can assume from experience will fall for him again: "Our nation has (...) unequivocally supported the sincere, unstoppable desire of the Germans for national unity. I am confident that you have not forgotten this, and I expect that the citizens of Germany will also support the aspirations of the Russians, of historical Russia, for the restoration of unity." The fact that Putin is making this analogy is perfidious. The citizens of the GDR first advocated the end of the GDR and then reunification. In the case of Crimea, the government of another country, Russia, initiated unrest to appropriate a territory that did not belong to it. Putin opposed German unification, especially the Monday demonstrations that paved the way for it.

The KGB agent experienced the last years of the GDR until its downfall in Dresden and went in and out of the district administration of state security there. He had a house pass that allowed him access to the offices at any time and is said to have kept an eye on the GDR's largest electronics manufacturer, Robotron. The Soviet secret service (the Federal Security Service) was interested in high technology from East and West Germany, which it wanted to smuggle into the Soviet Union with Stasi support (the Ministry for State Security). Robotron and Dresden served as hubs. Putin also experienced the Monday demonstrations in the Elbe metropolis in 1989. The fact that the GDR leadership did not deploy the police or the army and that Mikhail Gorbachev did not call on the Soviet armed forces contradicted Putin's understanding. After all, 380,000 soldiers from his country were stationed in the GDR. SED Secretary General Erich Honecker had, on the occasion of the celebration of the 40th anniversary of the GDR on October 7, 1989, increased combat.

The National People's Army was called into readiness, and the hospitals were asked to keep enough beds and blood on hand. Putin was determined to use weapons when demonstrators stormed the Stasi district administration in Bautzner Strasse in Dresden on December 5, 1989, and moved on to the KGB branch. He did not favor a united Germany but preserving the GDR, even by military means. Ukrainians can only understand Putin's speech after the Crimean referendum as a sheer mockery:

> We do not want to harm you in any way or hurt your national feelings. By the way, we have always respected the territorial integrity of the Ukrainian state. (...) Do not believe those who want to scare you from Russia and scream that other regions will follow Crimea. We do not want to divide Ukraine, we do not need that. As for Crimea, it was, and remains Russian, Ukrainian, and Crimean Tatar land. (...) Let me say quite frankly that it hurts our hearts when we see what is currently happening in Ukraine. Our worries are understandable, because we are not only close neighbors, but, as I have often said, one people. Kyiv is the mother of Russian cities. Old Rus is our common source, and we cannot live without each other

Putin is shedding crocodile tears. He has ruthlessly shaken the postwar order in Europe and is trying to redraw the previously inviolable borders. While the world community is still outraged and assures it will not recognize this annexation, his troops are already moving on and wreaking havoc in eastern Ukraine.

Sanctions as threatening as cotton balls

On March 6, 2014, the European Union imposes entry bans on 18 Ukrainians from the former Yanukovych government and blocks their accounts because of the decision on the Crimean referendum. Among them are the fled Ukrainian President Yanukovych, his two sons, the head of the Presidential Administration, the prosecutor general, several ministers, and advisers to the president. In addition, negotiations on visa facilitation with Russia and the EU-Russia Basic Treaty are suspended. One day after the referendum in Crimea on March 16, eight top Crimean politicians and 13 Russians are added to the sanctions list. The EU's foreign policy chief, Catherine Ashton, described these measures as the "strongest possible signals" to Moscow. In Brussels, there is enthusiasm for its decisiveness. The EU is celebrating itself, not only for these "strongest possible" signals but also for their unity and speed. By the end of the year, about a dozen people will be listed several more times each. In addition, exports of military equipment and dual-use goods to Russia are banned, as are investments in infrastructure, especially in the energy and raw materials sectors, and certain financial transactions. These measures ensure that the Russians "recognize the seriousness of the situation." However, US President Obama is prepared to go further and points out that the Crimean crisis can always be solved diplomatically. Sarah Wagenknecht, deputy leader of the Left Party, takes a hard line with the government after the celebration in the Kremlin of the treaty on Crimea's membership in the Russian Federation. Not with the Russian government, but with the German government, because for the Russia apologist, the situation in Eastern Europe is as follows: "A coup government, which includes neo-fascists, and anti-Semites, comes into office with the blessing of Merkel and Steinmeier, the relationship with Russia has deteriorated dramatically, a civil war is threatening in the region, and US diplomacy is rubbing its hands together. Even the most tolerant SPD voter could not recognize Willy Brandt's tradition in the GroKo's course. The fact that Putin is continuing the tradition of the Tzars and the Communists by stealing territory from neighboring countries does not seem to be a reason for her to question her attitude toward Russia.

The Russian commander-in-chief is unaffected by European and American sanctions and thus sees the West's reaction as a free pass. For him, the sanctions are about as dangerous as throwing cotton balls at him. If this is to be the price for Crimea, he can confidently continue with his expansionist policy, which he is doing. He sends more army units to the territory of Ukraine and again stages a hybrid invasion. As in the occupation of Crimea, the soldiers wear no insignia of sovereignty or are dressed entirely in civilian clothes. The target is the coal basin in the east, a large industrial region with defense plants, coal mines, and fields as far as the eye can see. Around seven million people live here, most of them speaking Russian. The most important major cities are Kharkiv, Donetsk, and Luhansk. Everywhere there is sudden unrest. New hotbeds of conflict are flaring up all the time. No one knows who exactly is stirring up the area.

In Donetsk, demonstrators, whom no one in the city knows, clash with local supporters of the Maidan movement. Two men died. Similar reports are from other places in eastern Ukraine and Mariupol, Kherson, and Odesa in the southeast and south, respectively. The provocateurs are brought across the border on buses from Russia. Their mission is to disrupt rallies and destabilize the situation. The masterminds in the Kremlin want to take advantage of the general power vacuum in the country. This is because the flight of Viktor Yanukovych and the replacement of many offices has led to a great deal of uncertainty at all levels. No one knows who is currently calling the shots in the country.

The new Ukrainian president, Oleksandr Turchinov, is taking the precaution of firing governors who, like the politicians in Crimea, are suspected of seeking "support" from Moscow. Oligarchs are seen as the final authority in the increasingly troubled region and are appointed governors, for example, the wealthy banker Ihor Kolomojskyj in Dnipropetrovsk. In his inaugural speech, he immediately takes on President Putin and displays an unexpected clairvoyance: "I cannot believe that Russians and Ukrainians should murder each other. I'm going to say something very undiplomatic now: If we already had a schizophrenic as president in Ukraine, then he was still harmless compared to the other schizophrenic in the Kremlin. His obsession to restore the old empire in the borders of 1991 will lead the world into a catastrophe." Kolomojskyj's Moscow private bank is placed under Russian receivership a day later.

Dozens of cities fall to pro-Russian separatists starting in March 2014, in addition to Donetsk and Luhansk, including Sloviansk, where Igor Girkin, known as Strelkov, takes over the regime. Girkin is known for his violence and was an employee of the GRU, the former Soviet and current Russian military intelligence. The pattern of occupation is the same as in Crimea: pro-Russian separatists and Russian foot soldiers, led by Russian intelligence operatives and backed by the military, occupy city councils, police stations, and other institutions and arrest anyone who resists: Mayors, deputies, priests, people who are among the most active in society, who embody a certain authority and organize peaceful resistance. They are abducted, mistreated, and killed. Human rights lawyer Oleksandra Matvichuk, who heads the Center for Civil Liberties in Kyiv, documents pro-Russian, and Russian terror against Ukrainian civilians to this day. "It is one thing to occupy a territory. And something else to keep it under control afterward. This happened from 2014 onwards with war methods. With a whole network of illegal prisons." Unlike the occupation of Crimea, the now-revitalized Ukrainian Army is not simply allowing itself to be taken territory by territory without a fight but is instead defending territory. Russia is sending fighters and weapons to the separatists, driving Ukraine into war over its eastern territories.

A meeting of the eight largest industrialized nations is planned for June 4 and 5, 2014, in Sochi on the Black Sea. Russia has been a group member since 1998 and will host the summit for the second time since 2006. For the US President, Obama, this is already no longer conceivable at the beginning of March; he calls his counterpart in Moscow and informs him that the US is withdrawing from all G8 events. France and Great Britain follow Obama's initiative. Berlin still hesitates to cut the channel of talks. "Reversal is still possible. A new division of Europe can still be prevented," says Foreign Minister Frank-Walter Steinmeier, who was confident after a telephone call with Russia's Foreign Minister Sergey Lavrov. He was disappointed; Moscow neither stopped support for the separatists nor did Putin ensure an end to human rights violations by the new rulers. The G8 will again become the G7, which will meet as planned in early June, but in Brussels.

On July 22, 2014, the EU announced further sanctions against Russia. The reason for this is the downing of MH 17. Two hundred ninety-eight passengers, including 80 children, were on board the international scheduled flight. The Malaysia Airlines Boeing, on its route from Amsterdam to Kuala Lumpur on July 17, crossed the Donetsk separatist area, where it fell into the trajectory of a Buk missile that had previously been brought across the border from Russia and deployed in Snishne. Russia denies any involvement—as it did in 1983 when a Soviet interceptor fired on a South Korean passenger plane near Sakhalin, causing it to crash and killing all 269 people on board. The international investigative research network Bellingcat does not specify whether Russian soldiers or pro-Russian separatists operated the Buk system but cautions that the weapon system is expensive and very complex, and it takes at least six months of training to know how to use it. They said that the decision to deploy a Buk-M1 system to the war zone was made at the highest level of Russian air defense. The defense minister or Supreme Commander Vladimir Putin only can permit sending military equipment to Ukraine.

The EU adopted the sanctions then imposed on July 25 unanimously. They include 15 additional individuals and nine companies but remain without major effect. They cannot rein in the war in eastern Ukraine in any way. On the contrary, in Ilovaysk, a war breaks out in August 2014, a heavy battle that lasts almost a month. Seven thousand Ukrainian fighters are encircled. President Putin reportedly personally advocates a security corridor, which turns out to be a deadly trap. The 1000 unarmed Ukrainian soldiers who use it come under fire—366 die. They are Putin's dead in the Ilovaysk massacre.

The war in eastern Ukraine is claiming new victims every day, yet most German politicians and journalists still call it a "conflict," trivializing it. Peace talks finally take place at the beginning of 2015.

The venue is the Belarusian capital, where on February 12, French President François Hollande, German Chancellor Angela Merkel, Petro Poroshenko, now Ukrainian president and Vladimir Putin negotiate the Minsk Agreement. The talks drag on for more than 17 hours. The three foreign ministers, Lavrov, Klimkin, and Steinmeier, are often present, but not always. There are constant interruptions. According to Hollande, the reason for the marathon was that Putin wanted to delay an agreement to give his troops in Debaltseve enough time to surround the Ukrainian Army. In the end, Putin did not sign the agreement because he does not consider Russia part of the conflict. Because Putin does not sign, Poroshenko does not either. Merkel and Holland are "only" the mediators; they do not put their names to the agreement. In the end, the document bears only the signatures of former President of Ukraine Leonid Kuchma, Russian Federation Ambassador to Ukraine Mikhail Zurabov, and the militia leaders of the self-proclaimed Luhansk and Donetsk "People's Republics" Igor Plotnitsky and Alexander Zakharchenko, respectively in addition to the OSCE representative, Heidi Tagliavini.

The result is more than mixed.

Kyiv can unreservedly agree to the ceasefire and the withdrawal of heavy war equipment, prisoner exchanges, and humanitarian aid. But the agreement also contains a toad that the Ukrainians cannot swallow. They must allow regional elections in the occupied Donbas to decide on self-government and the future status of the so-called people's republics. The outcome of these elections would be as predictable as in all Russian elections and referenda since Putin has been in power. His propaganda machinery would take care of that. Poroshenko cannot and will not allow this to happen. It would be tantamount to giving up these territories, and Moscow would have achieved its goal. Thus, the sides part exhausted and, at the same time, disgruntled, knowing that the agreement will never be implemented.

Only Putin achieved partial success in Minsk, apparently trying to buy time for the encirclement of thousands of Ukrainian soldiers in the embattled city of Debaltseve. He reached his target. Hence, according to François Hollande in his memoirs, the frequent interruptions during the proceedings. Putin, he said, had raised his voice several times and threatened his Ukrainian counterpart to crush the Ukrainian troops. In doing so, Putin admitted the presence of Russian forces in eastern Ukraine, Hollande writes.

Debaltseve became one of the battles with the highest losses. It broke out while the Minsk negotiations were still on and violated the ceasefire that had just been agreed upon. The ink on the document was not yet dry. The battle for the strategically important railroad junction between Donetsk and Luhansk also involves using T-72 battle tanks of the Russian Armed Forces, directed by Russian soldiers. Putin denies his army's involvement in the fighting. The city of Debaltseve is completely destroyed during the four weeks of fighting.

Let us pause for a moment: Russia annexes Crimea. The EU imposes sanctions on about 20 people. Moscow's troops occupy eastern Ukraine with willing pro-Russian stooges. The Ukrainian Army defends its territory, unlike in Crimea. The separatists receive military support from Russia. They shoot down a passenger plane over the battle zone. And the EU? The EU adds 15 people and nine companies to the sanctions list. It refrains from imposing harsh sanctions on the Russian economy. Hundreds of people die in the battles of Ilovaysk and Debaltseve, and one and a half million Ukrainians flee the war zone, where the pro-Russian occupiers established a regime of terror and arbitrariness. The Kremlin leadership is learning that there are hardly any consequences for its misdemeanors, that the Western community is letting it have its way, and that it is falling for Moscow's propaganda about Ukrainian fascists time and again.

Fascists, patriots, and pacifists

Ukraine has been at war since 2014, with Europe taking virtually no notice. Its army is so poorly equipped that civilians all over the country are taking care of the soldiers' equipment. In Lviv, female Ukrainians board buses to Poland to get bulletproof vests because each can only buy one; many must make their way there. In private cars, vests, helmets, binoculars, and food are brought to the volunteers and soldiers at the front in eastern Ukraine. Only on February 24, 2022, Europe is horrified to learn that there is war in Europe, revealing how blind the West has been in Ukraine for the past eight years.

Then as now, the military equipment of Ukraine is insufficient. Then as now, the aggressor calls its invasion a fight against fascists in Ukraine. At the same time, everyone who utters a critical word about Russia is called a fascist. It is a senseless fighting term with nothing to do with its original meaning. The Kremlin ideologues use it purely for enemies who are particularly on their minds. Politicians in former Soviet republics, for instance, committed to the independence and development of their newly created nation-states, are called fascists. By 2021, the term had a dangerous undertone but passed for Russian propaganda. In 2022, it becomes central to warmongering. Now an entire people, the Ukrainian people, must be "denazified."

For Russian propaganda, Dmytro Yarosh is enemy number one in Ukraine in 2014. Since 2021, he has again been an advisor to the commander-in-chief of the Ukrainian armed forces, as he previously was when he sat in parliament for Right Sector from 2014 to 2019. At the time, he was also a Verkhovna Rada's Defense Committee member. Yarosh is from Dniprodzerzhynsk and spent his childhood and youth in the Soviet Union. In the summer of 2014, he and his people are staying in a converted vacation camp in the forest, two hours from Kharkiv. His people are fighters in a volunteer battalion with the same name as the party he founded: Right Sector. They are a strange sight on the grounds, among playgrounds and yellow clinker buildings that resemble daycare centers. I wonder when the last children spent their summer weeks here? For the volunteers from the Right Sector Battalion, the retreat is ideal. None of them are professional soldiers, so they have to practice. Yevgeny, the instructor, spurs the men on with recent success stories: Under the command of Dmytro Yarosh, the 400-strong battalion has recaptured places in eastern Ukraine occupied by the pro-Russian separatists. Kalashnikovs were captured in operations with other volunteer battalions and army units. His Right Sector would often support the other battalions and the Ukrainian military, says Yarosh, yet he would not receive weapons from the Ministry of Defense. The parliament and government in Kyiv have been full of suspicion of Yarosh ever since he proposed arming the people. Because of this, he and his men were denied official volunteer battalion status.

This differs from the Azov Battalion, whose fighters have been revered as heroes since the defense of Mariupol in 2014, especially since their deployment in 2022. For weeks they hold out in the Azov steelworks, where thousands of civilians seek shelter, keeping Russian troops from other military operations. Many other volunteers have long since joined the Azov soldiers. In the end, there are around 3,000 men in Mariupol alone. President Zelenskyy wants to save their lives and finally orders them to surrender in mid-May, knowing it will be difficult to free them from Russian captivity. The Azov fighters, in particular, are considered by Moscow to be the epitome of fascist Ukraine and are the most important opponent in Russia's 'denazification' campaign. The Azov Battalion was founded in 2014 after the annexation of Crimea as one of the first volunteer battalions. Its name refers to where it was founded, located on the Sea of Azov: It is the southern Ukrainian city of Berdyansk, not far from Mariupol. Initially, it has the image of a right-wing extremist combat unit because members of the racist and neo-Nazi organizations Social-National Assembly and Patriot of Ukraine, Automaidan activists, and various hundred-man squads of the Maidan self-defense form the unit's core. The commander is Andrij Bilezkyj, a right-wing extremist from Kharkiv. He heads the fascist Social-National Assembly and Patriot of Ukraine, a splinter organization. It has hardly any followers, but its racist positions and symbolism reminiscent of the NSDAP make it stand out. Their torchlight processions also contribute to this. In 2013, Bilezkyj and two other men stand trial for the attempted murder of a journalist but are not convicted. The Azov Battalion is immediately subordinated to the Ministry of Interior. By the fall of 2014, it had grown to around 800 fighters, most of whom came from eastern Ukraine and spoke Russian. At the end of 2014, the battalion was given the status of a regiment and integrated into the newly created Ukrainian National Guard. Until then, its funding is mainly provided by the oligarch Ihor Kolomojskyj from Dnipropetrovsk. The so-called Wolfsangel contributes to the right-wing extremist image. It is the emblem of the regiment. The Azov leadership denies that it is based on a symbol of the National Socialists, which the SS also used. Instead, it depicts the stylized Latin letters N and I, representing "the national idea." Human rights organizations also record cases of violence against the civilian population and torture, contributing to the Azov Battalion's dubious reputation in its early days.

In 2014, however, it is not Biletsky but Dmytro Yarosh who is the most important face of the demonstrators on the Maidan, who are described as fascists. The reason for this is presumably the agenda with which he is running as a presidential candidate after Yanukovych's escape. The fact that he wants to smash the criminal systems of the oligarchs and strives for a socially oriented state with an efficient market economy has most likely left the ruler in the Kremlin cold, but not that he is declaring war on "the Kremlin's neocolonialism" in Moscow. As future president, Yarosh promises to end Russian aggression, significantly increase military spending, declare full mobilization, and restore Ukraine's nuclear status. They must have pricked up their ears in the Kremlin. The leader of his paramilitary bloc advocates a strict ban on anti-Ukrainian media, wants to provide comprehensive aid to the Crimean Tatar people, and combat all manifestations of separatism. He also wants to cut taxes, investigate civil servants, and educate young people religiously. On TV talk shows, he argues for taking back Crimea in a guerrilla war, with the help of the Crimean Tatars, and proposes physically eliminating the leaders of the popular militias in the separatist areas.

In Russia, the media supervisory authority Roskomnadzor then orders the blocking of all websites connected with Dmytro Yarosh and the Right Sector. Anyone who even prints an interview with him experiences the full rigor of the censorship apparatus. This happened to Galina Timchenko, the former editor-in-chief of the successful Russian news portal *lenta.ru*. She was forced to leave Russia because of a report on Yarosh's Right Sector. She then founded her media platform, *meduza.io*. In 2014, in her newly occupied editorial offices in Riga, the current managing director talks about the pressure from the Kremlin. Her entire reporting on the annexation of Crimea and the war in eastern Ukraine did not suit the Moscow leadership, she says, because it clearly deviated from the official line. Timchenko is convinced she can better provide her Russian-speaking readership with critical articles from afar. She chose the Latvian capital because Russian is also mainly spoken here, but freely, in a democratic environment. From May 2021, her work will become even more difficult because the Russian Ministry of Justice will include *Meduza* in the register of foreign agents. Those who are listed as such must note this in all their publications. *Meduza* will not only lose advertising revenue because this label scares off customers but also cut off journalists from important informants who move in the circle of the Kremlin, the government, the security services, and the Duma.

Yarosh enjoys the fuss about his person. Yet the small, wiry man is a bogus giant. In the presidential election in May 2014, he received a pitiful 0.7 percent of the votes. But he wants to run again in the parliamentary elections next time in October. He knows he is not trusted and that people in Germany are particularly skeptical of him and his Right Sector. He also knows that many people think he has discredited the entire protest movement on the Maidan. He is not interested in the reaction of the West. The rightwinger, a teacher in his early life, calls himself a patriot and law-abiding fighter. "Our volunteer units, of course, abide by the orders of the commander-in-chief." He can hardly understand that the organization's name alone contributes to the critical view of him and his movement. Right Sector's name has nothing to do with a political orientation. "It was the young people who suggested it to us. They are all soccer fans and wanted this term out of the stadium." The Right Sector was initially a rallying point for far-right groups. Yarosh joined it with his organization *Stepan Bandera All-Ukrainian Organization 'Tryzub'* — we have no relationship with the German national socialists or Italian fascists." Nationalism in Ukraine includes the love of one's country but not hatred of foreigners, he said. In his organization, he said, there are also Russians, Armenians, Georgians, and Jews. Also, here in the volunteer battalion. "We have a rabbi. We don't have conflicts because of these different nationalities. Nor is there any anti-Semitism. Russian propaganda has demonized us." It always reminds people of Stepan Bandera and his partisan struggle against the Red Army, proving that Ukrainians hate everything Russian. This spreads fear in the majority Russian-speaking population in eastern Ukraine. But you can see how people welcome them, even entertain them, when they liberate the places occupied by the separatists. The mood has changed. Not with everyone, of course, because some people have a negative attitude toward Ukraine. "But something is moving, here in the Donetsk and Luhansk regions."

The battalion chief fights for votes with a gun in his hand against the Donetsk and Luhansk militias and Moscow's special forces. The only chance to defeat the great Russian Army is partisan warfare, says Jarosch in 2014, sentences that could also have come from 2022.

The 0.7 percent for Yarosh in the presidential election in May 2014 and the 1.16 percent for Oleh Tyahnybok of the likewise radical right-wing and nationalist party Svoboda, with a voter turnout of just under 60 percent, clearly show how far right-wing extremists are gaining ground among the Ukrainian population. It is low. The fact that they are militarily influential seems to be a fact then as now. Yarosh and Tyahnybok of Svoboda did enter parliament, but neither Right Sector nor Svoboda had the strength of a parliamentary group; they received one and six seats, respectively. But with the "fascists on the Maidan, " a specter was painted on the wall, which the West, especially German politicians, fell for. In rows and for different reasons.

On December 5, 2014, former Chancellor's Advisor Horst Teltschik (CDU), former Secretary of State for Defense Walther Stützle (SPD), and former Bundestag Vice President Antje Vollmer (Greens) initiated the appeal "War in Europe Again? Not in our name!" Even the question in the headline is wrong: "War in Europe again?" should not have been a question but a statement. The war in eastern Ukraine is actually taking place 2,000 kilometers away. But the geographical proximity only comes to the attention of many Germans on February 24, 2022. Against the backdrop of this call, open letters like the one to Chancellor Olaf Scholz from May 2022, eight years later, feel like déjà vu. On closer inspection, what initially sounds like a noble concern turns out to be a relativization of the aggressor's guilt:

> The Americans, Europeans, and Russians have lost the guiding principle of permanently banning war from their relationship. (...) The German government is not taking a Sonderweg, not going out on a limb when it continues to call for prudence and dialogue with Russia in this tense situation. The Russians' need for security is as legitimate and pronounced as that of the Germans, the Poles, the Balts, and the Ukrainians. We must not push Russia out of Europe. That would be unhistorical, unreasonable, and dangerous for peace.

Those who call a spade a spade find themselves in a position that would not have been thought possible in Germany until then. The media are collectively insulted, their reports doubted, because the signatories of the appeal supposedly know better. Some are suffering from the development of the war in eastern Ukraine, wishing out of their pacifist convictions that the terrible events would stop. Others simply have not done their homework to finally get themselves up to speed on what is going on. Because of their lack of knowledge, they easily fall for Russian Internet trolls. Companies doing business with Russia suspect early on that the sanctions will harm their economic interests. They plead for leniency with Russia because they do not want to lose their business partners under any circumstances. This is probably true of Eckhard Cordes, for example, who signed the appeal as chairman of the Committee on Eastern European Economic Relations, and of Gerhard Schröder, of course, but also Hans-Joachim Frey. The founder and artistic director of the Semper Opera Ball awarded Putin the medal of his event association in 2009 and initially refused to take it away again after the war began in 2014. Were the signatories aware of the impact of their sweeping accusation against the media?

> We appeal to the media to fulfill their duty to report without prejudice more convincingly than before. Editorialists and commentators demonize entire peoples without sufficiently appreciating their history. Any journalist versed in foreign policy will understand the Russians' fear since NATO members invited Georgia and Ukraine to become members of the alliance in 2008. It's not about Putin. Leaders come and go. It's about Europe. It is about taking away people's fear of war again. Responsible reporting based on solid research can contribute a lot to that.

One would have wished for this "research" from the signatories. Did they know that with these completely unfounded accusations, they put themselves in the same row as the AfD and Pegida? That they were tooting the same horn as the right-wing extremists who spoke of "state broadcasting," "system media," and "bought journalists" of the "synchronized journalistic establishment"? This call was well-intentioned at best. In fact, it was malicious and hypocritical. It contributed little to social pacification and nothing to enlightenment. In 2014, the term *lügenpresse* [lying press] was named "Unword of the Year."

In the spring of 2015, the Kremlin-founded Rodina party hosted a "Forum of Conservatives" in St. Petersburg. It is a meeting of ultra-rightists and neo-Nazis, but Fyodor Biryukov, the host, vigorously denies this:

> European leaders and the Obama administration are embracing and kissing the true fascists of the 21st century. The ones from the Kyiv junta. They hail the annihilation of the Russians in southeastern Ukraine. Nazism, fascism, extremism, and terrorism are growing and flourishing there nowadays. We are acting as a peacekeeping force. Because the war in the Donbas is not only a genocide, but a war that the US administration has unleashed against Europe, against every European nation

In this roundabout way, the United Nations also gets something that would welcome terrorism and fascism in Ukraine and the OSCE.

Students protest in front of the conference hotel. Maybe a dozen; there are more police vehicles than demonstrators. Inside the hall, ultra-nationalist Chris Roman from Belgium mocks the few Petersburgers who have come to the Holiday Inn to oppose the neo-Nazi event. He mocks critical journalist Anna Politkovskaya, who was murdered in 2006, the Russian Jewish entrepreneur Boris Berezovsky and opposition politician Boris Nemtsov, who was shot dead a month ago. The extreme rightwinger shared with the audience in St. Petersburg a meeting he allegedly had with a former soldier. The latter admitted a mistake and made it clear that Germany should rather have invaded the USA than the Soviet Union. He, the Belgian Chris Roman, said he agreed with him. "The enemy today is Western democracy. America wants to invade Russia. I don't want to spend my future life with the USA but with Russia. Russia is our friend, America is our enemy. I thank Russia for finding the strength to prevent a third world war." Roman, who describes himself as a Russophile in his opening speech at the forum, describes Europe as a peninsula of the Eurasian continent and Russia as a great neighbor with whom Europe is linked not only by a geographical but also a spiritual project.

Most speakers address the audience in the hall with openly xenophobic, racist appeals. No one contradicts, no one relativizes; they rather reinforce each other. Representatives of eleven nationalist and right-wing extremist parties in Europe have gathered on the Neva. In February, they formed the so-called Alliance for Peace and Freedom, which includes Germany's NPD, Belgium's Movement Nation, Denmark's Danskernes Parti, Italy's Forza Nuova, Spain's Democracia Nacional, Greece's Chrysi Avgi, Sweden's Svenskarnas Parti, and individuals such as former National Front member Olivier Wyssa of France, Nick Griffin of the United Kingdom, and the aforementioned Chris Roman. Court or ban proceedings have been conducted or are being considered against almost all parties, including the NPD. Its European deputy Udo Voigt explains that the ultra-right gathered in St. Petersburg are united by a common enemy: the globalists, the banking capital, and the speculators. Voigt and his comrades-in-arms, he says, are not against Europe, only against a Europe along the lines of the United States of America and for a Europe of fatherlands. "Russia and Ukraine belong to that, but in no case the space alien power USA, which is today determining in Europe via NATO. And in no case Turkey, it does not belong to Europe."

Voigt visited seven members of the Chrysi Avgi party from Greece in prison at the end of 2014. They are accused of money laundering, murder, and organized crime. Both the NPD and Chrysi Avgi are known for their hatred of foreigners. It unites them. The Kremlin is not squeamish in choosing its friends; while it refuses to allow Green MEP Rebecca Harms to enter the country, NPD politician Voigt is a welcome guest in Russia.

The "Forum of Conservatives" is taking place with the knowledge of President Vladimir Putin, Russian political scientist Emil Pain is convinced because nothing happens without the Kremlin knowing about it

> They have invited [them] to a luxury hotel paid for the participants' stay. This is all the more interesting because nowadays nobody in Russia develops any initiative on their own. And if you ask now why there are so few protests, then that is also the answer. The religious associations, for example the Muslim ones, have understood perfectly that the government likes this event, but the protests clearly don't

But for the Kremlin, the right is not the same as the right. Right-wing extremists from Ukraine, Poland, and Latvia were denied access to the forum. The Kremlin more or less openly protects right-wing populist parties in Europe. According to Russian hackers, the French National Front, which later renamed itself Rassemblement National, received a million-dollar loan as a reward for Marine Le Pen's approval of the Crimea referendum after the annexation. Moscow's loan to Le Pen became known because the Russian opposition group "Anonymous International" hacked over 1,000 websites and messages belonging to Timur Prokopenko. That is the head of the Interior Department in the Russian presidential administration. In one email exchange, the hackers found a statement of intent that said that the politically good conduct of the party leader was to be rewarded. Nine million Euros of the loan were transferred to the National Front in November 2014, which Marine Le

Pen later admitted. However, she denies a political connection. The right-wing populist makes no secret of her admiration for Vladimir Putin, which does not bother her supporters in the presidential election in April 2022.

Conspicuous among the participants of the forum are the Cossacks because of their folkloric uniforms and high fur caps. Alexei Kapustin's face is red. He is sweating under his headgear in the well-heated conference hall but bravely keeps it on. He, too, follows the Kremlin's reading of the war in eastern Ukraine as a conflict between Ukrainians and Russians. Cossacks like him see themselves as preservers of Russian traditions. They are a paramilitary organization with many regional offshoots. One of their most important tasks is recruitment. The target group is children from socially disadvantaged families lured by sports. Some are even allowed to learn to ride, something their parents cannot offer them. The aim is to provide pre-military training for the youngest children to introduce them to the army early and prepare them for military service.

At Alexei Kapustin's side sits Anna Shilayeva. She, too, is wearing a uniform, a costume, and a Cossack cap. Shilayeva works in her own company in civilian life; in the Cossacks, she would like to establish a women's department. The Cossacks must support the army, she believes, even though the Russian armed forces have been modernized in recent years and are by no means underfunded. The weapons used against the Ukrainian units are easily recognizable as Russian because they are much more modern than the outdated Soviet military technology the Ukrainian Army has to make do with.

She confirms that Cossacks from all over Russia are moving to the Donbas: Kuban Cossacks, from Baikal, from Tversk, Orenburg, from the Amur, from the Urals, from Siberia. Cossacks are not soldiers. They would fight voluntarily, for example, in Luhansk. They also consider themselves indispensable in Crimea. "We just buried one of our own. He was a sniper in Debaltseve." The Cossacks are not plagued by any sense of injustice that they are fighting on Ukrainian territory. On the contrary, Alexei Kapustin is proud of the just war against the "fascists."

> I saw this on the Internet. Still this may be a small group, but such a thing must be fought from the very beginning. It's not just about Luhansk, it's about what kind of people they are: these Banderovtsy. Bandera, Hitler, Mussolini—they are all the same. We know what they do with little children in Donbas, in Kramatorsk. They torture and kill them. This is not propaganda, these are facts.

Over the years, Moscow has tried to divide Germany by no longer relying only on the SPD as a political partner but also by enlisting radical forces for its purposes. Both the far right and the far left are allies because they weaken the democratic camp in Europe.

Bahr, Eppler, Schmidt, and Schröder — the quartet of vain old men

Germany, which likes to consider itself the world champion in reappraisal, has many gaps in its knowledge about Ukraine, even among top politicians. This leads to misjudgments and false considerations that are both embarrassing and disastrous. When Russia began to act out its lust for conquest and war on its neighboring country in 2014, people in Germany thought they had to hold back on criticizing Moscow because of the Nazi crimes in World War II. But hardly anyone among German politicians has dealt with the Soviet Union's successor states since its collapse. The USSR was equated with Russia. The grid was so rough that Ukraine simply fell through. And this is even though it is almost twice the size of Germany in terms of area and has about as many inhabitants as Poland. The country has been criminally neglected. Even experienced political professionals generously overlooked the second-largest state on our continent for decades. Russia changed Europas' postwar order, shifted borders to Ukraine's disadvantage, and instigated a war in the east of its territory — but SPD politicians, in particular, primarily expressed misgivings about Kyiv. One look at the course of the front in the Second World War is enough to know that the enemy occupied Ukrainian territory for the entire Russian campaign.

For this reason, the destruction and casualties are higher than in today's Russia. That also suffered, but not to the same extent as Ukraine. Why, from a historical view, Russia must be taken into consideration and Ukraine is not, is not explained. Astonishingly, it is mainly top SPD politicians of the wartime and postwar generation who only remember the historic debt to Moscow. Is it really ignorance or intention? Is the space between Germany and Russia repeatedly crossed out of old habits? In Eastern Europe, these questions awaken unpleasant memories. Keyword Rapallo and keyword Hitler-Stalin Pact.

First to the Rapallo Treaty: Germany and Russia participate in the 1922 World Economic Conference in Genoa. As so often since the end of the First World War, the issue is German reparations. Russia is to list its claims against Berlin. Germany is outraged. The delegation from Berlin has a plan. It asks the Russian side for a meeting in Rapallo, 30 kilometers away, to propose something. What if Germany and Russia were to ally? Both are losers of the First World War and still international outlaws: Germany because it is blamed for the war alone, and Russia because of the revolution. The Russians like the idea. They agreed — outwardly quite harmlessly — to establish diplomatic relations and to assist each other economically and financially. Moscow renounces German reparation payments, which is a great relief for Germany, which is already groaning under the payment obligations from the Treaty of Versailles.

Conversely, the Germans drop their compensation demands. Damaged German property in Russia after the October Revolution does not have to be replaced. In addition, both sides agreed on how to help each other in the energy sector. As a reminder, the year is 1922! The Germans offer production facilities, the Russians oil, which reduces Germany's dependence on British and American oil cartels. A win-win situation.

The plans for military cooperation, however, are delicate. The German Junkers-Werke is to set up an aircraft factory in Fili near Moscow, and the Germans are to train Russian pilots — and many of their own — at a secret flying school near Lipetsk. There are also plans to build a poison gas factory. The Treaty of Versailles expressly forbids Germany to do all this, especially to build up German air forces. With Moscow's help, it is undermined. The spin doctor of the secret cooperation between the Reichswehr and the Soviet Red Army is the Chief of Army Command, General Hans von Seeckt. He is ready to go one big step further. Seeckt finds the very existence of Poland intolerable and wants it to disappear. With energetic German support, the best way would be through its weakness and Russia. Poland had to be destroyed so Germany and Russia would become immediate neighbors again, as they had been in 1914. There was no mention of this later in the Treaty of Rapallo, but when this became known, there was great indignation in France and Great Britain. Germany was accused of having revanchist intentions. Rapallo became the epitome of distrust against the Berlin-Moscow axis.

On August 23, 1939, Germany and the Soviet Union again agreed on a secret pact. Foreign Minister Joachim von Ribbentrop and Foreign Commissar Vyacheslav Molotov negotiated it. It contains the agreement on how the two dictators will subjugate Europe and the world. Officially, it is a non-aggression pact. For his planned invasion of Poland, Hitler secured the neutrality of the Soviet Union, which did not change his war plans against it. Stalin, for his part, intends to cooperate with Germany as long as possible to avoid war. Both sides agreed that Moscow would support Hitler's arms industry by supplying raw materials and receive machinery in return.

But what is explosive is the additional secret protocol providing for a division between Europe and the world between Hitler and Stalin. A good week after the signing in the Kremlin, Hitler's troops invaded Poland from the West, and about two weeks later, Stalin's Red Army troops invaded the East. On September 22, 1939, the infamous victory parade of the Wehrmacht and the Red Army takes place in BrestLitovsk, celebrating the German-Soviet brotherhood in arms. Poland had to capitulate on September 27. One day later, the two invaders decide on the German-Soviet Friendship and Border Treaty, which regulates a precise division of territory. According to it, western Poland, including Lublin, and Warsaw, would go to the German Reich, and the rest of Poland, Finland, Estonia, Latvia, Lithuania, and today's Romania to the Soviet Union. The German, Ukrainian, and White Russian minorities will be resettled into their sphere of power from the affected areas. Together Hitler and Stalin violate the right of self-determination of five countries. With the German invasion of the Soviet Union in June 1941, the Hitler-Stalin Pact is rendered obsolete.

In Russia, the reasons why Stalin entered into the pact still change today—sometimes it was a non-aggression pact, and sometimes it was to delay the war. The truth is that the Soviet Union was not only a victim but also a perpetrator in the

Second World War, which Germany started. Russia is not interested, and most recently, Putin even blamed Poland. The Red Army invaded Poland in 1939, only when the government in Warsaw was no longer in control of the country. This was done only to defend the security of the USSR. Why the Soviet forces killed thousands of members of the Polish elite was not explained by Putin in his remarks at his 2019 annual press conference.

When Berlin and Moscow work closely together, when German politicians even today speak of Russia as a neighbor and ignore the countries directly bordering it, the people of Eastern Europe rightly become very vigilant. All the more so when Russia and Germany conclude treaties across them and at their expense. At the end of 2014, Erhard Eppler, the very peace-minded Social Democrat, has only contempt and condescension for Ukraine and knows how to deal with the Eastern European country almost a year after the Russian occupation and annexation of Crimea. First, he is outraged that Ukrainian parties are "outdoing each other in anti-Russian nationalism" in the election campaign. Apparently, it escaped Eppler's notice that Russia is fueling the war in eastern Ukraine, which has already cost thousands of lives. Moreover, he finds Ukraine

> economically and financially so run-down that neither the European Union nor Russia will be able to rehabilitate this huge country on their own. Only together could they manage it. (...) So sooner or later, the realization that the European Union must come to an agreement with Russia will become inevitable. In this process, a Ukrainian government will have a say, but will not be able to dictate the terms

In other contexts, such an attitude would probably be called colonialist. Eppler does not utter a word of sympathy for the war victims, whose number is already in the thousands, and not a syllable of solidarity with the civilians fighting for their country's modernization and democratization. It is the quartet of vain old men who simply cannot warm to Ukraine. The youngest and, at the same time, the most present in the media in this group spoke out even before the Crimean referendum on March 16, 2014, when Russia was in the process of annexing Crimea. Gerhard Schröder excused

Putin's invasion, saying there had been a breach of international law but that one should be careful about pointing the finger "because I did it myself." For him, what Putin did with Crimea was Germany's participation in the war in Kosovo, and he also made the same mistake. That is why Putin should not be demonized. The parallel that Schröder generously draws here is not quite so straightforward. Germany or other NATO countries did not occupy Serbia during and after the bombing raids in 1999.

Moreover, the military action was preceded by months of negotiations and did not take place unannounced. The NATO intervention was justified in averting a growing humanitarian catastrophe, which was a shaky argument at the time, because the so-called responsibility to protect, which allows interventions in urgent cases, only found its way into international law after the Kosovo war. NATO also did not seek the approval of the Security Council because it was clear that Russia and China would veto it. NATO's deployment in Kosovo was highly controversial in Germany; Schröder's foreign minister, Joschka Fischer, came under particularly heavy pressure from his party, Bündnis 90/Die Grünen. He agreed to the deployment because he wanted "never again war, never again Auschwitz, never again genocide, never again fascism." Schröder undercuts the most important thing in the comparison: Ukraine was not guilty of any crime. The Putin friend blames the EU for pushing Ukraine into an association agreement. The country, he argues, which is culturally divided into Europe-oriented nationalists in the West and Russian thinkers in the East and South, was thus faced with an either-or situation. Ukraine only had the choice of deciding against ties with Russia.

In Germany, knowledge of the sensitivities and actual conditions in Ukrainian society and the extensive network of Ukrainian NGOs is, to put it mildly, in need of development. The willingness to get to know the country tended toward zero for a long time. Many are under the misapprehension that if they know Russia, they know enough about Ukraine. But there are major differences, especially in the citizens' commitment to their country. Whether it is the reform of electoral laws and the judiciary, the fight against corruption, or transparency in the economy, curtailing the power of the oligarchs, transparent income declarations for members of parliament and government, the decentralization of power, and the strengthening of local parliaments and administrations—there is hardly a policy area that the activists in the NGOs have not helped negotiate. Mostly young men and women are getting involved in transforming their country on such a large scale that cannot be rudimentarily found in Russia. This is also because this political part of civil society is being massively suppressed there. Ukraine had free and fair elections at the end of 2014, which Russia has not experienced since Putin took office. Oligarchs dominate both countries, but their degree of freedom has differed since the end of the Yeltsin era. Yet Germans still sympathize with authoritarian Russia and remain estranged from Ukraine, which has a strong civil society.

German politicians and journalists have no problem admitting they are writing about and judging a country they still do not know from their own experience. At the same time, a flight to Kyiv took less than two hours, and outside occupied eastern Ukraine, travel to the remaining regions was completely safe until 2022.

Another sought-after interlocutor is SPD driver Egon Bahr. The architect of Willy Brandt's Ostpolitik is already certain in March 2014, in the run-up to the vote in Crimea, that the peninsula would be part of Russia in the future. Bahr is repeatedly asked to answer in interviews whether the Cold War has returned. This is a strange question given the ongoing hot war in eastern Ukraine, but a good occasion to turn again to his favorite topic, change through rapprochement. He praises the eastern policy he helped establish in the highest terms retrospectively because no one had wanted to convert the other side at that time:

> I now have the feeling that people basically resent Putin for not being a democrat in our opinion and in our way of doing things. (...) Russia has to develop according to its traditions, and its traditions, as we know, do not include democracy. This means that neither Putin nor his children nor his grandchildren will be democrats according to our way of thinking and understanding. (...) No, it will be a democracy à la russe and that should actually be enough for us

For decades, German foreign policy was based on the principle that peace was only possible with and not against the Soviet Union or Russia. This expressed hope and a desire to make amends for the guilt in World War II. In return, the SPD was prepared to overstep boundaries that it would sometimes have been better off maintaining.

Some GDR citizens still remember Bahr's policy of "change through rapprochement" as "change through ingratiation." Beginning in 1982, representatives of the SPD, led by Eppler and Bahr, regularly met the SED. They discussed ideological disputes between East and West, the two systems' ability to achieve peace and reform, democracy, and human rights. Beginning in 1984, SED comrades from the Academy of Social Sciences and members of the SPD's Fundamental Values Commission spent weekends together, which, on Eppler's initiative, soon led to stringent work. The goal was to present a dialogue paper with the totalitarian state party. On August 28, 1987, it appeared simultaneously in the SED's central organ, *Neues Deutschland,* and *Vorwärts,* the SPD's party newspaper, under the title "Der Streit der Ideologien und die gemeinsame Sicherheit" ["The Dispute of Ideologies and Common Security"]. The SPD opposed the CDU/CSU and FDP-led government, but also to the arms policy of US President Ronald Reagan and the NATO dual decision that its own Chancellor Helmut Schmidt had pushed.

In 1987, the Social Democrats celebrated themselves for the fact that the paper linked common security with the domestic demand for openness and the ability to engage in dialogue and that the SED recognized the principles of pluralist democracy with its signature. However, the SED leadership was as far away from this as before. It did not even think of a dialogue with its critics within the GDR but called them to order, unimpressed, and in a time-honored manner. Those in the GDR who read the text more soberly than the SPD comrades could also understand it as a promise of eternity for preserving the GDR, which disappointed many greatly. "Our hope cannot be for one system to abolish the other. It is directed to the fact that both systems are capable of reform, and competition between systems strengthens the will to reform on both sides." If there were to be reforms, then only within a defined framework that did not touch the system itself. The freedom of the East Germans and Eastern Europeans fell by the wayside for the primary goal, peace. Bahr followed up a year later: "There must be peace, even without a solution to the German question. The powers that be will not come to blows over a question that has become small."

Once again, the SPD feared any shaking of the status quo, as it had in 1980 with the Polish Solidarność movement. And once again, it preferred stability to breaking up the dictatorship. In 2014, it should come as no surprise that it also had little to do with the Ukrainian democracy movement.

Helmut Schmidt knew best in the quartet of vain old men. The policy of the West is based on a great error, namely that "there is one Ukrainian people, one national identity. In reality, there is Crimea, eastern Ukraine, and western Ukraine. And while Crimea is in any case only a 'gift' of Nikita Khrushchev to Ukraine, western Ukraine would consist largely of former Polish territories, all Roman Catholic. " By contrast, he said, eastern Ukraine, predominantly Russian Orthodox, was in the territory of Kyivan Rus, once Russia's heartland. Perhaps the former chancellor had followed Putin's speech in March 2014 on the celebration of the treaty on Crimea's affiliation with Russia a little too closely; in any case, he used its argumentation. The last census in Ukraine in 2001 says something quite different: 78 percent of the population say they are Ukrainian when asked about their nationality.

If one thing has undoubtedly happened, it is that no one has welded Ukraine together as a nation as much as Putin has.

Bahr is certain that Ukraine does not belong to the East and not to the West. "Ukraine is the terribly durable country through which the border between Latin and Orthodox Christianity runs. And it will remain so. (...) Ukraine cannot become a member of NATO." The American and Russian presidents would determine where it may sort itself out geopolitically in the future. Bahr's words make it clear that it is by no means only Putin who is wedded to thinking in terms of spheres of influence. The additional secret protocol of the Hitler-Stalin Pact, which became known only after the fall of the Iron Curtain, spoke of "spheres of interest." Are those who criticize the eastward expansion of NATO today, which does not allow sovereign states the free choice of an alliance, aware that they are still stuck in this totalitarian thinking in spheres of interest?

On March 18, 2022, Egon Bahr would have turned 100. On that day, the Russian war against Ukraine will be almost four weeks old, and even some SPD comrades will have realized by now that time has passed by the inventor of change through rapprochement. Change through trade is not a recipe for eternity, nor can Germany, with its special relations with Russia, continue to achieve a balance of interests with Moscow. Unlike the Soviet Union, imperial, chauvinist Russia is not interested in preserving the status quo but rather in changing it.

In Willy Brandt's day, Germany's defense budget was a good four percent of the gross domestic product, more than twice as high as when SPD Chancellor Olaf Scholz took office. At that time, the Soviet Union could be sure that Germany's strength would not be neglected despite all the détente policies; on the contrary, soft power was possible because no compromises were made on defense capability.

German business in the interests of the Kremlin

In 2015, one can only marvel at how extremely short the memory of federal politicians is and how quickly they are willing to forgive and forget the Crimean annexation. In the fall, then Economics Minister Sigmar Gabriel flies to Moscow. His trip begins on October 18. Germany and Europe are in a state of emergency as over a million people flee to Europe from the war in Syria. In their wake are Afghans, Pakistanis, and migrants from various African countries. The initial welcoming culture tips over. Asylum seekers' homes are attacked, and a xenophobic mood spreads. Angela Merkel's "We can do it" is not taken as an incentive by everyone. The Moscow propagandists, who seize on and additionally fuel every controversy in Germany, are spreading the so-called Lisa story. According to this story, Syrian asylum seekers raped a German girl. Nothing about it is true; the story is a lie, as it later turns out.

The Kremlin is exploiting the explosive potential of the asylum issue in the EU. Poland and Hungary are at loggerheads with Germany and Brussels because they refuse to accept new arrivals, many of whom are Muslim. Warsaw and Budapest accuse the German government of not being asked for its opinion in advance. Germany has decided over their heads that the refugees are allowed to come, so Berlin is to cope with the onslaught independently. Moscow, incessantly on the lookout for such cracks in the Western wall, has become a master at finding and exploiting even the smallest, most subtle ones. Everywhere, the corrosive propaganda hooks in to sprinkle salt in open wounds. This is also the calculation when Putin's henchman Lukashenko sends migrants from Belarus to Poland, Lithuania, and Latvia in 2021. It does not succeed in destabilizing the situation because the EU has finally realized that this is precisely the Kremlin's intention.

The war in eastern Ukraine almost completely disappears from the radar of politics and the media during the refugee crisis in 2015. It is almost lost in Germany that Vice Chancellor Gabriel, in

Moscow of all places, speaks out in favor of the gradual lifting of sanctions, which had only been imposed at the beginning of the year following the annexation of Crimea and the occupation of eastern Ukraine. The Minsk Agreement of February 2015 has by no means been implemented. For that to happen, Ukraine would have to be able to control its border with Russia again, which it is a world away from doing. With his willingness to compromise, the Social Democrat is stabbing Kyiv in the back. This backtracking is unfriendly even toward the chancellor, who helped negotiate the Minsk Agreement for 17 hours. Or perhaps not? Is her vice chancellor on a mission to coordinate with her? After all, Gabriel is meeting the Russian president in Moscow, which would actually be the boss's business. It is about Nord Stream 2, two additional pipes through which even more natural gas is pumped from northern Siberia to Western Europe. At his meeting with Vladimir Putin at his residence in Novo-Ogaryovo, Gabriel plays the role of Schröder. Like the former chancellor Schröder he lacks any distance when he asks the Kremlin chief and warlord for an autograph for a dental assistant Oksana, who works in his wife's practice. He combines his request with a declaration of surrender: "If you look back into the past, into the year 2000, it is not at all clear why our two countries developed in completely different directions."

The annexation of Crimea was less than a year and a half ago. There is no end in sight to the war in eastern Ukraine. It claims lives daily. Regardless, the German vice-chancellor Gabriel is pushing the next major German-Russian project. Another affront to Ukraine and the Eastern European member states in the EU. Germany had already antagonized all of them with Nord Stream 1, the first direct pipeline from Russia to Germany. Warsaw, in particular, resisted the project, fearing that the Yamal pipeline on Polish territory could also become superfluous. Moscow's main concern is transit through Ukraine, which it would like to end sooner rather than later.

Officially, because the gas pipes and the stilts on which they stand are ready for the scrap heap, Gabriel is pro forma in favor of renovation or renewal, but this is no more than lip service for Kyiv, given the new German-Russian project worth billions of Euros. The

SPD slogan "change through trade" takes on a whole new meaning for the Ukrainian government: the change forced by the Germans will stop Ukrainian trade. They are to be squeezed out of the gas business and are accordingly worried about their income from transit fees. These amount to around two billion US dollars annually. But something else is even more important to Kyiv than the money: Ukraine will not be destroyed as long as Russia needs the pipeline. So for Ukraine, it is a kind of life insurance. This is an argument that the German government ignores. It is not being heard at all in Berlin.

Frank-Walter Steinmeier and Sigmar Gabriel are Schröder's most important allies in Angela Merkel's cabinet, says Christoph Heusgen, who was her foreign policy advisor until 2017. The chancellor gives both ministers in her cabinet a free hand. Even her decision in 2005 was difficult to comprehend when she embraced the Schröder-Putin Nord Stream 1 project. The first two pipes end in her Vorpommern-Rügen-Vorpommern-Greifswald I electoral district. This is exactly where the Russian natural gas arrives. Now a third and a fourth pipe are to follow, which are unnecessary for the security of supply and only put more money into Russia's coffers.

The fact that the objections of Ukraine and the transit countries of Poland and Belarus have once again received scant attention is leading to criticism at home and abroad. Members of the Bundestag are demanding that the government disclose a list of all meetings between representatives of both sides, politics, and Nord Stream 2. According to this list, between January 2015, and October 2017, there were 62 gatherings in which Ministers Gabriel and Steinmeier or the German ambassadors in Brussels and Moscow met Nord Stream 2 representatives. Speaking to the *New York Times*, former Social Democrat Economy Minister and later Foreign Minister Gabriel said that he came together with representatives of Russia and Gazprom during this period to "avert a threatened cutoff of Russia's supplies to Ukraine." How many times he conferred with Kyiv on the matter is unknown. Gabriel threatened the newspaper: "If you put my visits and meetings in Russia in a different context, I would like to inform you now that I will take legal action." That sounds nervous. Gabriel has to deal with one partner in particular.

It is Matthias Warnig. The ex-Stasi man is considered the most important German in Russia, even more important than Gerhard Schröder. Putin awarded him the "Order of Honor" in 2012. Matthias Platzeck also joins the group of Russia lobbyists after the end of his political career. For six months, he succeeded Schröder as SPD chairman. After resigning as party leader due to illness, he resigned again as minister-president of Brandenburg in 2013 for health reasons. But only shortly after leaving politics, he took over the chairmanship of the German-Russian Forum, which is much more homogeneous in composition than the Petersburg Dialogue, because critics of the Russian leadership have no place in the Forum from the outset. This is a policy that the supposed bridge-builder, Platzeck, is continuing. Platzeck appears conciliatory and understanding on the outside, but he sorts things out behind the scenes. Whether from social organizations or journalists, critics of Russia are neither invited to the Forum's events nor granted interviews. The message is unmistakable: they want to keep to themselves. Platzeck is a prominent guest at the first "Russia Day," launched in Mecklenburg-Western Pomerania in 2014 by his ex-minister president colleague Erwin Sellering. Nord Stream AG is the main sponsor of Russia Day, and former Chancellor Schröder will speak at the opening.

Matthias Platzeck made a name for himself as a new Russian lobbyist in a flash. In 2014, he demanded that the annexation of Crimea be settled retroactively under international law. All the spotlights were on Platzeck. The SPD man defied Ukraine, the EU, and the West by being prepared to support Russia's expansion with "financial benefits, a referendum rerun under OSCE control, and more." The new Kremlin friend back peddled somewhat when protests arose in his party. Now it no longer has to recognize the annexation of Crimea, which is against international law, the Crimea problem must be settled between Moscow and Kyiv under international law—this is the only way to solve blockades. He justifies his proposal by saying that he wants to finally take a step forward in the entire crisis and not let a regional conflict become a conflagration.

The damage to the SPD is obvious. Niels Annen warns that a subsequent recognition of the annexation would set a precedent with destabilizing effects far beyond Ukraine. However, anyone who thought that Germany would hold back on such demands in the future after Platzeck's advance has been proven wrong. Putin supporters can be found even in the highest ranks of the Bundeswehr. Kay-Achim Schönbach, vice admiral and inspector of the German navy, even outed himself as such in January 2022. "What Putin really wants is respect. And — my God — showing respect to someone (...) costs nothing. So, if you would ask me: it's easy to even give him the respect he really demands — and probably deserves." While the EU has been struggling for its credibility and cohesion for years, a German general, of all people, is giving up on Crimea: "The Crimean peninsula is gone, it won't come back, that's a fact." Like Schönbach, Gregor Gysi sees it, understanding that Ukraine is outraged, but, "Nevertheless, the admiral is of course right that Crimea will not return." The general, a devout Catholic, sees Russia as a Christian country and considers China to be by far the greater threat. Russia is needed against China, he said. Pure wishful thinking! Why should Russia join the side of the West? The two dictatorships are closer today than before the Russian war of aggression, and both regard the West as their enemy.

Schönbach is also backed by the former Inspector General of the German Armed Forces, Harald Kujat, and the two AfD members of the Bundestag, Rüdiger Lucassen, and Joachim Wundrak. Schönbach says what many realpolitik politicians know, says the retired general. The two right-wing extremists also have a lot of empathy: "Moscow sees the eastward expansion policy of NATO and the EU as a threat. Now it is a matter of self-confidently staking out one's own interests while at the same time respecting legitimate Russian security needs."

So much applause from the far left and the far right cannot be surprising when even former Foreign Minister Frank-Walter Steinmeier and other SPD foreign policy experts are calling for the gradual scaling back of sanctions against Russia even before they have been in place for a year. Rolf Mützenich believes that the sanctions are not an end in themselves and should therefore be gradually lifted when the ceasefire in eastern Ukraine is observed and other conditions are met. Steinmeier was already worried in December 2014—when the Minsk peace negotiations were not even in sight—that Russia would be destabilized if Europe did not ease the sanctions.

As foreign minister, Steinmeier should have known better: The economic restrictions had been imposed primarily because of the annexation of Crimea, which was illegal under international law, not because of the war in eastern Ukraine. In Kyiv, Steinmeier can be heard singing Putin's song and concluding one thing above all: the Germans cannot be relied upon. They are only tying themselves more closely to Russia.

In 2015, Merkel allowed important infrastructure in Germany to fall into Russian hands when BASF sold all its gas storage facilities to Gazprom in exchange for shares in a natural gas field in Siberia. A quarter of Germany's storage facilities now belong to a Russian state-owned corporation. The German government has no intention of setting up a strategic German natural gas reserve along the lines of the petroleum reserve. On the other hand, the chancellor is not considering easing sanctions against Russia at any time. She gathers the EU member states behind her every six months and organizes the extension. But she counteracts her sanctions policy by waving through the Nord Stream 2 project in 2016. For years, the chancellor has repeatedly fobbed off critics with the same sentence: this is a purely private-sector project in Germany's interests.

She knows better than anyone that she will not convince anyone. Many, not only in her party, feel dumped. They do not understand why the Christian Democrat is brushing off her partners' fears, putting EU cohesion at risk, and throwing to the wind the warnings of one-sided energy dependency that are also coming from the United States. The usually so deliberative head of the cabinet is in neutral gear. Nor does she intervene when Schröder arranges the oil refinery sale in Schwedt to the Russian oil giant Rosneft, for which he has been on the board since 2017. The deal will be signed and sealed in November 2021. The largest deployment of troops on the Ukrainian border is taking place then. Kyiv is more than nervous about this, but Berlin is obviously not. On the contrary, it allows yet another piece of Germany's economy to fall into Russian hands. In Mecklenburg-Western Pomerania, they have gone even further.

Russia Day and climate foundation

Nowhere else in Germany has the Russian state-owned Gazprom company spread its wings as much as in Mecklenburg-Western Pomerania. "Russia Day" is a major event for business and politics that has been held every two years since 2014 and for which the Schwerin state government does not even have to dig deep into its coffers. The so-called "Entrepreneur Days: Russia in Mecklenburg Western Pomerania" are mainly financed by the companies that profit from Nord Stream. Gascade in Lubmin, for example, connects the Baltic Sea pipes with the pipelines. Gascade is a subsidiary of Wiga Transport Beteiligungs-GmbH, which Gazprom and Wintershall Holding own. The port of Rostock and Mukran Port near Sassnitz on the island of Rügen, both economically linked to Nord Stream, also give money to the economic event. It is also part of the tradition that the Gazprom-Russia Days, because that is what they are really about, are always honored by top SPD politicians.

In 2016, then-Federal Minister of Economics Sigmar Gabriel delighted entrepreneurs and lobbyists with his demand that Russia sanctions be gradually dismantled, as he had done in Moscow in 2015. Two years later, Thomas Oppermann will be there, the head of the SPD parliamentary group. Matthias Warnig, who, until the end of the GDR, was a captain in the Ministry of State Security, is a regular participant and most recently Deputy Head of Department Five of Division XV of the MfS District Administration Berlin — now "Managing Director of Nord Stream 2 AG".

Erwin Sellering, at that time prime minister of the extremely structurally weak federal state of Mecklenburg-Western Pomerania, hopes that Nord Stream will help him pass the final torch. That is how development aid goes *pa Russki* [so Russian]. In political parlance, he says: "In recent years, the economy has been one of the pillars of relations between Germany and Russia," a euphemism for the fact that the Russian state economy has captured the German northeast. Manuela Schwesig also holds fast to the tradition of Russia Day, as Erwin Sellering places his co-offices in her hands in 2017, that of prime minister and that of SPD chairman. Matthias Platzeck will again participate in the next regular meeting in October 2018, but no longer only as chairman of the German-Russian Forum, but also as a recipient of the Order of Friendship, which had been presented to him a few days earlier by Foreign Minister Sergei Lavrov on the instructions of President Vladimir Putin.

Platzeck, Sellering, Schwesig, Schröder, and, in their shadows, Warnig are pursuing a kind of sideline foreign policy. Angela Merkel does not put her foot down but defends the superfluous new gas pipes, albeit not very emphatically.

Does she not have to assume that Putin understands this continuation as a sign that he is not even threatened with serious consequences for a blatant violation of international law? The German interest in clarifying these wrong decisions is noticeably low, perhaps because all political forces are somehow involved in the dilemma, even the Greens, although they are the only ones who have always kept their distance from the Kremlin and Nord Stream. But even they prefer not to ask so loudly because they want to save the environment and push through the nuclear phase-out and, later, the coal phase-out at all costs.

In search of a reason why Merkel always stuck to Nord Stream 2 but did not really explain this, it is worth looking at March 11, 2011. In Japan, the Tohoku earthquake occurs in the afternoon, shortly before three o'clock. It begins more than 30 kilometers under the sea and triggers a tsunami just under 400 kilometers east of Tokyo. The waves tower ten meters high. They were smaller and less violent in 1960, 1933, and 1896. The wave that hits the Fukushima nuclear power plant site is as high as 14 meters. Japan, considered the country with the best tsunami protection system, has to watch many of its important coastal protection structures being washed over. The tidal wave destroys the seawater pumps at the Fukushima Daiichi nuclear power plant. The diesel generators of the emergency power supply are also no longer able to withstand the tsunami and thus produce no energy for cooling the reactor units, which have now been shut down, and the decay pool. The cooling water evaporates in two reactors, causing explosions that release radioactivity, which the wind carries to the Pacific Ocean. Eleven reactor units in four power plants are shut down. News of the triple catastrophe—earthquake, tsunami, nuclear power plant disaster—reaches Germany in the morning hours. The news broadcasts are full of reports of giant waves on the east coast of Japan. Over 20,000 people are killed, and over 200,000 evacuated. Many buildings are damaged, as are roads, rails, and bridges, and even the top of Tokyo's tower is bent. The power goes out. Although the nuclear catastrophe occurs on the other side of the world, it immediately awakens all the familiar fears in Germany. The black-yellow federal government comes under pressure to act because the CDU/CSU and FDP have overturned the nuclear phase-out of the previous red-green government only six months earlier. Greens and Social Democrats see their 2001 nuclear phase-out plan confirmed because they had always justified it with the lack of nuclear waste repositories and, since Chornobyl, a lack of safety.

After the opponents' victory over nuclear power, the economy had just, of necessity, come to terms with the nuclear phase-out. Then black and yellow decided to phase out nuclear power. But now the chancellor surprises with yet another about-face. The reactor accident in Fukushima transforms the level-headed scientist into an ad hoc politician. Angela Merkel, of course, has other reasons for this change of heart. Even if there are continents between Fukushima and Stuttgart, it is clear that from now on the Japanese disaster will be the main topic for the state elections in Baden-Württemberg in two weeks. In Rhineland-Palatinate, March 27, 2011, and one week later in Saxony-Anhalt. But the first of the three, in CDU's home state, is particularly important because it is in danger of being lost to the CDU/CSU.

During the election campaign, top candidate Stefan Mappus clearly positioned himself in favor of longer operating times for nuclear power plants, which now seems out of step with the times. The CDU leader Merkel has very fine sensors for the moods of the electorate. That is why she is sensitive to the reactivated nuclear fears of most Germans; however little she probably shares them herself. After all, as a physicist, she has by no means demonized nuclear power in the past. Merkel's solo act so close to the elections triggers criticism and astonishment. Her Environment Minister Norbert Röttgen cannot follow her lead, and abroad, too, she is mainly met with incomprehension. Is Germany in an earthquake zone? Is there a latent tsunami danger? Her reaction seems to many to be exaggerated. But for the time being, her calculations are working. The CDU becomes the strongest party in Stuttgart in 2011. However, it is three votes short of a majority with the FDP, so the Greens, who come second for the first time, win. In Baden-Württemberg, a green-red coalition governs for the first time in the state's history.

The end of nuclear energy use has already been decided. On March 14, the German government decided to take the seven oldest nuclear power plants off the grid and shut them down. In 2021, 14 power plants will be shut down, and the remaining three will cease operation at the end of 2022. It happened in the spring of 2023.

In 2011, the first Russian natural gas will also come from Vyborg to Lubmin through the pipeline on the seabed. Instead of nuclear power, gas is increasingly used as transitional energy. Since the pipes are being laid deep in the sea, only a few special ships can be seen on the surface of the huge construction site, and the large-scale project always disappears from view. Almost unnoticed, the first plans for Nord Stream 2 began in 2013. The following year, the grand coalition passes the Renewable Energies Act. By 2035, 60 percent of energy is to come from renewable sources.

At the end of 2015, just a few weeks after Sigmar Gabriel had spoken to Putin in Moscow about Nord Stream 2 and Horst Seehofer had given Angela Merkel a 13-minute lecture on upper limits for immigration at the CSU party conference, which the chancellor listened to on stage like a schoolkid, the Paris climate conference was taking place. There, it was decided to limit global warming to well below two degrees and to phase out coal by 2030. In political circles in Berlin, the abandonment of fossil fuels is being discussed solely from a climate perspective. The ever-increasing dependence on Russia that goes hand in hand with this does not play any role at all. Objections are immediately dismissed by pointing out that Russia is at least as dependent on fossil fuels. Moscow, after all, would need the export revenues. The question is not discussed. Gas is flowing, and it is cheap. The industry considers sun and wind to be uncertain canonists and fears supply shortages if, after nuclear power, coal-fired power is also to be eliminated. The plans for renewables are correspondingly unambitious. Nord Stream 1 and soon Nord Stream 2 are Merkel's assurance that the country and its economy will have enough energy. As chancellor with the authority to issue directives, she does not want to be held responsible for a possible power blackout.

Presumably, she would not have wanted to see what Robert Habeck, the federal minister of economics and climate protection, would have to prepare the country for just six months after the 2021 parliamentary elections, should Putin turn off the gas tap or the coalition finally agree to a boycott. By declaring an early warning stage, the green realist has installed a crisis team of authorities and energy suppliers in his ministry, which must determine in an emergency who will no longer receive gas and in what order. Feeling responsible for the security of supply of an industrialized country like Germany is actually a legitimate motivation. Merkel could explain that. Instead, she fobs off the public repeatedly with the platitude that Nord Stream 2 is a commercial project. The noise from the Germans amuses the gentleman in the Kremlin:

"You don't want nuclear power? No gas? What do you want to heat with then? With wood? But for wood you have to go to Siberia, too." Supporters of Nord Stream and those friendly to Russia are also in other parties. They do not waste a thought on the consequences of cozying up to Putin for Ukraine.

In the 2017 Bundestag election campaign, reproaches hailed from all sides when Christian Lindner proposed accepting the Russian annexation of the Crimean Peninsula for the time being. Wolfgang Kubicki, FDP member of parliament and then vice president of the Bundestag, declares in 2018 in a tone of deep conviction that Nord Stream 1 has not done any harm and Nord Stream 2 will not do so either. The losses suffered by Kyiv and Warsaw do not count. If Kubicki had his way, the sanctions regime could be ended step by step. For he sees "with great concern that NATO needs an enemy again, firstly to justify its own existence and secondly for Mr. Stoltenberg to be able to implement his idea of spending two percent of gross domestic product on armaments." The liberal offers clear orientation difficulties in locating allies and opponents. He sees the latter in the US, in the form of 39 US senators "who come from fracking [hydraulic fracturing] states and promote the idea that American gas should be processed in Europe." They are linking this quite dishonestly with political attacks and economic sanctions.

Despite all objections from Kyiv and the Eastern European capitals, the pipes will be laid on the Baltic Sea floor in 2018 as a silent construction activity if disputes do not break out in the EU with each new stage. The pipeline has a far-reaching destabilizing effect. The EU Commission, Parliament, and European Council have opposed its construction from the start because it contradicts the goal of diversifying supply sources, routes, and suppliers and undermines climate targets. The Russian pipes also provoke trouble with the US, which advises less dependence for security policy reasons and — quite selfishly — wants to sell its fracked gas in Europe. The Committee on Eastern European Economic Relations [Ost-Ausschuss der Deutschen Wirtschaft] even sees the sanctions and blockade attempts by the US, which are increasingly shrill under President Donald Trump, as a threat to the democratic processes in Germany and Europe.

Putin can feel like a winner all the way because he has achieved one of his goals: he has divided the West. He does not need a united European and transatlantic community. He benefits from dissenters, especially when they come from the middle of society, allowing themselves to be harnessed to his agenda. Prime Minister Manuela Schwesig, for example, still rejects any political pressure on the Nord Stream 2 project when Russian opposition activist Alexei Navalny is poisoned with the chemical agent Novichok. On the day of the assassination, she attends a works meeting in Mukran and, while calling for the crime to be investigated, immediately qualifies that it should not be used to prevent the Baltic Sea pipeline. "We are close to completion. Germany needs this energy supply, and the federal government must not allow American politicians to threaten German jobs." *Druzhba* – Friendship!

In Schwerin's Schlossstrasse, people are annoyed by the interventions from the US. The state government finds that they are becoming increasingly foul-mouthed under Trump. Several US senators openly threaten German construction companies with sanctions. The Kabinett chief and her predecessor seek a solution before the punitive measures kick in. A way out is found with the help of Nord Stream 2. Schwesig proposes to the state parliament that a *foundation for climate and environmental protection MV* be set up, with former state premier Erwin Sellering as chairman, who, like Matthias Platzeck, left office for health reasons and now works as a Russia lobbyist. Sellering is virtually a specialist in the field, having already founded an association, the Deutsch-Russische Partnerschaft e.V., of which Nord Stream spokesman Steffen Ebert is also a member. On January 7, 2021, the parliament decides with the majority of SPD, CDU, and Left Party to create this state-owned foundation. At the time of the vote, the deputies do not know that it was set up on the initiative of Nord Stream 2 boss Matthias Warnig, who proposed the idea to Schwesig as early as August 2020, i.e., at the time of the attempted murder to Navalny. Members of the state parliament also did not know the actual purpose of the foundation, which was traded as a top secret. Nord Stream 2 explained in a secret classified document to the state government how the foundation could be used to circumvent possible US sanctions. Among other things, the foundation would use bogus employment relationships in which employees of the previous companies would be employed pro forma by the foundation but, in reality, complete the pipeline.

The state politicians acted "like a branch of Nord Stream 2 AG," summarized *Welt am Sonntag* on April 10, 2022, which first had to invoke the Freedom of Information Act to obtain the correspondence on establishing the state foundation from the State Chancellery of Schwerin. The papers show that Energy Minister Christian Pegel (SPD) and State Chancellery Head Heiko Geue were responsible for contract negotiations with Nord Stream 2. Both received regular instructions from a close associate of Warnig, Nord Stream 2's communications manager in Germany, who did not want to leave anything to chance, including the language used to present the foundation to the public. The state government even had to submit the press release wording to Nord Stream 2's PR representative in advance. On top of that, an employee of the PR agency in Berlin was to be allowed to secretly listen in on a press background discussion "in order to record statements as well as questions and answers." An official justification for continuing construction should read, "Russia has a far greater interest in the pipeline and thus remains amenable to German-Russian dialogue."

The new state foundation will have an initial capital of 20.2 million Euros. The state of Mecklenburg-Vorpommern is responsible for the two behind the decimal point, the 200,000 Euros. Nord Stream 2 AG is donating the hundredfold amount of 20 million Euros. Russia has pledged another 60 million Euros and Gazprom another two million Euros each for 20 years. Lots of money for environmental protection, the stated purpose of the foundation. "These 60 million are available exclusively for climate and environmental projects," assures foundation chairman Erwin Sellering. Publicly effective, children are allowed to plant trees, and a seagrass meadow research project is promised because the water plants can absorb carbon dioxide from the atmosphere and thus help to stop climate change. When asked, Erwin Sellering mentions the much more important task only in passing. "Of course, we also set up the foundation to finish building Nord Stream 2." With its help, raw materials and construction machinery will be delivered to Nord Stream, but the German companies involved will always remain hidden. Only the foundation appears in the public eye. Environmental associations speak of greenwashing because nature conservation is only a "fig leaf." Others are bothered by this deal because of the ongoing human rights violations in Russia. Tens of thousands of Russians are currently arrested and detained in the Navalny protests, which are taking place simultaneously as the foundation is being set up and sentenced in fast-track trials.

What the Schwesig–Sellering foundation planned could be called deliberate undermining of sanctions. Fortunately for those responsible, they were never imposed. Hardly anyone in Mecklenburg-Western Pomerania has given solidarity with Ukraine a second thought. No one in Schwerin is asking about the possible economic end for the Ukrainian pipeline.

Dangerous amateur historian
— Putin declares the unity of Russians and Ukrainians

Anyone talking to Ukrainians in the late summer of 2021 will sense their vulnerability. No wonder, given the gigantic Russian troop deployment on the Ukrainian-Russian border, the large-scale maneuvers in the immediate vicinity, and, above all, Vladimir Putin's ominous history article. Historians such as Sergei Kot and his colleague Tetiana Sebta in Kyiv or Polina Barvinskaya from Odesa understand the danger posed by the pamphlet and the extent to which the Kremlin ruler distorts historical facts. Putin's essay appears on the Kremlin's website in Russian and Ukrainian. "On the Historical Unity of Russians and Ukrainians" is the headline under which he presents his Ukraine doctrine, which includes familiar material from earlier writings.

Regarding radicalism, however, the treatise surpasses everything that has gone before. Putin denies the neighboring country the right to exist. He refers to the Soviet Union, with which all misfortune had taken its course. The following are the core messages of the amateur historian:

> The Declaration on the Union of Socialist Soviet Republics and later the constitution of the USSR of 1924 contained the right of the republics to freely break away from the Union. Thus, the most dangerous 'time bomb' was placed in the fundament of our statehood. It exploded when the security mechanism in the form of the supervisory role of the CPSU disappeared. A 'parade of sovereignty' began. On December 8, 1991, the so-called Belovezh Agreements on the Establishment of the Commonwealth of Independent States were signed, in which it was declared that 'the USSR no longer exists'. (...) It was the Soviet national policy that created a tripartite nation of Velikorussians, Lesser Russians, and Belarusians instead of a great Russian nation, which established the position of three separate Slavic nations — Russians, Ukrainians, and Belarusians — at the state level. (...) In 1954, the Crimean region of the RSFSR [Russian Federative Soviet Republic] was transferred to the Ukrainian SSR — a blatant violation of the law in force at the time. Ultimately, it does not matter what the Bolshevik leaders were guided by when they chopped up the country. One thing is clear: Russia was indeed robbed. Step by step, Ukraine was drawn into a dangerous geopolitical

game aimed at making Ukraine a barrier between Europe and Russia, a bridgehead against Russia. An 'anti-Russia' was needed, which we will never accept. And the most despicable thing is that Russians in Ukraine are forced to deny their roots and their ancestors and believe that Russia is their enemy. It is not an exaggeration to say that the course toward forced assimilation, toward the formation of an ethnically pure Ukrainian state that is aggressive toward Russia, is comparable in its consequences to the use of weapons of mass destruction against us. Such a crude, artificial separation between Russians and Ukrainians could decrease the Russian population by hundreds of thousands or even millions. (...) It is also logical that Ukrainian representatives have repeatedly voted against the UN General Assembly resolution condemning the glorification of Nazism.

With the protection of the official authorities, marches and torchlight marches are held in honor of the unharmed war criminals from the SS units. They threatened ethnic cleansing and the use of military force. And the residents of Donetsk and Luhansk took up arms to defend their homeland, language, and lives. After the pogroms that swept through Ukrainian cities, after the horror and tragedy of May 2, 2014, in Odesa, where Ukrainian neo-Nazis burned people alive, they staged a new Katyn. The supporters of the Banderists in Crimea, Sevastopol, Donetsk, and Luhansk planned the same massacre. (...) The coup and the subsequent actions of the authorities in Kyiv inevitably led to confrontation and civil war. The United Nations High Commissioner for Human Rights estimates the total number of victims related to the conflict in Donbas at over 13,000. (...) Terrible, irreplaceable losses. Russia has done everything to prevent fratricide.

Russia is open to dialogue with Ukraine and ready to discuss even the most complex issues. We respect the Ukrainian language and traditions. We respect the desire of Ukrainians to see their country as free, secure, and prosperous. I am convinced that real sovereignty of Ukraine is possible only in partnership with Russia. Our kinship has been passed down from generation to generation. It is in the hearts, in the memories of people living in today's Russia and Ukraine, and in the blood ties that unite millions of our families. Together we have always been and will be many times stronger and more successful in the future. Because we are one people. And I want to say one thing: Russia never has been and never will be 'anti-Ukrainian'. And what Ukraine will be, its citizens will decide

What did the author want to say to the world, especially his compatriots and Ukrainians, in about 20 pages? Putin suggests in his essay that the Soviet Communists broke up the unity of Greater Russians, Lesser Russians, and Belarusians and voluntarily gave up the great Russian nation, which did not secure its existence. Accordingly, Great Russians are the Russians, and Little Russians are the Ukrainians. Added to this is the assertion that Crimea was given away. It gives the impression that the West is forming an anti-Russia out of Ukraine, in which forced assimilation is taking place that is tantamount to the use of nuclear weapons. He attributes the 13,000 deaths in the war he instigated in eastern Ukraine to Kyiv. Putin's most important statement is: We are one people. With this statement, the Russian president makes the dangerous announcement that any attempt to separate Ukraine from Russia would be considered using weapons of mass destruction. All the declarations of intent in the text about dialogue, respect, sovereignty, and the Ukrainians' decision-making sovereignty no longer need to be explained. The Russian invasion of Ukraine on February 24, 2022, has created cruel clarity here.

Alarm bells are ringing in Kyiv following the publication of the article. Ukrainian Head of State Volodymyr Zelenskyy reacted to Putin's article in a written and video-read greeting message on the occasion of the 1033rd anniversary of the baptism of Kyivan Rus:

> Today we celebrate the Day of Baptism of Kyivan Rus — Ukraine. This is the official and, above all, historically just name of the holiday, which emphasizes the inseparability of the two states. Between Kyivan Rus and Ukraine lie a thousand years and a mark. In the text of the corresponding decree of the Ukrainian president, a bindestrich is put in between. And it is not only an interpunction symbol. It is a sign that Ukraine has inherited one of the most powerful states of medieval Europe. In its capital, today's Ukraine, the history of Christianity in Eastern Europe began when Grand Duke Vladimir of Kyiv baptized Kyivan Rus 1033 years ago. Kyivan Rus — Ukraine.
> It is not part of our history, it is our history. We do not have to prove it with historical treatises, works, and articles. Because our evidence is not on paper, but in metal, and in stone. Not in myths and legends, but in our cities and on our streets.

The Ukrainian Minister of Culture, Oleksandr Tkachenko, found Vladimir Putin's interpretation of history "not particularly original." In his opinion, the Russian tsars began to rewrite history. Zelenskyy, before making his written statement, first expressed surprise that the Russian president was doing historical research but did not have time to meet him, his Ukrainian counterpart. After all, he said, there was a ceasefire, prisoner exchange, or a peace treaty to discuss. Instead, history talks about times long past.

Ukrainian historian Polina Barvinskaya, a member of the German-Ukrainian Historians' Commission founded in 2015, is not only worried about the pamphlet's purpose but also afraid of it. For Russian Defense Minister Sergei Shoigu immediately made it compulsory reading in the military and political training of the army. Professor Barvinskaya teaches at the National I. I. Mechnikov University in Odesa. Her postdoctoral thesis on the instrumentalization of history during the period of National Socialism is of topical importance. That Russian soldiers should read Putin's so-called historical writing is typical of the system, she said, because totalitarian regimes use history to legitimize their actions. "It was the same in the USSR as in the Third Reich. General Secretary Stalin, after all, saw himself as a historian and linguist. And Vladimir Putin is a product of the Soviet era." The scientist recalls the Eastern European studies of the German historians Albert Brackmann and Hermann Aubin, whose brochures were distributed to Wehrmacht soldiers. Both were among the co-authors of a memorandum on the National Socialist policy of conquest and extermination in the East, which propagated the "repatriation of German people to the regained eastern provinces," the "removal of Jewry from Polish cities," and the "establishment of a closed German national soil in these areas."

Polina Barvinskaya takes issue with Putin's arbitrary and manipulative compilation of alleged facts. Many of them are untrue, such as the fairy tale, repeated a hundred times, that Crimea was a gift to Ukraine from General Secretary Nikita Khrushchev. "At that time, Crimea had acute water, and electricity problems, as it does today. The Supreme Soviet of the USSR decided Kyiv should take care of Crimea. And thus it belonged to Ukraine. At some point, people started to present it as Khrushchev's gift to Ukraine. But no document of that exists."

Russian author Sergei Lebedev has long since written his novels from abroad to be on the safe side. They thematize the structure of the multi-ethnic state of the USSR and the aftermath of Soviet totalitarianism. In an interview for Deutschlandfunk on July 18, 2021, a scene from kindergarten in the mid-1980s comes to mind. "At a party, we children represented the different Soviet republics.

I was Russia because I was tall and blond. Everything national was promoted in a strictly Soviet manner. As soon as a nation broke away, it was whistled back. When the Soviet Union collapsed, the friendship of nations ended, and all the conflicts that had been frozen until then immediately came to the fore."

Putin has called the disintegration of the USSR the greatest tragedy of the 20th century, but in their nationality politics, the tsars, who brutally subjugated the peoples, are much closer to him than the comrades. Sergei Lebedev points out that in his essay, Putin denies the existence of Ukraine—as a state, country, nation, and people. "This is an absolutely aggressive undiplomatic action based on a very dubious interpretation of history." The writer believes it is entirely possible that Lithuania, Latvia, or Estonia could become the subject of similar Putin articles, presumably with reference to their shared Soviet years. They have gone down in the historic memory of the Baltic States as a time of occupation.

Putin is not concerned with history but with politics. Volodymyr Fesenko, head of the Kyiv Center for Political Studies Penta, reads the Russian president's July 2021 message as a declaration of war:

> If Putin himself draws our attention in this way, it means at least a new Cold War, a thorough ideological and propagandist offensive in which the article is to be the basis, the main argument. Obviously, we are being targeted. The Russian president does not recognize the borders of 1991, as the Soviet Union collapsed. He has already justified the annexation of Crimea with that. But if he comes up with it again now, it can be understood as a justification of new territorial claims, a new aggression. So, of course, there are fears

Blank spaces
— Stalin's terror and the unknown holocaust

The fact that Ukraine was never a separate state, as Putin claims in his essay "On the historical unity of Russians and Ukrainians" in July 2021, is already not true. On January 26, 1918, Ukraine declared its independence. It formed its national consciousness at the same time as other European countries, such as the successor states of the Habsburg monarchy. At that time, Russia was not a nation-state but a multi-ethnic empire. Much cited by Putin, the Kyivan Rus did not lead straight from the Middle Ages to today's Russia; it was a multi-ethnic entity consisting of Eastern Slavs, Vikings, Balts, and other ethnic groups.

After the October Revolution of 1917, the tsarist empire was initially in chaos. This was an opportune moment for Ukrainian nationalists to break away and found their own state. Everything Ukrainian is suddenly in vogue. Especially the language. Speaking Ukrainian, even teaching it, had been forbidden by a succession of tsars. Alexander I ruled in 1804: Ukrainian is not a language but a dialect. (If that were true, Spanish would be a dialect of French.) His successors, Alexander, and Nicholas II, also upheld the strict Ukrainian language ban, rightly sensing that a nation identifies itself through language. Ukrainians were taught Russian in school.

Ukrainian peasant children did not understand this language well, so they could not follow the lessons. This led to analphabetism. Those who spoke Russian made a career in the tsarist empire. Without a tsar as head of state, the Ukrainian language experienced a revival. Dictionaries were printed. Taras Shevchenko, the poetic Ukrainian peasant son and one of the first to write literature in Ukrainian, posthumously became a national poet and hero. But on February 9, 1918, only two weeks after the Ukrainian Declaration of Independence, the Red Army occupies Kyiv. The Soviets want to end the dream of Ukrainian independence before it becomes a reality. The few communist Bolsheviks in the Ukrainian capital receive powerful support from Moscow in fighting the nationalists. Anyone still speaking Ukrainian in public risks being killed. All Ukrainian symbols are destroyed, even street signs in Ukrainian. In the party, Stalin is in charge of nationality issues. He considers nationalism a distraction from socialism. Nationalism was especially strong, with many peasants, a thought that must already be worrying Ukrainian farmers.

In addition to Ukraine, Estonia, Lithuania, Livonia, Courland, Finland, and the Caucasus also became independent states between December 1917 and February 1918. Poland, which had been part of Russia until the end of World War I, becomes a separate state again after the Brest-Litovsk Peace Treaty. Moreover, Soviet Russia is forced to recognize the independence of Finland and Ukraine. The German Empire looks favorably on the breakaway countries because they must fear the reversion by Russia and could therefore turn to the German Empire as an ally. Consequently, the Germans help the Ukrainians to get rid of the Bolsheviks.

On March 1, 1918, German troops occupied Kyiv and advanced to the Donetsk region and Crimea. The Soviet Army is pushed back. Lenin, the revolutionary leader, is interested in Ukraine mainly as a granary. Kyiv is again occupied by Soviet troops in February 1919 and is given a Soviet government. Ukraine is to supply grain as much and as fast as possible because Petrograd, the city of his October Revolution, and many other regions in Russia are starving. Lenin's logic is that he who gives bread keeps power. He calls for confiscating all grain, including seed, which prevents the peasants from sowing the next crop. Grain production falls from 20 million tons in the tsarist era to eight million tons in 1920 and to just under three million tons in 1921.

In addition, there was a shortage of male workers in agriculture due to the First World War and the civil war after the revolution. The Council of People's Commissars established a food army, and Stalin demonstrated how to proceed in Tsaritsyn and its surroundings: Red Army soldiers rob traders in the city and peasants in the countryside of their grain; those who are robbed are tried by the Cheka secret police, which ends with mass executions. The method is too brutal even for Lenin. He had Stalin removed from

Tsaritsyn. In 1921, after the Polish-Soviet War, Poland, Romania, and Czechoslovakia divided western Ukraine among themselves.

The east becomes part of the newly founded Soviet Union. In 1923, the USSR adopts a constitution, which comes into force in 1924. The individual Soviet republics could theoretically withdraw from the Union, but from the beginning, they had no say in foreign, economic, and defense policy. Moscow calls the shots here.

In 1924, Lenin died of a second stroke. The cause of the 53-year-old's death was "cerebral sclerosis as a result of excessive intellectual activity." The "New-type party," an uncompromising functionary apparatus founded by Lenin that has monopolized all power in the state and thinks nothing of inner-party democracy, is without a leader.

In 1925, Tsaritsyn is called Stalingrad. Josef Vissarionovich Dzhugashvili, known as Stalin, won the power struggle to succeed Lenin.

In 1928, the Soviet government, which had already decided three years earlier to make the transition from an agricultural to an industrial country, launched the first five-year plan. It called for industrial production to increase by 20 percent each year. To achieve this goal, labor is needed. They come mainly from Ukrainian villages, not due to a recruitment campaign but because of collectivization, in which ten million peasants are driven off their land. The expropriated kulaks flock to the Donbas, where they are taken into the mining and heavy industries with a kissing hand. The peasants who do not voluntarily cede their land, farm, machinery, and livestock to the collective farm are forced to do so. Those who nevertheless resist are summarily deported. In the best case, they are deported to Siberian villages in sparsely populated areas, which they are not allowed to leave; in the worst case, the gulag awaits them. A kulak is a prosperous farmer; however, everyone is quickly considered a kulak, not only those who defend their property but anyone who says a word against the kolkhozes at that time, even if they are poor.

At the end of the collectivization of agriculture, most small farmers work as day laborers on foreign land with often less fertile soil. They must hand over their horses and cows — if they have not been slaughtered beforehand—and transfer their tractors to the national machine-tractor stations.

They no longer live in their houses but in communal barracks and are paid their wages in naturalia. After the forcible socialization of agriculture, only half of the pigs, cows, and horses, and only one-third of the sheep and goats, are still alive. In the now Soviet villages, the clocks tick completely differently. No church bell rings anymore because, little by little, they are all taken down, smashed, and melted down. Icons and liturgical utensils are confiscated and sent to a depot for one of the many anti-religion museums springing up, sometimes in a church. Most of the more than 10,000 closed places of worship are converted into movie theaters and warehouses or fall into disrepair. The priests often only have a future in production, and many are deported.

The hardship in the Ukrainian Soviet Republic is great. And it is mainly homemade. Because of collectivization, agriculture has collapsed so much that grain exports are out of the question. There is not enough food even for self-sufficiency. In 1921, during the civil war that followed the October Revolution, there was already a great famine. After the crop failure of 1924, the people starved again; in 1928, they were starving again. Industrialization has its price. Therefore, the most valuable art objects are gathered. Since all museums are already nationalized, confiscating the best pieces is not a problem, but accepting this action among the people is.

The Ukrainian art historian Serhij Giljarow offers bitter resistance against the art sellout. He defends the treasures of the Chanenko Museum in Kyiv. Gilyarov is a local celebrity. When he gives his lectures, the hall is always packed. The students love him, as dazzling as he looks: slim, well-groomed, with gray hair, "always shaven like an Englishman" because he always speaks freely, using a pointer, like a conductor, he is full of passion, inspired. He captivates his audience, infecting them with his enthusiasm for art. All the more so when he succeeds in making a sensational find for the museum in 1928. He made it in the Kyiv Lavra.

All the monks disappeared from the cave monastery, victims of the Red Terror. Ten years after the October Revolution, the monastery serves as an anti-religious museum with a depot for church art from the emptied places of worship. There the communists store crosses, liturgical utensils, cups, incense burners, and icons. In the Lavra, Gilyarov finds a panel almost two meters high and almost one meter wide. It is damaged and smeared. Under the dirt, he discovers a layer of paint. At first, he can hardly make out what is depicted on it. Two nudes that much is clear. On the left is a male, and on the right is a female — Adam and Eve. A diptych. He learns from a priest that it and many other valuable art objects were confiscated from the Trinity Church in Kyiv in 1927. The opponents of religion want to show it in the cave monastery as a deterrent example, as proof of the frivolous double standards of the priests, who would have secretly looked at the unclothed figures of Adam and Eve beforehand.

But Gilyarov makes another discovery in the double painting: under an old layer of varnish on the tree trunk, he uncovers a snake — with a comb on its back and a ring through its nose. The "Dragon." The signature used by Luke Cranach the Elder. The 41-year-old from Kyiv has unearthed a world-famous masterpiece. But in Bogdan and Varvara Chanenko's Museum of Western and Eastern Art — it is the third most important in the Soviet Union — the joy over the valuable Cranach diptych painted in 1556 lasts only a few weeks as The Politburo of the Communist All-Union Party under the leadership of General Secretary Josef Stalin has decided to sell abroad the most profitable Western artworks from the museums of the newly founded Soviet Union. The cash-strapped regime is so desperate for foreign currency that it has already sold Catherine the Great's tsarist crown. The tapered headdress, dating from 1762, weighed two and a half kilograms. In total, the Soviet government sold $250 million worth of tsarist jewelry. On November 6, 1928, Russian works of art from Leningrad castles and museums were offered for sale in Germany. The auction house Rudolph Lepke achieves the fabulous proceeds of 2,650,000 Reichsmark at the auction. Russian emigrants in Berlin are outraged to find their property among the paintings and precious objects. The police confiscate individual exhibits.

Initially, the Kyiv Museum is to contribute 20 paintings. Serhij Giljarow resists tooth and nail, acts, and raises objections. Ultimately, the museum had to give up only four works, but among them was the Cranach painting. The Bolsheviks speculate on the 30,000 rubles they want to earn with the 400-year-old work of art at the next auction. When they later auctioned it off in Berlin, it did not even fetch half that amount. The precious masterpiece changed hands for a mere 10,000 dollars. Because of the world economic crisis, the prices are in the basement. A large part of the art offered by the communist negotiators was returned to the Soviet Union unsold.

Russian works of art fetched only around 40 million rubles at auctions in Western Europe in 1929. Only one major industrial project could be financed with these funds. For the communist planned economy, this was a meager result, for the museums an irreplaceable loss. Gilyarov had to pay for his resistance. He is imprisoned because he is said to have had contact with foreigners.

As the work ethic in the collective farms falls, so do the yields. But the communist officials demand ever higher levies without regard to the summer drought of 1932. Stalin does not like the recalcitrant Ukrainians. They oppose the collectivization of agriculture, so they are punished. But he is even more greedy for Ukrainian grain, which he wants to turn into gold abroad. He ignores the misery in the agrarian republic caused by his policies. Officially, no one is allowed to say the word "hunger". In Germany, the newspapers are suddenly full of news of the Soviet food disaster, as British foreign correspondents in Berlin report what they have seen with their own eyes in the Soviet Union. Gareth Jones is one of them. The 28-year-old has boarded a train in Moscow for Kharkiv to investigate rumors of famine. He listens to dozens of farmers, not just Ukrainian "kulaks," the alleged scapegoats for hunger in the Soviet Union. He talks to them, always alone, in Russian, which is common in eastern Ukraine, and hears about their complaints about Soviet agricultural policies. He ends his talk at a press conference in Berlin on March 29, 1933, with a bitter final sentence: "May I conclude by congratulating the Soviet Foreign Ministry on its skill in concealing the true situation in the USSR? Moscow is not Russia, and the sight of the well-fed people there obscures the real Russia."

The fact that millions of people have died of malnutrition, especially in Ukraine, and that desperation has led to cannibalism is not said aloud by anyone in Ukraine who cares about their life. But in the meantime, it is obvious that in the Soviet Union, the food supply is not as good as it used to be.

Everything is going according to plan. In the Soviet Socialist Republic, hunger has reached dramatic proportions. *Delo*, the oldest Ukrainian newspaper published in Galicia since 1880, reported on February 14, 1934, that 140,000 Germans died of starvation in Ukraine, referring to the journal of the Union of German Ethnic Groups in Europe *Nation and State*. It presented the number of Russian Germans who perished in the various catastrophes of the Bolshevik period:

> Of all the Germans in Russia, 360,000 live in Ukraine. Of the 45,000 Germans who lived in the swamps of Volhynia, four percent died of hunger. The 70 000 Germans who lived near Odesa suffered far more losses. In the districts of Mariupol, Myko-Layiv, and Melitopol, with 100 000 Germans, ten percent died

In the Crimea, the famine was the worst. In both districts, where there were 25 000 Germans living in a large village five years ago, there are now barely 15,000. In the Donbas, where there is coal and factories, people are also starving, but the government has an interest in keeping these factories running so that the food supply is secure. Of the 12,000 Germans in the Artemivsk district, only five percent have died. In 1937, Stalin "purged" the party; millions were shot or imprisoned in camps. For years, the red terror covered the Soviet republics.

In a quarter of a century, Ukraine experienced, first, the denial of independence and, second, the starvation of almost four million citizens. There is a word in Ukraine for this killing by starvation: *Holodomor*. Third, the worst excesses of Stalin's terror were in people's bones. Ukraine had already suffered all these crimes of the Zaren Empire and the Bolsheviks when the Wehrmacht invaded the USSR on June 22, 1941.

At first, the German units were supposed to advance to Moscow. But then Hitler changed his mind and first occupied the whole of Ukraine. On September 19, the 6th Army of the Wehrmacht took Kyiv and fought a days-long encirclement battle with the Red Army, which cost the lives of about 600,000 people. But the killing continued. During the German occupation of Kyiv, 100,000 Ukrainian victims were buried in the Babyn Yar ravine on the capital's outskirts alone.

Ukrainian soil is full of mass graves from World War II, 2000 experts estimate. French priest Patrick Desbois, whose grandfather was killed in the Lviv region, is researching where exactly the many pits full of mortal remains are located. He came to western Ukraine in 2002 with a former prisoner of war. He told him that he had to work at the Lviv airport. There were many holes in the runway. Desbois wanted to know how they were filled. With Jews, the ex-prisoner told him. There are 49 mass graves in and around Lviv alone, the largest in the Lesinichi forest. In 1945, the bodies of Italians and Jews were burned there to cover up traces. Today there is a park on the site.

Desbois has made it his life's work to honor the dead. "The quieter we go, the more we talk to the people in charge on the ground, the more we achieve." One thousand seven hundred mass graves, each containing 500 to as many as 2000 dead, have been located thanks to Patrick Desbois' help. He and his volunteers interviewed more than 4000 inhabitants of Western Ukraine. Mostly historians, teachers, and sometimes students. Often people in the villages know that there is a mass grave, but not exactly where. Using scanners that measure soil density, which is lower in the earth that has been dug up and mixed with bodies, experts can accurately trace the boundary of a grave.

They are supported and supervised by Joe Shik and Maurice Herszaft, sent by the Committee for the Preservation of Jewish Cemeteries in Europe. The two rabbis with temple curls, long beards, and wide-brimmed hats travel from grave to grave. Their job is to prevent the dead from being treated in an undignified manner again and to ensure that they are buried in accordance with Jewish law.

The Holocaust, through mass shootings, is only gradually becoming known in Ukraine. With the end of the Euromaidan movement, attention began to be paid to these victims. Over the decades, it was almost forgotten where the mass graves were located; now, they are being identified as such.

For years, Marieluise Beck has not been at peace because crimes of this unimagined magnitude have not made it into European historical memory. "It concerns a huge area in Eastern Europe, a strip from the Baltic countries down to the Black Sea, the settlement area for the Eastern European Jews. There, the Shoa took place through shootings, during which towns and villages were systematically emptied of the Jewish population. Almost no Jewish family survived this. And thus, there are virtually no testimonies and no narratives." The Green politician would like to remember these hitherto little respected victims and erect monuments to them wherever possible. The former parliamentary state secretary and commissioner for foreigners and refugees has repeatedly left the political spaceship Bonn or Berlin and ventured to the scenes of various wars. She wants to understand better the victims fleeing to Germany so that she can help them more effectively.

Beck has a keen eye for the needs of others. In Bosnia, where a particularly large number of people suffer from eye injuries by snipers, she presented the doctors with a large box of glass prostheses from her hand luggage during a stay in Sarajevo in 1994 because they were in short supply in the civil war country. The war in the Balkans shook her basically pacifist attitude. Since the occupation of eastern Ukraine in 2014, she has been traveling to the contact line repeatedly. In the gynecology department of the Bilovodsk clinic near the front line, she learns in 2015 that many pregnant women are going into labor prematurely because of the fighting and that there is an increase in premature births. Back in Germany, she initiates an appeal for donations for an incubator for premature babies. But her understanding of effective help goes further. As early as May 2014, but even more so since the Russian troop build-up on the Ukrainian-Russian border, she has been advocating for arms deliveries. "To protect those who are under attack, military means are needed if necessary."

In 2013, under the impression of Russian allegations that fascists were dominating the protest movement on the Maidan, the Green Party campaigned for a German-Ukrainian commission of historians because it sensed the explosive potential of a shared history that had been little examined. The working group, formed in 2015 with equal representation, is dedicated to topics such as research into the First and Second World Wars in Germany and Ukraine, German occupation policy, and the Holocaust. It also focuses on the history of Ukraine under state socialism. From her work with the Russian human rights organization Memorial, which the Greens have supported for decades, Marieluise Beck knows how difficult these issues are in post-Soviet society. She raises her voice all the more frequently against the Russian government's repression of the NGO. At the

December 28, 2021, Memorial in Russia was dissolved by order of the Supreme Court. Beck and Ralf Fücks, her husband and co-founder of the joint think tank Liberale Moderne, protested: "Such a verdict is unthinkable without political directives from the very top. Authoritarian uniformity on the inside and an aggressive policy on the outside go hand in hand. What is needed now is a thorough assessment by the German government and the EU of the impact of the verdict against Memorial on German-Russian relations."

With her interventions as her parliamentary group's representative for Eastern Europe, the self-confessed Putin critic repeatedly caused trouble in Berlin's political establishment, so much so that even her own party did not even dare to discuss the idea of some CDU representatives proposing her as a candidate for the office of the first woman president. No one doubts that as Federal President, she would represent Germany in the best possible way on the international stage and stimulate important debates. But instead of sending the woman with the precise political compass into the race, the Greens and Christian Democrats chose the comfortable "business as usual" with the SPD. Everyone agreed on Frank-Walter Steinmeier, who had announced his renewed candidacy a year before the 2021 federal election when an SPD election victory seemed beyond anyone's imagination.

The Russian invasion of Ukraine was just a month ago, and Beck was traveling to Kyiv and, in May 2022, to Odesa. As in the capital, rockets are already hitting there, too. She has felt a particularly close bond with the port city on the Black Sea since 2014, visiting it countless times and forming close friendships, such as with Mikhail Saslavsky, who died in 2019, and Roman Schwarzman, whom she is now meeting again during the war. Schwarzman heads the Regional Association of Former Prisoners of the Ghetto and Nazi Concentration Camps. Saslavsky was an important contemporary witness, one of the few to survive the city's greatest tragedy.

In October 1941, Romanian soldiers, in collaboration with the Nazis, killed over 22,000 Jewish inhabitants of a port town. The Romanians initially imprisoned him, his family, and Jewish neighbors. When the Red Army blew up the headquarters of the Romanian and German occupiers during their retreat, the occupiers launched a retaliatory action. All Jews were taken away and herded in several columns to nine army ammunition depots, including Mikhail Saslavsky, who carried his frightened brother on his shoulders. At first, the little boy held on to him, but they were separated in the crush and under the kicks of the guards. They drove more and more people into the barracks and locked all the doors. They sent one hail of bullets after another from the outside through the wooden walls. Later, the Romanians set fire to the barracks. Walls and ceilings collapsed, and many escaped into the open, like the then 16-year-old Mikhail, who ran toward a cornfield. Behind him, he heard the volleys of guns and the screams as people fell to the ground dead. "There must have been hundreds, maybe 500, or even 800. Behind the field at the junction with the forest, I turned around, saw flames leaping up from the barracks. I fell to the ground, completely out of breath."

Saslavsky lost his mother, four siblings, an aunt, and many neighbors that day. The war was to last almost four more years. Nothing shook him later as a soldier, like the mass shooting in Odesa. "When I was fighting at the front, sometimes the images would suddenly come up again: the fire in the warehouses and in it my mother, sisters-in-law, my brother, aunt, and neighbors. All of them were burned alive." Like Mikhail Saslavsky, Roman Schwarzman spent his life in Odesa. If he were to draw a map of the city, it would look somewhat different from one for tourists. "Until a few years ago, eyewitnesses called me, some of whom observed crimes from their windows during the occupation. One described a massacre at the trolley bus stop and said: dig in the ground there. We know so many such places in Odesa and its surroundings. In Bohdanivka there were 54,000 Jews, in Domanivka 18,000, in Berezivka 12,000. The smell of people burning in the warehouses lingered for a month for miles around."

Today, the various Jewish communities in Odesa have around 5,000 members, only a quarter as many as in 1941; visible Jewish life is once again stirring in the southern Ukrainian city on the Black Sea. It flourished with the collapse of the Soviet Union and the independence of Ukraine. Julia Gris joined a liberal branch of Judaism in 1991. Her rabbi predicted that she would one day make a very good wife at the side of a rabbi. But Julia Gris wanted not only to marry but to become a rabbi herself. At the first memorial service in Odesa in October 2018, dedicated to the 22,000 victims of the munitions camp, she says the Kaddish.

The rabbi handles the prayer a little differently than usual. Unlike the Christian prayer of remembrance, the Kaddish does not contain the words mourning, regret, sorrow, or loss but the praise of God because death is a natural process in the Jewish faith. "However, it is something else if it was brought about by unnatural means. That's why I preceded the Kaddish with a prayer." Marieluise Beck did not leave it at the memorial service, also attended by the RathsChor from Bremen, where her constituency was. Bremen and Odesa have been twin cities for a long time. The Odesa Chamber Orchestra and the choir of the Hanseatic city opened the evening with Felix Mendelssohn Bartholdy's "Elijah" oratorio.

Next, a memorial is planned around the stone with the Star of David. There are garages and a playground nearby, which trees, benches, and stylized flames will join if Odesa survives the current war of Russia against Ukraine.

In many places in Ukraine, there is still no evidence of the Holocaust by bullets. But little by little, Ukrainian partners, the federal government of Germany, and the American Jewish Committee are inaugurating new memorials. Ulrich Baumann of the Memorial to the Murdered Jews of Europe Foundation observes that these changes are being met with a positive response. The first memorial to be inaugurated is in Rawa Ruska. In this small town near Lviv, no one has sung a Yiddish song for a long time. Boris Dorfman experiences this July 3, 2015, as a day of joy because, finally, some of his ancestors have received a dignified resting place, as far as this is possible, with a mass grave. No more tractors roll over the remains, and no more playgrounds or cultural palaces are built on the graves, as it happened for more than 70 years since 1945 in Rawa Ruska, Kyssylyn, Ostroschets, Prochid, Bachiv, and many other places.

Since the Second World War, only half the village of Kyssylyn is left. First, the Jews were shot, then in one service, 70 Poles. In other villages, Poles killed Ukrainians. The Nazis sowed discord among peoples and forced the population to collaborate.

The Germans have almost completely blanked out the Holocaust by bullets, but Ukrainians must also face it because collaboration is still an issue. Parliament passed a law in March 2022, a few days after the war began, that makes collaboration a punishable offense today. In 2014 locals cooperated with the Russian Army. The current government has drawn its conclusions from this. But the participation in the crimes of the Nazis, forced or voluntary, is still not readily talked about in Ukraine.

Volodymyr Kravchuk, a Kovel resident 200 kilometers north of Lviv, speaks out at the dedication of the memorial to the Jews murdered there. The former teacher is disturbed by the inscription on the memorial, which states that local forces were also involved in the mass murder. Ukrainians, he says, were not involved. "That was the Jewish police." An argument ignites because another visitor corrects Kravchuk: "The Germans didn't know who was Jewish. The local people here showed them." "Who?" asks the teacher. "Well, who do you think? The Ukrainians." After the Kaddish, the argument continues.

When talking about the involvement of the local population in the crimes, Anatoly Podolskyi warns us to be careful. The Holocaust expert does not deny collaboration but considers it inadmissible to speak of purely Ukrainian collaboration. In his opinion, it should be called Soviet collaboration. After all, Ukraine did not exist then, and Soviet citizens from other republics were also involved, not only Ukrainians. The new monuments fulfill their purpose: The discussion with history begins.

At the Euromaidan in Kyiv, red and black OUN flags were waved alongside many European flags. Few, but enough to recall an ominous past. The Organization of Ukrainian Nationalists was founded by Stepan Bandera, a nationalist who pandered to the German occupiers. Together with Einsatzkommandos 5 and 6 of Einsatzgruppe C, the Bandera Battalion participated in numerous mass shootings. In Lviv, they were also joined by a self-proclaimed Ukrainian militia and ordinary Ukrainians and Poles. Together they shot or otherwise killed some 20,000 Jews in a few weeks. Bandera's OUN wing and the Ukrainian underground army UPA also murdered some 100,000 Christian Poles because they wanted an ethnically cleansed territory as the basis for a homogeneous Ukrainian nation-state. Polish and Ukrainian nations participated in the crimes against the Jewish population. In up to 140 places in Western Ukraine, Ukrainians and Poles murdered between 13,000 and 35,000 Jews during the German occupation. And they also killed each other.

In Ukraine, the role of Bandera is either glorified or suppressed by many. That he fought against Soviet power is merit enough to revere him as a hero.

His name is particularly common in Lviv. No fewer than three streets are named after him, and there is also a monument in the city through which hundreds of thousands have fled since February 24, 2022. In the historical square around the town hall, the "Kryivka" has become famous. Kryivka means hideout and is the name of a pub that pays homage to the Ukrainian partisan movement. Before you can enter, you have to knock. Only then does a window in the heavy wooden door open, and a voice asks for the slogan *Slava Ukrajini*! [Glory to Ukraine!] The answer to this is *Herojam*

Slava! [Glory to the heroes!] This slogan goes back to Stepan Bandera. The Euromaidan movement adopted it in 2013 and thus also unsettled several Ukrainians.

Times of war are conceivably unfavorable moments for a differentiated view of history, which made the renaming of Moskovsky Prospekt in Kyiv to Stepan Bandera Prospect. In Kyiv, people have reacted allergically to everything Russian since the Crimean occupation, which is why the so-called decommunization law was passed. It was high time, as Vitali Nakhamovich of the Kyiv History Museum thinks. Finally, the Soviet symbolism, which until then no one had taken offense at, was being cleared up. He states calmly that Bandera is experiencing a renaissance. He is merely a symbolic figure for the resistance against the Soviet power and, thus, against Russia. Bandera himself had not participated in any crimes during the war; after all, he had served time in a concentration camp. That is an astonishingly lenient statement for a historian; like everything about the figure of Bandera, his imprisonment in a concentration camp is complicated.

In Lviv on June 30, 1941, the Ukrainians proclaimed an independent Ukrainian state alongside Hitler's Germany. This arbitrary act went much too far for the Nazis. They took Bandera into "honorable custody" in the Sachsenhausen concentration camp because they did not see the fanatical Ukrainian loyal to Germany as a mortal enemy. Bandera's defenders say today that there is no blood on Bandera's hands, all the more so on those of his fighters. After the end of the war, they organized fierce resistance against Soviet rule. In all this, Bandera's name was only on the flags, nothing more. Nakhamovich agrees that he should not be equated with his organization.

"Collaboration is when someone cooperates with the regime of the enemy. Bandera personally didn't do it. It was his organization."

The partisans, which included not only but also Bandera supporters, fought for an independent Ukraine until the 1950s. The Soviet power responded to this perseverance with brutal violence. It killed 150,000 Western Ukrainians and deported another 200,000 Ukrainians. The Soviet crimes contributed to a secret cult of heroes and victims around Bandera. In this context, it was certainly not insignificant that he died on October 15, 1959, shot dead in Munich by a KGB agent with a poison pistol. From his German exile, he had allegedly agitated against the Soviet Union's enslavement of Ukraine.

Many Ukrainians believe that Bandera is the lesser of two evils, so the outrage over the renaming of streets and squares is limited. The historian blames the Soviet power for far greater crimes than the Ukrainian nationalist. Bandera took up the fight against the Soviets and allied himself with the Nazis. He could not know where that would end. "Bandera is not my hero, nor would I have wanted to live in a state that Bandera established." Vitali Nachamovich experienced in Soviet times that a differentiated approach to the history of the 20th century can be impossible. Many people proud of their non-Russian nationality were defamed as a fascist at that time. The prospects for a new critical engagement with Bandera and the nationalists have not improved with the war, especially since Putin constantly brings up the name against Ukraine. Ukrainians are currently painfully experiencing the toxic effects of unquestioned narratives. Their struggle to come to terms with history is rarely discussed in this country. And even in the Federal Republic of Germany, many a misjudgment would not have been made if the past of the country in which Germans caused so much harm had been dealt with thoroughly.

One-sided consideration due to selective memory

Even in 2021, seeing Russia as a good partner is still a widespread attitude in Germany — not only in business but also in politics.
One man in particular stands for this position: Federal President Frank-Walter Steinmeier. He has shaped German policy on Russia longer than any German politician since the fall of the Berlin Wall: first at Gerhard Schröder's side as his head of the Chancellor's Office and inventor of the "modernization partnership with Russia," then as chairman of the SPD's parliamentary group, twice as foreign minister, and even now as Federal President, he has an enormous amount of creative leeway. Steinmeier sets the tone, ushers in phases of rapprochement with Moscow, and does not let human rights violations or a breach of international law stop him. He even brushes aside Germany's security interests if he has to. And he even ignores warnings that Russia is demonstrably becoming more and more threatening, not only for Ukraine but also for the Baltic countries and Poland. In June 2016, the foreign minister even qualifies NATO's need to strengthen the defense of its immediate border with Russia as "saber-rattling." He, of all people, who regularly takes part in the hours-long and inconclusive negotiations of the Minsk peace process and the Normandy format should have been aware of Russian aggression in the Donbas and criticized the maneuvers of NATO allies in Eastern Europe at the time, in which Germany itself was involved. Steinmeier instead calls for more dialogue and cooperation with Russia. "What we should not do now is to further inflame the situation by loud sow-belching and war-howling." History teaches us that.
Six months later, at the end of 2016, Steinmeier gives a speech at Boris Yeltsin University in Yekaterinburg, which had awarded him an honorary doctorate on a previous occasion. At this time, Russia supports the war in eastern Ukraine and fights in parallel to keep Syrian dictator Bashar al-Assad in power. After Russian bombardments, Aleppo in northern Syria resembles the Czech capital

Grozny in 1999. Russian forces also commit human rights crimes here, as civilians are again targeted and displaced. Meanwhile, Steinmeier asks the student audience in Yekaterinburg:

> When should we worry and when should we not? (...) Russia's military intervention [in Syria] came as a surprise to the West; we could not assess with what goals, with what means (...) and with what armament. Or let's take the Crimea: at the beginning there was no sign of the so-called "green men", and even later it was said that special forces had also been deployed. (...) I think it is important (...) to ask these questions honestly. And I'm sure there are also questions about German or European foreign policy from the Russian side.

The then-foreign minister walks on eggshells in order not to criticize the Russian Army and the Wagner mercenary force financed by the oligarch and Putin's friend Yevgeny Prigozhin too clearly – not for their actions in Ukraine or their deployment in Syria, which serves a ruler who has his people subjugated and tortured. Steinmeier says nothing wrong in Yekaterinburg but leaves out far too much. Nowhere does he really take a stand. There are no clear words of criticism at any point, but instead, a series of relativizations. The German foreign minister treats the Russian regime with kid gloves: "But all this is no reason to turn our backs on each other. On the contrary, it is all the more reason to make every effort not to lose or even alienate each other, but to seek dialogue, even if it has become more difficult."

It gets even trickier when, as in 2020, in his speech on the 75th anniversary of the liberation from National Socialism and the end of World War II in Europe, he invokes "Never again!" "This 'Never again!' means for us Germans above all: Never again alone! And this sentence is nowhere more valid than in Europe. We must hold Europe together." It is a reminder that his party, in particular, is studiously ignoring, especially regarding Nord Stream and Ukraine. Moreover, no one has thrown it to the wind as often as Steinmeier himself.

Then the federal president surprises the public, if not with insight, then with an admission. In the fall of 2021, he will travel to the small Ukrainian town of Koryukivka on the Ukrainian-Belarusian border. As head of state, he is out of current politics; this visit is about history. Steinmeier mentioned Koryukivka before in his speech on the 80th anniversary of the beginning of the war in the USSR on June 22, 1941. He held it in the Museum Berlin-Karlshorst, then called the German-Russian Museum Berlin-Karlshorst.

The Ukrainians reacted sniffily because they found a German-Russian museum for the commemoration of this anniversary inappropriate. In the meantime, the museum has renamed itself because it wants to remember all Soviet victims of the German war of extermination, regardless of their nationality. On the day of Steinmeier's speech, June 18, 2021, Ukraine once again felt that its independent history, detached from Russia, had been ignored. That is why the Ukrainian ambassador in Berlin, Andrij Melnyk, was upset about the venue. The flags of the successor states of the Soviet Union raised in front of the memorial were of no use.

So much for the back story; in Koryukivka, something very rare in German politics happens almost unnoticed. Steinmeier, who has already declared that he would like to be reelected as federal president, publicly draws attention to a mistake. In the small Ukrainian town, the Jewish inhabitants were first killed in 1941; two years later, in 1943, almost all the remaining 6700 people died. Given this number of victims, one might have heard of the place in Germany.

In Koryukivka, the tragedy was also kept quiet for a long time. It was only in recent years that people began to talk about it. A contemporary witness, Halina Popova, describes to the German politician how she survived the massacre as a six-year-old. Apart from Steinmeier, many children listen in the local school auditorium. Some of the girls and boys are the great-great-grandchildren of a few survivors from that time. The youngsters know the stories of fleeing and hiding in the swamps. They know what happened in 1943 and tell the guest from Berlin about it with selected politeness and that they would be happy about a monument in Koryukivka. Perhaps, with German help, it could be erected where the mortal remains, first buried in the gardens, were buried a second time.

In the evening, Frank-Walter Steinmeier repeated his confession in Kyiv. At the solemn commemoration of the 80th anniversary of the Babyn Yar massacre, he once again admits that Germans are too little aware that the human crime of the Holocaust did not begin in the German death factories of Auschwitz, Treblinka, Sobibor, Majdanek, or Belzec, but before that on the campaign of conquest toward the East. He asks, "Who in my country, in Germany, knows today about this Holocaust by bullets?" His public confession nourishes the hope of not repeating this past mistake. It testifies to a failure of the supposedly so thoroughly reappraised history of National Socialism when many German citizens still cannot make sense of even the name Babyn Jar. "There is no comprehensive reappraisal of the German war of aggression in Eastern Europe," Martin Schulze Wessel also makes clear. The historian of Eastern Europe at Ludwig Maximilian University in Munich is the spokesman for the German section of the German-Ukrainian Historical Commission

> We have of the Holocaust primarily the idea that it happened in concentration camps, in extermination camps. We have less of an idea that there was also the Holocaust by shootings, by bullets, which took place, for example, in Ukraine, in Kyiv. That is, our idea of the Holocaust is incomplete. (...) We have little understanding of the fact that (...) of course there was also a policy of extermination, which was directed primarily against Belarus and Ukraine. Also against Russia. But Russia was not occupied to the same extent as Belarus and Ukraine, where the German occupation was extensive, and the destruction was therefore much greater

159 Germans took part in the Babyn Yar massacre. On September 29 and 30, 1941, the occupying forces ordered all the Jewish men, women, and children from Kyiv to the ravine, then at Kyiv's gates, where they shot more than 33,000 people. Volodymyr Pronichev's mother almost died in the pit on the city's outskirts. She had accompanied her parents to Babyn Yar. She suspected disaster when she saw that people had to put their valuables on one pile and their clothes on another. She tore up her passport, which stated that she was Jewish, and showed only her trade union card and work paper, which did not state her nationality. Her married surname was Russian because Volodymyr's father was Russian. So she pretended to be a non-Jewish companion. It was useless because these persons were also to be executed before nightfall. What happened then, her

son Volodymyr listened to again and again. First from her personally, later in a documentary film about his mother. She says

> I closed my eyes and jumped under the shots. I fell on top of the bodies. Then the shots stopped, and the Germans came down into the pit, climbed over the bodies, and checked who was not dead yet. I kept as quiet as I could. Then it went dark. They shoveled sand onto the bodies. I understood that I was buried alive. At night I moved my left hand and felt that it was on the surface. Then I shoveled myself free that I could get more air. And finally I crawled back out of the earth over the bodies. It was pitch black. They were still firing down into the pit in the dark. On one side, I climbed up

Still at the ravine, she was discovered and arrested. She escaped not once but many times, jumped from a moving prisoner transport, hid in cellars and on rooftops, was caught again, and locked up in prison, where a German soldier helped her escape. Her husband, Volodymyr's father, was arrested by the Gestapo. He was supposed to say where his Jewish wife was. They were looking for her because they knew she had seen what happened in Babyn Yar. The father did not return home from the Gestapo prison. Volodymyr and his sister were placed separately in children's homes because they were no longer safe with their grandparents and friends. The mother's escape lasted two years. Only a few weeks after the liberation from the Germans that Dina Pronicheva found first her daughter, then her son. To this day, he admires his mother, a famous Ukrainian puppeteer, for her will to survive and her courage.

A year after the end of World War II, on January 24, 1946, her eyewitness testimony during a Kyiv trial caused a sensation throughout the Soviet Union. The defendants were Germans involved in Babyn Yar, who had been caught and sentenced to death. Dina Pronicheva publicly described how exactly the German massacre of the Jewish population of Kyiv had taken place. The film clip in which she was among the first to report on the Holocaust by firing squad can be seen in the Ukrainian capital's History Museum.

The fact that around two million Jews were killed by Germans with rifles in Eastern Europe is almost absent from the German culture of remembrance. The supposedly comprehensive reappraisal of the Nazi era has not yet focused on the thousands of Wehrmacht soldiers and members of the SS task forces involved in the mass killings. They returned home as perpetrators with the knowledge of their crimes from Poland, Belarus, Romania, the western parts of Russia, and Ukraine. The leaders are known by name, but not the individual shooters, each of whom alone destroyed hundreds of lives.

In the Soviet Union, these massacres were also hushed up, especially in small towns. Nobody was allowed to talk about them, and nothing was supposed to remind them of these victims. The fact that these people could not be protected would have diminished the victory in the Great Patriotic War. Thus, these traumatic events were forgotten because there was hardly anyone left who could tell about them.

For at least ten years, anyone can read about what happened in the Soviet "Bloodlands," as Timothy Snyder calls them. The historian lists precisely the German crimes committed in the regions against the various population groups. Unfortunately, German politicians, and society as a whole, hardly take notice of this meticulous research by the American author, which was bitterly avenged as of 2014. There, people in Germany thought they had to hold back on criticizing Moscow after the annexation of Crimea because, after all, German ancestors had done many bad things in Russia. Out of the frightening ignorance that the former Soviet Union is not only today's Russia, German policy sought for years a closeness to Russia that it denied to Ukraine. It turned a cold shoulder to the hundreds of thousands of Ukrainians who demonstrated their country's democratic path to the EU. The obliviousness to Ukraine's history is still shameful today.

More than just art theft
— the Nazi foray through Ukraine

Steinmeier's admission in Babyn Yar in the fall of 2021 that the Holocaust by bullets is not yet anchored in the collective German memory could build new mutual trust. But for that, Germany must turn to other, completely unnoticed chapters of its history in Ukraine. Because Putin denies that their country is a nation of its own, many Ukrainians have been remembering since February 24, 2022, that they were once supposed to be wiped out as a nation. They fear that, in addition to losing many lives, they will now also lose their cultural heritage again. Volunteers are trying to bring art and cultural treasures to safety, but it is too late in many places. Numerous museums, galleries, theaters, churches, and libraries have suffered severe damage. Others face the same fate with each passing week of the war. This is one of the reasons why it is so important that Ukraine gets weapons that can effectively push back the enemy. People everywhere suspect their homeland is once again being culturally bled dry, as happened 80 years ago when the German occupiers wanted to create so-called living space for 15 to 20 million Germans on Ukrainian territory.

The Nazi occupiers looted everything they liked; the plundering of Ukraine served not only for enrichment. Wagon after wagon of books, archival material, files, and documents were loaded and transported by the Reichsbahn to Germany. Mountains of documents. A service report dated 27. September 1943 in Kyiv notes what was packed into wagon 22743 to Munich: "42 boxes of books for the Rosenberg East Library, 7 boxes of catalogs and card indexes, 1 box of volumes for the High School (eleven other boxes had to remain in the wagon in Kyiv because of lack of space), 21 boxes of periodicals, 12 boxes of the picture folders, 9 packages and 7 rolls of Bolshevik pictures (but 8 packages had to remain in Kyiv), and 22 pairs of Bolshevik ideological films." Many others followed this wagon.

Based on the material, the essence of the enemy was to be researched post-mortem because, before that, the enemy was to be exterminated in the form of Jews and Bolsheviks. The Nazis wanted to study the communist Bolshevik social system, as Tetiana Sebta, who has been researching the German occupation period from 1941 to 1943 since Ukraine's independence in 1991, discovered, "They wanted to know how ideology was put into practice, in medicine, or agriculture in the Soviet Union. What was it about the collective farms? It was about how the Soviet Union was structured."

Dictator Adolf Hitler had appointed the NSDAP chief ideologist Alfred Rosenberg as Reich Minister for the Occupied Eastern Territories. Rosenberg was a Baltic German who had learned Russian as his mother tongue. He had harbored a deep hatred for the Soviet Union since the October Revolution. He saw Jews and Bolshevists as the worst enemies of the German people. Rosenberg was intent on their legacies as objects of study. The longtime Hitler confidant wrote in his diary: "There are still about six million Jews living in the East. The Jews question will be solved for Germany only when the last Jew has left German territory, and for Europe when there is no Jew left on the European continent as far as the Urals."

The art robbers closely followed the murdering units. When people talk about Nazi raids in Eastern Europe, they often refer only to Russian losses. Yet the bloodletting in what is now Ukraine was far greater, corrects Bremen-based looted art expert Wolfgang Eichwede, who has worked for decades on restitution between the countries. "According to all counts made in the Soviet Union and according to all information [from] German files (...) two-thirds of all Soviet cultural losses are Ukrainian losses." The fact that the majority was stolen in Ukraine was due to the course of the front. The Soviet Republic was occupied during the entire campaign against the USSR. Here the German occupiers had time.

The construction of Rosenberg's Eastern Library began at the end of 1941. In Kyiv, the Central Oblast Library, today's Wernadsky National Library, had to bleed for it. All its Soviet literature was confiscated. Within two years, vast quantities of books were gathered, including 10,000 volumes from Dnipropetrovsk. All Jewish writings were given to the Frankfurt "Institute for the Study of the

Jewish Question". For its library, books were stolen from all over Europe. One hundred and sixty-seven thousand volumes in Hebrew and Yiddish and manuscripts came from Kyiv. The Soviets had already hoarded most of them in the 1930s when the synagogues and churches were closed. Now the Germans took these books with them.

In Ukraine, German occupiers also stole paintings, for example, from the Museum of Western and Eastern Art in Kyiv, which stood in a row with the Tretyakov Gallery in Moscow and the Hermitage in St. Petersburg. In honor of the founding couple and collectors Bogdan and Varvara Chanenko, it is still called the Chanenko Museum. It is housed in their villa, a homely Italian-style city palace in the Ukrainian capital. Serhiy Gilyarov, whom the Bolsheviks had imprisoned for trying to prevent the Soviet state finances from being boosted by the sale of art from the Chanenko Museum, lived in Kyiv during the occupation. He was 54 years old, had spent his entire professional life at the museum, and was almost part of the inventory. Now the German occupiers harnessed him for their services, for which he was arrested again by the Soviet Communists after the war. In 1946 he officially died of pneumonia. His family reported that he had refused food in prison.

Nothing was safe from the German marauders. They also used them privately, and many pictures have still disappeared. Loot art expert Tetiana Sebta names the biggest thieves: "The Reich Commissar for Ukraine, Erich Koch, stole 16 paintings from the Chanenko Museum and one painting from the Russian Museum entitled 'Girl in Red Costume'. Most of the pictures were taken by the Commissioner General Waldemar Magunia. 48! 27 have reappeared, 21 are still missing."

The employees were able to hide part of the collection from the Nazis. The occupiers took what they could from the museum's collection. Some of it was sent to Germany, and others were used to decorate their administrative rooms and service apartments in Kyiv. They documented everything in notes that can still be found today in the museum archives. After the war, the list of lost artworks included 25,000 works of art, including 20,000 copperplate engravings by Rembrandt and Dürer, among others. In addition,

450 paintings are missing. The museum, or more precisely, Olena Zhivkova, the vice-director responsible for restitution issues, has been searching for these works to this day. Only four paintings have been returned, two of which Olena Zhivkova discovered at international auctions. She looks through the catalogs of auction houses every month. She knows all the paintings that the museum is missing. She has almost 500 black-and-white photographs of the paintings and other works of art in her house.

When the Red Army launched its counteroffensive in 1943 and pushed back the German occupiers, the stolen goods were hastily transported westward. There were countless interim storage facilities, including one in a castle near Königsberg. After the end of the war, it was said that much of the art had been destroyed in a fire. But now and then, works of art from precisely these transports turn up. Eighteen million Germans belonged to the Wehrmacht, and many were involved in the operations and, thus, often in the raids in Eastern Europe.

After 1945, almost 100,000 works from the Dresden Picture Gallery were stored in the emptied Kyiv museum rooms. The Soviet trophy brigade had confiscated art, mainly in East Germany, as compensation for their previous losses in the Soviet Union. The Picture Gallery got its paintings back starting in 1950 as a gesture from the USSR to its brother state, the GDR. For the Chanenko Museum, the return was far less successful. The museum has entered what it looks for into the Lost Art database, an online directory of mislaid artworks. There are currently 477 works.

In February 2014, Olena Zhivkova was reminded of the horrors of World War II for the first time. When Russia annexed Crimea, she and her team seriously considered evacuating the museum. "Because it was absolutely not clear what Russian President Putin had in mind for our country."

The colleagues decided against it because the experience from the war said that the damage caused by transportation and storage in places unsuitable for art treasures could be even more devastating in case of doubt. They moved the paintings to the basement of the museum.

From February 24, 2022, Olena Zhivkova and her colleagues will again pack exhibits day and night. Paintings, plastics, busts, fine Chinese and Japanese porcelain, fans—all valuable pieces are to be secured against possible Russian attacks on Kyiv. In an email from March 2022, she writes, "There is such a saying: hope for the best, but assume the worst. This has come to pass."

Alfred Rosenberg was obsessed with a so-called high school. He had already been nagging Hitler since 1936 about the elite party university. In order to equip the 17 planned institutes of the High School, Rosenberg enlisted the help of numerous German specialists for his raid: archivists, librarians, historians, archaeologists, musicologists, folklorists, economists, microbiologists, geologists, and psychologists. For the future party school, he had stolen from all over Eastern Europe "what is suitable to vividly portray Bolshevik life in the Soviet Union".

Troops of his task force were also on the move in occupied Dnipropetrovsk, today's Dnipro. The industrial city was in German hands from August 25, 1941. After the fighting, universities, factories, party organizations, archives, and museums were occupied. What survives is how meticulously a commission of experts from Germany first combed through the inventory lists of the institutions. Valentina Sazuta has worked at the National Historical Museum in Dnipro for 45 years, making her the longest-serving. "The Germans closed the museum to visitors, and the specialists began to study the inventory books very thoroughly. They compared the lists and checked what was left after the evacuation by the Soviet authorities." Mrs. Sazuta remembers how astonished her colleagues, who had experienced the occupation themselves, told her about it. That is German thoroughness, they thought, and they were not wrong. But what diabolical plan the Nazis had come up with, that they would first exterminate Jews and Bolsheviks in Ukraine and only then study them, the Museum employees did not know at the time. Those who survived the German occupation discovered that the occupiers had brought a large part of the archaeological collection and museum paintings to Germany.

Because the Nazi High School was also to have an institute for North Germanic history of the Eastern region, the area around

Dnipropetrovsk was particularly interesting to Rosenberg's task force. But not only for him, because the ideologist had competition. From 1941 to 1944, four rival Nazi art robbery units hunted down cultural treasures in Ukraine, or what the Wehrmacht soldiers had not yet destroyed, devastated, or looted. It was not only the NSDAP's looting organization, i.e., the Reichsleiter Rosenberg task force, that had its sights set on pictures, books, and other cultural assets. The Wehrmacht's so-called "art protection" units also confiscated entire libraries, such as the Mining Institute in Dnipropetrovsk or the Soviet military history archive in Kyiv. In addition to the Sonderkommando Künsberg of the Foreign Office, named after its leader, SS-Sturmbannführer Baron Eberhard von Künsberg, Himmler's "Ahnenerbe" was also on the move. These four organizations often engaged in a regular race for the treasures.

The Reichsführer of the SS, Heinrich Himmler, had a penchant for the occult, which earned him great sympathy among many NSDAP members. Together with the private scholar Herman Wirth from the Netherlands, he founded the Forschungsgemeinschaft Deutsches Ahnenerbe in 1935, the "Study Society for the History of Ideas." The "Studies" included medical experiments on humans and excavations on the territory of the Ukrainian Soviet Republic, where the would-be archaeologists searched for evidence of Germanic ancestors. Himmler's people were also sent on excavations on the Dnipro River. They were supposed to use "German traces" in Ukraine to justify the violent expansion of the so-called Third Reich. The fact that Goths had lived around Dnipro was nothing new for the local archaeologists, but it was for the Germans. They regarded it as evidence that Aryans had lived here, from which they derived a right to these territories.

Oksana Rudkovskaya is the archaeologist at the National Historical Museum in Dnipro. She finds the ideological fixation of the fascists on alleged German traces indisputable and extremely strange from a scientific point of view. The whole romance of the Goths has not given them any peace. "They were looking for some kind of capital. But there is no such Gothic capital here. Instead, there are plenty of archaeological monuments that are still untouched in the ground today. Expeditions are still busy excavating them." During the migration of peoples 300 to 600 years after Christ, many tribes mixed in the region, and all of them have left numerous testimonies, including the Scythians, who lived in southern Ukraine just over 2,000 years ago, whom the Nazis also considered early ancestors, like the Goths later. The scientist also tells that archaeologists familiar with the area had to accompany the Nazi expeditions of Himmler's Ahnenerbe.

Also, the then-Ukrainian director of the Museums, Pavel Kosar, was forced to go on a three-week excavation tour. After the war, the Soviet power accused the archaeologist of nationalism and being bourgeois. He was forced to leave the museum and was politically persecuted for collaborating with the occupiers.

On the square in front of the museum building are about 50 stone figures in a circular area; thirty-eight female and male figures from the Kipchaks from the 9th to 13th century and the Scythians from the 5th or 6th century before Christ. These archaeological treasures also aroused great desire among the Nazis, says Oksana Rudkovskaya. The statues were found in or on tumuli, called kurgans, often richly decorated. At least 15,000 are spread across the mostly flat landscape of eastern Ukraine.

In the meantime, the figures, which weigh several tons, have been wrapped in sandbags and encased in wooden scaffolding. Oksana Rudkovskaya hopes this will protect them from the Russian attacks on Dnipro. She has already secured the remains of a missile that hit a neighborhood in the east on March 25, 2022, as an exhibit. Some of her colleagues still at the museum in the summer of 2021 have fled abroad. Oksana Rudkovskaya remains, organizing smaller archaeological exhibitions but also painting circles. Everything takes place in the basement. One of her cell phone videos shows a small workshop where refugee children from Kharkiv paint Easter eggs with elaborate patterns in April 2022. An activity that calms the nerves.

Since the invasion on February 24, 2022, Russian troops have left a trail of devastation in Ukraine. As ruthlessly as they treat the population, so too is art destroyed. The list of damaged or destroyed objects is growing longer every day and is far from complete. The Kyiv History Museum hopes it will be spared the fate already befallen dozens of cultural sites. These include the Drama Theater and the Museum of Art in Mariupol and the Museum of History and Local History in Ivankiv near Kyiv, where the works of the famous Ukrainian folk artist Maria Prymatschenko were exhibited. Residents were able to save them in due time by hiding them in their houses. The building of the Babyn Yar Holocaust Memorial was damaged on the first days of the war, on March 1. In Kharkiv, the legendary Slowo House, which looks like a Russian S from the air, suffered from the Russian attacks. Ukrainian artists who disappeared during Stalin's terror lived there in the early 1930s. Later, more and more places in the east are evacuated, which is also felt by the staff of the History Museum in Dnipro, and the city becomes increasingly crowded. Where the wrapped stone figures from the burial mounds now stand, the monument to Catherine the Great had its place until the German occupation during World War II. Oksana Rudkovskaya hopes that her figures will not suffer the same fate as Catherine because there is no trace of her to this day. The Germans took everything with them that had a connection to German culture. Catherine came from Germany, as did the sculptor, so the monument was a kind of beacon of German art. In the summer of 2021, museum director Julia

Pischanska drew parallels between the German occupation and the aggressive Russian military, preventing peace in eastern Ukraine since 2014. "Signs are being sought that Russians lived here. Not Slavic peoples, but precisely Russians. At the same time, it is claimed that Ukrainians never existed. This unscientific, ideological, and fanatical approach is typical of totalitarian dictatorships that wage wars of occupation. They seek right manufacturing because a war of liberation sounds better than a war of occupation."

The phantom pain about the lost St. Catherine's monument is limited, similar to the painting of the tsar by Mikhail Panin. He was the first director of the art museum in the city on the Dnipro. He depicted "The secret departure of *Ivan the Terrible* from Oprichnina". The painting is three and a half meters long, and with its height of two and a half meters, it almost touches the ceiling of the restoration workshop in Kyiv, where it has been standing since the end of 2019. It should have returned to Dnipro long ago, where it was awaited with some anticipation, especially since a wild art theft story surrounds the imposing painting. It has been on an odyssey. Before it arrived in the Ukrainian capital of Kyiv at the end of 2019, it was first in St. Petersburg, then in the art museum in Dnipropetrovsk, and finally in the US in Ridgefield, Connecticut. There, the couple Gabby and David Tracy had purchased a fully furnished house in 1987, including *Ivan the Terrible*, the painting of whose history they knew nothing during the 30 years they lived in the house. When they wanted to sell the house again in 2017, including the furnishings, the auction company hesitated because the obviously Russian work looked suspiciously like looted art. The signature was on the back. Someone had folded the canvas to fit into a smaller frame. It shows Tsar Ivan Grozny in a fur coat and fur cap on a powerful white horse. Rider and horse trot out through an archway from a fortress into the snow with heads bowed. Armed figures and beggars gaze after them. A church with onion domes shines distantly in the evening glow.

Mikhail Panin was not an unknown painter but a graduate of the Tsar's Art School and came to Ekaterinoslav in 1925, which was the name of the city on the Dnipro at the time. Such an obvious Russian painting in the USA smelled like picture theft, so the origin of the painting, the provenance, had to be clarified before the sale. In 2017, the current director of the art museum, Tetjana Schaparenko, received an inquiry from the auction house, the Potomack Company in Alexandria in the US state of Virginia, as to whether the work in the photograph sent along had ever been in the inventory of her museum. Mikhail Panin's work of art is one of 1002 paintings the German occupiers removed from the museum during their looting campaign. It is number 417 of the confiscated works listed by the occupiers. Thanks partly to the pedantic Nazi bureaucracy, Tetjana Shaparenko proved with numerous documents and photographs that Panin's *Ivan the Terrible* belonged to her museum. In a note from July 17, 1942, for example, there is the following evidence: "Brigadier Tatz was handed seven exhibits: a porcelain vase, a bust, several paintings, including Panin's 'Ivan the Terrible.'" The US intelligence services immediately became interested in the previous owner of the painting and followed the trail of the ominous

Brigadier Tatz. He entered the US in 1946 under a false name, posing as a Swiss border guard and adopting a new identity. The small piece of paper with the list written in Russian does not say much about the art robber Tatz. Also, his rank "brigadeführer" does not allow a safe conclusion as to which of the four rival Nazi art theft associations he belonged to. Brigadeführer Tatz, the thief of the Tsarist painting, should have died long ago. The last owners of the painting, the Tracy couple, did not hesitate for a moment to release the work of art free of charge, as required by US law. No problem for Gabby Tracy, who is a Hungarian Holocaust survivor.

Nevertheless, *Ivan the Terrible* did not return to Dnipro immediately. First, the painting had to be restored. The layers of paint had changed due to heat because it had probably hung over a fireplace or heater for a long time. Moreover, someone kept painting over it, completely unprofessionally, noted Olena Kravchenko, who restored the damaged image of the tsar. Since February 2022, it has been restored to its former glory. After 80 years, it was to return to Dnipro as the first and so far the only one of over 1000 paintings of the Dnipro Art Museum, which the Germans stole. As the Russian war was already raging outside Kyiv, the transport was postponed as a precaution.

Other, very few pieces were returned from Germany in time. Archaeological exhibits, books, and a tsarist document. They were stolen from the Wernadsky National Library in Kyiv, where the Einsatzkommando Künsberg had been up to mischief. It was mainly after documents and maps. Künsberg's men confiscated the manuscript section of the library, including an original document of Tsar Peter I. After the Second World War, this tsar's document hung in the University of Tübingen for everyone to see. But it was not until more than 70 years later, as of 2014, that people there began to wonder what it was all about. In 2019, the University of Tübingen returned the tsar's deed to the library.

In Kyiv, the jubilation about the restitution was limited because the German-Ukrainian restitution dialogue is a disappointment for the Ukrainians. According to historian Serhij Kot, this was also due to expectations that were far too high in 1993 when the talks began. He died on March 28, 2022. He was a member of the

Ukrainian-German Restitution Commission and described himself as an idealist at the beginning of the restitution talks. "We thought that if we could find some, Germany will do the same because that's where everything we're missing is. Instead, only individual pieces came back. Practically nothing, compared to Ukraine's losses." Serhij Kot was one of Ukraine's most important experts on looted art. The Nazis held Ukraine for two years. Then the Red Army inexorably approached, which was once again accompanied by massive destruction and losses for Ukraine. The Germans were not the only ones who stole from Ukraine during the Second World War. When the Red Army expelled the Nazis, they confiscated the stolen goods from their depots. The most valuable pieces were distributed among Moscow and the then Leningrad, now Saint Petersburg. There, for example, hangs a painting from the Chanenko Museum that clearly belonged to those that Erich Koch had stolen in Kyiv.

The US Army seized the largest stashes of looted art. In so-called collecting points, it brought together all looted art from dozens of Nazi depots and sent large quantities back to their countries of origin in Eastern and Western Europe. According to American data, 530,000 museum exhibits, archives, and library exhibits were returned to the Soviet Union. Of these 530,000 exhibits, 350,000 came from Ukraine. That is 70 percent of what was looted by the Germans and eventually recovered in Germany and Austria. And of these, 170,000 objects came from the city of Kyiv. But they often did not end up in the places from which the Nazis had stolen them, something Serhij Kot regretted for the rest of his life. The US forces handed over the seized stolen property in Berlin to the Soviet Military Administration in Germany, to which Ukrainian experts were not allowed before to sort out the Ukrainian exponents. Only specialists from Moscow and Leningrad had access, according to Serhij Kot. "Ukrainians were allowed to join only when everything was already packed in boxes." Thus, many precious exhibits, such as the famous frescoes from the Mikhailovsky Church in Kyiv, went first to Pavlovsk, then to Novgorod, and from there were taken to the Hermitage or the State Russian Museum. "That is why we speak of double robbery, once by the Germans, and then by the Soviet institutions, which secured the most valuable." Until the very end,

Serhij Kot fought for the return of Ukrainian artworks from German and Russian stocks, kindly but firmly. When Putin's troops were outside Kyiv, he fled. He had to leave behind his computer, which contained his collected records. For the scientist, a terrible loss. Finally, he asked the Germans to look around in their living rooms, where they were sure to find one or another work of art that their grandfather or great-uncle had taken from Ukraine. If their descendants returned this booty to Ukraine, they would certainly be able to contribute to the cultural heritage of the Ukrainian nation. In his opinion, this would have been part of the historical responsibility the Germans supposedly care so much about.

Merkel's cold farewell, Chancellor Scholz's tough start, and a scuttled joker

Until the end, until the farewell visit of the chancellor in August 2021, Kyiv hopes for the end of the superfluous pipeline. The Ukrainians know that Putin's history pamphlet published in July is, in fact, a threat of war, especially as more and more Russian forces are taking up positions along the Ukrainian border. No Ukrainian believes that they are only holding maneuvers. But they are optimistic that the future ex-chancellor has a parting gift in her luggage after all. They want Nord Stream 2 or weapons to be stopped. But the German head of government is also passing up this last opportunity, which many Ukrainians see as a betrayal. Merkel, who was Germany's face abroad for 16 years, is far too emotional about all this. This is far too emotional for Merkel, who was Germany's face abroad for 16 years. Objective, bureaucratic, and true to herself to the end, she points to a new German-American agreement that she has concluded over Zelenskyy's head with US President Joe Biden. It states that Ukraine's gas supply will be guaranteed in an emergency, even without Russia. In addition, Ukraine is promised a "green fund," with the help of which it should be able to start producing hydrogen. Given the imminent danger from the East, this is future music to which the young president has no ear. He has to control himself visibly next to the crisis-experienced politician, who routinely carries out her farewell visit and has neither a feeling for her host nor the people in Ukraine. They are waiting for a signal of solidarity, of compassion, however small. They would have been most pleased with weapons because they know they would soon need them urgently. The chancellor holds out no such prospect. Instead, she hands over 1.5 million vaccine doses against the coronavirus. But in Ukraine, unlike Germany, the pandemic is by no means the greatest of all worries.

While Angela Merkel's commitment to the Minsk Agreement was still credited, the Ukrainians only waved it off at the end of her term in office. The agreement was already obsolete, a political solution for eastern Ukraine as little in sight as peace. On the contrary, almost one million eastern Ukrainians have Russian passports.

The chancellor, of all people, who usually showed consideration for the smaller countries in Europe, remained intransigent to the end with regard to Ukraine. Without telling the public why. Did she want to save Nord Stream 2 as a last trump card to stand up to Putin? If so, she should have played this card in the Crimea crisis. Chance missed. The next opportunity would have come after the poisoning of Russian opposition politician Alexei Navalny. Again, she does nothing. Did she want to show that with Moscow, not much, but still, something is possible? What for? It is not in Europe that the will to cooperate is lacking but in the Kremlin. The pipeline is Merkel's biggest mistake in European policy. From the start, the gas pipeline was a climate policy dinosaur that divided the continent and harmed Ukraine—to Putin's delight. Werner Schulz, a former member of the Bundestag and the European Parliament for Bündnis 90/Die Grünen, described Gazprom's westward expansion as a far greater threat than the east expansion of NATO. As chancellor, Angela Merkel remained silent about the benefits of the Nord Stream project for Germany. She explained herself in the euro and refugee crises but not in the pipeline, which is important for Moscow. In doing so, she offended her European partners and compatriots for years. Many have turned their backs on her; others have learned from her gruff style and are copying it.

Instead of reducing Russian imports for climate protection reasons alone, Germany is importing more gas than ever at the end of Merkel's chancellorship, thus filling the Russian treasury. According to official figures, Moscow's revenues from the export of fossil fuels account for a good third, and according to Western estimates, at least 40 percent of the state budget comes from the sale of fossil fuels. Military experts have noted for years that the Russian Army is becoming better and better equipped and that expensive armament projects are being implemented. Putin does not miss the opportunity to personally demonstrate the latest military achievements, such as hypersonic missiles, never forgetting to mention how effortlessly they can reach targets in the West. Why, in the face of his increasingly strident rhetoric against NATO, the US, and the EU, did no one in the Chancellor's Office, the Ministry of Defense, or the Foreign Office become uneasy? Why did no public reflection begin that German Euros were being used for dangerous purposes? Why did Germany continue to believe in the peace dividend and allow itself an increasingly poorly equipped Bundeswehr? Why did it take war for Germany to be ready to rethink?

As the troops build up in the north, east, and west of Ukraine takes on ever more frightening proportions, many mediators are busy in the Kremlin. But they cannot reach the president, who is lecturing after his history essay about the past rather than listening to the guests' concerns. Thus, the visitors leave the richly decorated halls without having achieved anything.

Germany's new chancellor, Olaf Scholz, is in no hurry. His trip to the Kremlin on February 15, 2022, will also be his inaugural visit to Moscow. Political Berlin is more interested in how the new head of government compares to his predecessor Angela Merkel than in what he achieves. Scholz is celebrated for the four-hour conversation, but the public hardly hears anything about it. Did he get a lecture series on historical revisionism? We do not know. Scholz is also praised for showing backbone in the press conference that followed. But did he really do that? In any case, he did not announce the end of Nord Stream 2 — not in the Kremlin or even a week earlier during his first visit as chancellor to the White House. There, the Hanseatic assured that he would stand firmly with the transatlantic partner, "saying the same things together, acting together," but he did not. US President Joe Biden speaks plainly in the direction of Moscow: "If Russia, for example, crosses the border to Ukraine with tanks and troops, Nord Stream 2 will no longer exist." Unlike Biden, the words Baltic Sea pipeline or Nord Stream 2 do not cross Scholz's lips. He prefers to refer to the resuscitated NATO-Russia Council and the Normandy format, which "hasn't emitted much life for years." Scholz is riding a dead horse.

Joe Biden gives the new, almost rudely short-tempered chancellor a considerable leap of faith. This is met with great incomprehension in the US Congress. They have far less patience with the dithering German, who, like Angela Merkel, is trying as little as possible to use the pipeline to generate political pressure on Moscow, but also ignores Kyiv's imploring pleas to supply weapons for self-defense. The new government in Berlin is continuing the mistakes of the old one. The learning curve remains flat.

When the Winter Olympics in China ended on February 20, 2022, Russian President Putin surprised the world one day later with an announcement. Russia recognized the independence of the so-called Donetsk and Luhansk People's Republics. He also announced that they had asked for help. Translated, this means that on the 21st of February 2022, there is war. The only question is: what kind? Should the war in eastern Ukraine be extended? Could the pro-Russian separatists advance to the oblast borders, i.e., occupy an area more than twice as large as the one occupied so far? Or should the entire Ukraine even be subjugated?

The answer is not long in coming. On February 22, 2022, Putin orders Russian soldiers to enter embattled eastern Ukraine. Now German Chancellor Olaf Scholz halts Nord Stream 2, putting the approval process on hold. The situation today is fundamentally different. The international community must now react, Scholz stresses. He has gambled thoroughly. The pipeline, Germany's last wild card, now lies at the bottom of the Baltic Sea, worth billions and a useless investment ruin. So much for a bridge, so much for leverage. It is a political ruin, a monument to German appeasement policy that—fortunately for German politics!—no one sees so deep in the water.

On September 26, 2022, the sea surges at one point, and natural gas rises to the surface. Because gas leaks from the pipes are very rare, the suspicion immediately arises that someone has deliberately destroyed them. Footage of a bubbling Baltic Sea that seems to be boiling at this point goes around the world. For safety reasons, shipping routes are immediately changed. Speculation about who could have blown up three of the four tubes is rife. To find out, it is necessary to consider who could have had the greatest interest and who else had it at the time. Seven months after the invasion of Russian forces, Ukraine is more than stretched with its defenses against Russian attacks. If it had destroyed the pipelines, some of which are owned by German companies, the already strained relationship of trust between Berlin and Kyiv would again be disturbed, and discussions about Berlin's now extensive military and financial support could take on a risky momentum of their own.

On the other hand, many Ukrainians would presumably want to damage Russia severely; retaliation for the many dead and the destroyed cities is certainly a possible motive. Research by the German media in March 2023 suggested that the trail did indeed lead to Ukraine, at least to a Ukrainian company that had rented the boat in which the assassins had gone out to sea. Since they, in turn, had used forged passports to identify themselves when renting the yacht, the evidence is extremely thin. In Moscow, blowing up the tubes was certainly the work of American specialists acting on behalf of President Joe Biden. The American investigative journalist Seymor Hersh confirmed this thesis in February 2023 but referred only to an unnamed source. He followed up on Biden's threat in May 2022 when he warned that Nord Stream would no longer exist if the Russian Army crossed the Ukrainian border. Economically, the pipeline had lost its importance by then. Russia had already stopped supplying gas since July 2022. Export revenues from Germany had dried up, and, for the first time, the Kremlin was proving unreliable; contrary to what it had claimed for decades, Moscow was not fulfilling its supply contracts. Was it perhaps imminent recourse for the claims to be minimized by blowing up the pipes? According to the motto: If there are no more pipelines, no gas can be sent through, and contracts cannot be fulfilled. It is unlikely that Germany would blow up its facilities; it could be that Ukrainian or Polish forces did it to take revenge for Germany's long hesitation, but that would not be a particularly strong motive.

Germany feared getting into an energy emergency with the sudden lack of gas. That is why the German Minister of Economics looked for substitutes for cheap Russian fuel worldwide and found them in the USA. Would they have an interest in a destroyed Nord Stream plant? The fracking gas the Americans had wanted to sell to Germany for years was already sailing across the Atlantic in special LNG ships.

A so-called false-flag action that Russia wanted to blame on Washington or Kyiv is still being discussed. As long as the opposite is not proven, it cannot be ruled out that the pipeline was destroyed to preclude its restart later. In any case, the fact that the project, which seemed to have finally been buried on February 22, 2022, would once again be remembered in such a spectacular manner was a big surprise.

Before the possible war scenarios have even been played out, the world learns on the morning of February 24 that Putin has chosen the worst of the options: an attack on *all of* Ukraine. The joint military exercise with Belarus was a deception. It grew into an invasion. From the beginning, the Russian air force attacks Ukrainian cities in many parts of the country; ground troops invade from the south, east, and north. At six in the morning, Vladimir Putin addresses the public in a televised speech. He speaks for almost half an hour. He devotes the first half of his speech to NATO, which he claims threatens Russia. He does not mention during the 30 minutes that Russia has already invaded Ukraine or that the war has already begun. Nor does he utter the words war or invasion even once. Only at the very end does he talk about a special military operation whose purpose is to end the nightmare—"the genocide of millions of people who live there [in the Donbas] and whose only hope is Russia, i.e., us." To achieve their goals, the leading NATO countries would support extreme nationalists and neo-Nazis in Ukraine, and kill people in Crimea, just like the punitive columns of Ukrainian nationalists, Hitler's collaborators during the Great Patriotic War. The nationalists would even claim to possess nuclear weapons. The special military operation aims to protect the people subjected to eight years of mistreatment and genocide and to demilitarize and denazify Ukraine. In addition, those who committed numerous bloody crimes against civilians, including citizens of the Russian Federation, would be brought to justice. Finally, Putin threatens, "Whoever tries to interfere with us, let alone endanger our country and our people, must know that Russia's response will be immediate and will lead to consequences that you have never experienced in your history." To ensure everyone understands how serious he is about the warning, he has the nuclear "deterrent forces" in readiness. The German public is learning what the different escalation levels mean for the readiness of Russian nuclear weapons: level 1—

peacetime with parked nuclear weapons, level 2—increased alertness through permanent staffing of the barracks, level 3—arming of nuclear missiles, level 4—war with nuclear weapons. Accordingly, the third stage proclaimed by Putin means that the weapons are armed, i.e., the warheads, including nuclear ones, and missiles are brought together.

This is the third time that Putin has threatened the world with the worst weapons. As early as 2014, he was ready to put the nuclear forces on heightened readiness, and he told the Rossiya One television audience about a year later. In 2020, he expanded the possibilities for the first use of nuclear weapons, which may also be used in the event of aggression against the Russian Federation with conventional weapons if the state's existence is in danger.

His repeated accusation of genocide is pure nonsense. If there had been genocide in Ukraine, as Putin claims, the UN Security Council would have been the appropriate body to which Russia—especially as a permanent member—could have appealed. Moscow did not make this attempt. Putin's so-called "denazification" of Ukraine is a chimera. He insinuates that Nazis threaten Ukraine, whereas he wants to eliminate Ukraine as a nation.

On February 24, 2022, Europe's history divides into a time before Russia's war against Ukraine and a time after. The EU and the West must act now. Germany's refusal for so long to abandon Nord Stream 2 is already doing immense damage to the new government's reputation. The image loss continues regarding Russia's exclusion from Swift's international payment system. Germany is once again not going along.

Foreign Minister Annalena Baerbock announces sanctions for President Putin and Foreign Minister Lavrov but rejects a complete suspension of Swift because a granddaughter in Europe could no longer transfer money to her grandmother in Russia because of possible "massive collateral damage." Germany's reputation has slumped. Baerbock actually meant the threat to Germany's energy supply and that Germany must be careful "that we don't choose instruments where Putin ends up laughing at them, because they hit us much harder." But she didn't say it like that on February 28, but only two weeks later, on March 8.

In Kyiv, in addition to the message that Berlin does not want to exclude all Russian banks from Swift, a second one arrives: Germany is not considering a gas boycott either. Not even then, when Ukraine is sinking into rubble, and civilians are being tortured and murdered by a violent soldiery, does Germany want to correct its mistake and immediately turn off the gas tap. Because now, the German economy, which has always found a willing accomplice for its interests in politics, fears for its existence. Cheap gas from Russia has made them dependent on it. It hangs on the needle like a junkie. If the withdrawal is too sudden, there is a danger to her life.

The neighbors to the east are talking to the new chancellor in Berlin. To do so, they are coming to Berlin in person. Polish prime minister Mateusz Morawiecki wants to ask Scholz face-to-face whether he is serious about the helmets. He said German aid was far from what was needed now: "What kind of aid was delivered to Ukraine? Five thousand helmets? That must be a joke." On the evening of the second day of the war, with his Polish counterpart on his way home, the German government finally makes its first course correction. It promises Ukraine 1000 anti-tank weapons and 500 surface-to-air missiles from the arsenal of the Bundeswehr. Chancellor Scholz now speaks of a "duty" and, for the first time, of a "turning point" that the Russian invasion of Ukraine marked. "Germany stands closely by Ukraine's side. "Ukrainian President Volodymyr Zelenskyy holds no grudges, welcoming the German decision on Twitter as recently as Feb. 26: "Keep it up, Chancellor Olaf Scholz!"

This seems to end the months-long standoff over arms deliveries to Ukraine. Again and again, Berlin has blocked them because, 20 years ago, the Red-Green government prohibited arms deliveries to crisis regions. This doctrine is no longer tenable in the face of the Russian invasion.

Some pacifists do not go along with this step. The younger ones, however, have far fewer problems with the new reality than the older ones, shaped by the peace movement in the 1960s and 1970s. Anna-Nicole Heinrich, elected synod president of the Protestant church at only 25, faces a new challenge, which she describes with an image. It is like playing a board game together, (...) and maybe there are people who break the rules a bit, but the board is on the table the whole time. And all of a sudden someone comes and just throws the board off the table. That's an aggression that didn't exist before, and that now catches us off guard in our naivety, but it's so new that we have to learn to deal with it in a whole new way. Personally, politically, diplomatically

Politicians have great problems adapting to the changed situation, which is also evident from the fact that Berlin continues to distinguish between defensive and offensive weapons, which must sound like a gray theory to the Ukrainians since every offensive weapon is a means of defeating the enemy.

The *Zeitenwende* (turn of the times) speech

Three days after the start of the war in Ukraine, members of the Bundestag are invited to a special session in Berlin. Many things are different than usual—not only that it is taking place on a Sunday, but also what Chancellor Olaf Scholz has to say.

He begins with a package of unprecedented sanctions agreed upon by EU leaders. It announces excluding important Russian banks from the Swift banking communications network. In addition, the export of future technologies to Russia is to be banned, and punitive measures are to be imposed against the oligarchs and their financial investments and Putin and the people in his direct entourage. This is the first time Russia's president has appeared on a sanctions list. The catalog of punitive measures has a scope that Ukraine had hoped for right after the annexation of Crimea. After the Russian invasion of the entire country, it still does not go far enough. All Russian banks should have been affected by the Swift exclusion. Above all, the Ukrainian side misses Germany's support for an immediate EU oil and gas embargo. That has not happened. Scholz made a big splash by announcing a "special fund" of 100 billion Euros for the German armed forces. "Bravo!" shouts someone from the CDU ranks, and loud applause comes from many directions. The special fund is to be set up as early as the 2022 federal budget is only for the new budget, and it is intended to cover overdue investments and armaments projects and will be secured by an amendment to the Basic Law. In this way, the government wants to send out the signal "that the medium to long-term upgrading of the Bundeswehr will be implemented on the basis of a permanently secured funding basis and thus in a way that is visible and credible on an international scale."

In addition, Scholz pledges to permanently raise military spending to two percent, thus meeting NATO's target for defense spending by member states. Everything that Scholz presents on this Sunday morning must be measured against the new reality that the war has created. Many things stand up to the test. The two percent of economic output for the defense budget is not only the due implementation of a promise to allies but also serves Germany's own security. The long-neglected Bundeswehr is to be brought back into shape; there is applause for that, too. Scholz has even considered the danger of cyber attacks and disinformation campaigns, defending against attacks on critical infrastructure and communication channels. He promises a new generation of combat aircraft and tanks to be built jointly with European partners, especially France and the Eurodrone. Scholz also ends the long discussion about acquiring the armed Heron drone from Israel on this day; it is to be purchased.

The reserved 63-year-old chooses a broad term for the federal government's plans: turnaround. It should also take place in energy policy to overcome the dependence on imports from individual suppliers because the energy policy is now also understood as a security policy. Two liquefied natural gas terminals in Brunsbüttel and Wilhelmshaven, which have so far been prevented by years of disputes, are now to be built quickly.

Many members of the Bundestag follow the speech as if electrified; the enthusiasm for this overdue course correction is great, and several CSU representatives clap, standing up, some colleagues from the SPD who notice this also rise. After all, the opposition should not appear more euphoric than the coalition. Only Rolf Mützenich's face grows longer, and his mouth narrows. What his chancellor is presenting here was not agreed with him. He would have opposed it because even after the Russian invasion of Ukraine, the chairman of the SPD parliamentary group opposed any kind of rearmament. Some of his comrades feel that they have been overruled. Others are enthusiastic. Within half an hour, Scholz has named and, more importantly, corrected the mistakes of the past. He has pointed German security, energy, and environmental policy in a new direction. On February 27, 2022, he made good on his pithy campaign slogan from the Hamburg civic election campaign: "Those who order leadership get it! The message is going out from Berlin now: We have understood.

Even before Scholz removes his black FFP2 mask and begins his speech, the Ukrainian ambassador is greeted with long applause. However, he gets on the nerves of many with his persistent demands for weapons deliveries. Andrij Melnyk bows in all directions but applauds much less often than the members of parliament. Scholz makes the same mistake as many German politicians before him. His speech lacks balance: even now, at the beginning of the war, the chancellor goes into much more detail about the sensitivities of the Russians than about the plight of the Ukrainians. While the Ukrainians' lives are in danger and dozens of people are already dead, Scholz spent much longer and in great detail discussing the courage needed to protest against the war.

There is much applause from the plenary for these brave Russians. Not a word about the men and women in Ukraine who immediately enlisted in the army or the National Guard or formed territorial defense groups in which residents protect their towns and villages from the attackers, about the volunteers who cook food for the soldiers, weave camouflage nets, and bring fleeing people to safety, about those who risk death defying the Russian missiles and tanks. Scholz refers to the Ukrainians with one standard sentence: "They are fighting for freedom and democracy, for values that we share with them." Nothing more. In contrast, there is a detailed passage about the Russian people, who allegedly do not want Putin's war. You do not have to be Ukrainian to feel that the relations are not right again, that German politics does not look into Ukraine and has only a rough knowledge of what is happening there.

The fact that the Bundestag wants to provide the war-torn country with all possible political, economic, financial, and military support measures is honorable. But the fact that now "it is to be examined whether further military equipment can be made available" sounds much more timid.

Sighs of relief are lost in the loud applause for the chancellor. Scholz, who had virtually disappeared from the scene since his government declaration in December 2021, has not only reappeared but has performed a feat of strength that hardly anyone thought he could pull off. The AfD, the Alternative for Germany, is saving its applause as expected. For them, the West shares responsibility for the Russian invasion because "hardliners clung to the NATO accession perspective for the country, arrogantly accusing Russia of being a great power," says Alice Weidel. For the leader of the parliamentary group, the historic failure of the West consists "in offending Russia," but that does not change the reprehensibility of the Russian invasion.

Compared to the right-wing extremists, the chairwoman of the left-wing parliamentary group, Amira Mohamed Ali, is much more self-critical, admitting that she had misjudged the Russian president. He is the aggressor and must be stopped immediately. The Russian attack cannot be relativized or justified by anything. Nevertheless, her group rejects arms deliveries to Ukraine and the rearmament of the Bundeswehr. It could not and would not support this armament build-up, this militarization because only disarmament and democracy were the way to peace.

Just how drastically the Berlin Republic perceives the turn of the times is also clear from the FDP finance minister's changed view of renewable energies. He now calls them "freedom energies," just as the billions in support for the German armed forces is a "freedom investment."

Confusion reigns above all in the SPD parliamentary group, for the chancellor had not even hinted at the drastic policy change in an internal video conference that morning. He surprised them all, as he did the Greens and the FDP. He is resented for this in his own ranks, even if many basically agree with the new course. Scholz knows he will have to do some work in the parliamentary group to smooth the waters. Two days later, he took the time to explain his ideas to his comrades. He wants to convince them not to stop the discussion. His SPD is a cosmos all of its own, in which meteors can suddenly hail down. Just as they did not want him as party chairman, they could also make life difficult for him as chancellor. That is why he is stroking souls. Only the party friends from the Forum Democratic Left are unimpressed. They continue to reject his special fund and the two percent target. But they make up only 30 of 206 deputies.

The course the German government must set after Scholz's appearance is tantamount to a departure into a new German foreign and security policy. The response in the NATO countries has been consistently positive, and the commitment to the two percent target for defense was overdue. Only Volodymyr Zelenskyyj is still waiting for an answer. He had tweeted the day before the special session that NATO membership would have to be reconsidered because of the war against his country. Scholz did not respond to this request with a syllable. Ukraine does not feature in the security architecture the German chancellor wants to strengthen. Nor did he mention a gas or oil embargo even once because it was not a blood, sweat, and tears speech with which Scholz swore for the Germans into the near future. If he spoke of energy, then only in connection with supply independence, security, and price development. He also avoided any reminder of the billions of Euros that have filled Russia's coffers and helped to finance its rearmament.

The head of government is sparing his fellow citizens all this, partly because prices are rising rapidly at the gas stations. March 2022 will be the most expensive month ever for motorists, with 2.069 Euros for a liter of Super E10 and 2.140 Euros for diesel. An increase of 49 and 30 cents, respectively, since the start of the war.

But the demands to stop importing Russian fuel are coming from Kyiv with unabated clarity. The chancellor and vice chancellor jointly argue why they cannot give in to the pressure. Robert Habeck sets off for the United Arab Emirates and Qatar, where he wants gas and, in the long term, hydrogen as a substitute for Russian supplies. He explains how difficult it is for him to trade with countries that neglect human rights. He comes across as credible and authentic. Habeck also takes time for the Ukrainian ambassador, who does not relinquish his stoic demands for weapons. The Green Party is one of the few who take the trouble to speak directly to Andrij Melnyk. Others keep their distance or mock his Twitter tweets. With its fickleness, the federal government provides him with ever new occasions.

It takes Germany two months to clarify which weapons Ukraine will get. It is a petty, partly incompetent, and contradictory squabble. In any case, it is a new embarrassment on the world stage.

Berlin sends bazookas, hand grenades, and machine guns but no battle tanks, infantry fighting vehicles, warships, or combat aircraft, and initially, no armored vehicles, or artillery pieces, not even from Bundeswehr stocks. However, if other countries deliver Soviet-designed heavy equipment to Ukraine, Germany is willing to fill the gaps with its allies.

The Netherlands wants to deliver howitzers to Ukraine. Estonia can send the nine howitzers from GDR stocks on their way now that the approval papers have finally arrived from Germany. Slovakia hands over its only S-300 air defense system. The Czech Republic is in with T-72 combat tanks and Soviet-designed BMP-1 infantry fighting vehicles. Lithuania has supplied heavy mortars. Poland is offering combat aircraft, but the matter is convoluted. In the end, there is the word ring exchange for what Warsaw proposes. Soviet-made armaments will be delivered to Ukraine and replaced with new, Western technology by other NATO countries. It is good that NATO's eastern partners need far less time.

Unlike Germany initially, the US is not secretive about its military support. The list on an open website includes eleven Russian Mi-17 helicopters, 200 armored personnel carriers, 90 howitzers and ammunition, and 120 new Phoenix Ghost drones. France has been rather cagey about which weapons it is giving Ukraine. Among them are anti-tank missiles and Caesar howitzers, i.e., heavy artillery pieces.

Even before the war, Turkey sold Bayraktar TB2 combat drones to Ukraine, of which twelve are said to have been delivered. Great Britain has promised Kyiv 150 "Mastiff" armored vehicles. Nowhere, it seems, are the allies having as much trouble as in Berlin. After Scholz's turn-of-the-tide speech, Germany needs two months to decide on delivering heavy weapons. On April 28, 2022, a roll call vote will take place in the Bundestag, with 586 deputies in favor, 100 against, and seven abstaining. The promise to finally supply Kyiv with Gepard anti-aircraft tanks and twelve self-propelled howitzers could boost the Ukrainian president's confidence in German policy if everything did not go so slowly. In the Rhineland-Palatinate, Ukrainian soldiers are being trained on the howitzers, but 100 days after the start of the war, no heavy weaponry from

Germany has reached Ukrainian territory. The German government lists what has been sent instead: several thousand bazookas, anti-tank mines, Stinger and Strela anti-aircraft missiles, artillery, other ammunition, machine guns, anti-tank mines, and hand grenades.

Scholz hardly participates in the discussion about what can be delivered to Ukraine and how quickly, directly, or via detours. The confusion is considerable. The Hanseatic from Osnabrück is drawing more and more ire for not explaining himself enough. In this, he follows ex-Chancellor Angela Merkel. When he does deign to make a statement, he acts arrogantly. Asked in an rbb radio interview about his claim to leadership and the reactions to his current actions, he replies: "To some of these guys and gals I have to say: Because I don't do what you want, that's why I lead." The "boys and girls" are outraged. In Kyiv, one can only wonder about this German debate; another is about the whole thing. Two questions are at the center: Does Ukraine *have to* win the war? Or: *Should* Russia *not* win the war? A quibble, one might think, or a kind of shibboleth: Only those who pronounce the word correctly, or in this case, say the right sentence, are truly on Ukraine's side in its fight for freedom and believe in its victory. But you do not hear from the defense minister or the chancellor himself: Ukraine must win the war. Just as little as Scholz wanted to say Nord Stream 2, let alone announce the end of this project before February 24, 2022.

Olaf Scholz does not explain why he says, "Russia must not win this war." Instead, he calls Emmanuel Macron and holds an 80-minute conversation with Vladimir Putin — when neither the Russian nor the Ukrainian side shows interest in peace negotiations. It is an untimely attempt at mediation, and Scholz, in particular, is resented for it. The fact that the German, of all people, speaks to the Russian president but does not visit Zelenskyy in Kyiv is considered a faux pas.

On June 1, 2022, the chancellor informs the Bundestag that Germany will provide Kyiv with a tracking radar and the most modern air defense system that the Federal Republic of Germany has. It is the Iris-T SLM, with a delivery period of several months, as with the Gepard, for which ammunition must first be found.

Meanwhile, the Polish government reports that Poland is sending 18 howitzers to Ukraine and has already trained Ukrainian soldiers to use this weapon. Germany always remains in second place. Compared to the late delivery of weapons, the discussion is certainly the lesser of two evils. However, the German government's miscommunication contributes to Germany's continuing loss of reputation in Europe and the world and, more importantly, is costing lives in Ukraine. Scholz's undertone is all the more inappropriate: "Let me do it, you'll see."

Ursula von der Leyen, the President of the European Commission, is much more sure-footed. She senses that in these difficult hours, the Ukrainians want, above all, to be given the feeling that Europe stands by their side, that they are not alone, and that they are welcome in the EU after the war. That is why it responded to Kyiv's request on February 26. Volodymyr Zelenskyy knows it; she knows it; everyone and anyone in political Brussels and Berlin knows that candidate status is only the beginning of a long road to the EU. Those in power warn of the hurdles and express their doubts that the former Soviet republic will overcome them, given the corruption and a judiciary needing reform. Millions of Ukrainian war refugees see these objections as rejection. Solidarity looks different. However, the European Commission president is concerned about the community's credibility. On April 8, 2022, she will travel to Kyiv to meet Zelenskyy and shake both his hands in greeting. She has brought something with her that would be moaned about elsewhere: forms. The Ukrainian happily accepts them. This is the first time the country has applied to join the EU. Von der Leyen has held out the prospect of a much slower accession process, knowing that after the end of the war, reforms will have to be made in parallel with reconstruction: The judiciary must become independent, and laws must apply to Oligarches. Within a few days, the Kyiv presidential administration sends the completed papers back to Brussels, where the commission president now has her say. It usually takes years for the EU Commission to issue an opinion and recommendation, von der Leyen said during her visit. However, the German is moving quickly and promises a decision within weeks. The EU chief is also taking time for Bucha, where many serious war crimes have become known. Her sympathy is good for the Ukrainians, the EU, and Germany.

Ukrainian trust in Germany is far from having a solid foundation. Steinmeier's admission of guilt in Babyn Yar impressed the Ukrainians. It was both overdue and correct. Unfortunately, it was not entirely convincing because the Ukrainians find the Germans' rethinking too selective. They fear there has been no lasting change in attitude toward their country. When Ukraine's existence was once again threatened, the support of German leaders was not enough. It came neither unhesitatingly nor quickly but rather hesitantly, dithering.

He names Jens Plötner, foreign policy advisor to Chancellor Olaf Scholz, and Andreas Michaelis, state secretary at the Federal Foreign Office. He says that the Germans have always tried to wring concessions from Ukraine in negotiations with Russia and Ukraine. "My President Zelenskyy once said: We are being led around like horses in the ring." The interview divides the public. Many think it's outrageous. An ambassador should not speak like that. Where is the diplomatic restraint? At last, someone is saying it, think others who are publicly reticent in their approval. More than a few miss the gratitude for the refugee aid provided, the money from the federal and EU budgets, and the arms deliveries. In Steinmeier's political home, the SPD, all the defense reflexes immediately jump into action. The accusations also hurt so much because many of them are true. Melnyk pokes his finger into the wound. The usually accommodating ambassador remains consistent in his rejection of Steinmeier. Melnyk did not buy Steinmeier's speech on his re-election as German president, in which he settled accounts with Putin as clearly as never before. "He has no connection to us Ukrainians. Steinmeier doesn't know what to do with us, even though he himself was in Kyiv and even in Lviv. (...) Sensitivity is a foreign word for Steinmeier, at least with regard to Ukraine."

Most do not want to hear the long list of German-Russian mistakes that Ukraine is paying for with thousands of lives. Especially since Melnyk's Twitter frequency is extremely high, he speaks out more often than his president with video messages, and he seldom goes off without new reproaches. Having pushed the Germans for years regarding support for the war against Russia has left the diplomat deeply annoyed. He admits that he is thinking about going back to Ukraine soon. Acquaintances in Kyiv would now guard block posts and set up roadblocks. "When I feel that there is nothing left in Germany, I will say, dear German friends, goodbye. In many cases, I can achieve more in my homeland than in Berlin, with these deaf ears here."

Thomas Geisel was mayor of Düsseldorf until 2020 and is one of those who cannot deal with this criticism. Under the headline "Enough, Mr. Melnyk! President Zelenskyy's ambassador a pretentious PR professional", the Social Democrat makes up his very own account of the war crimes in Bucha:

> 410 civilians have — according to Ukrainian data — fallen victim to the atrocities of Bucha. Of course, every civilian casualty of a war is a tragedy and one too many. But doesn't the Ukrainian genocide rhetoric ultimately trivialize the war crimes of Srebrenica, My Lai and Babiyar (...) and perhaps also the Dresden night bombing, which allegedly claimed 30,000 victims?

Apart from that, as the SPD politician Geisel writes Babyn Yar, there are different possibilities, but the entry on his blog is a single monstrosity. For example, he indirectly insinuates that the number of victims may be false because it is Ukrainian data. The professional politician might know that international forensics have investigated and counted the victims in the meantime. He also accuses the Ukrainians of "genocide rhetoric." Genocide has been a criminal offense under international criminal law since 1948. It is characterized by the intention to destroy, directly or indirectly, a national, ethnic, or religious group in whole or in part. The SPD local politician insinuates that the crimes in Bucha are linked to the others he listed as massacres because more people fell victim to them. He "forgets" about this cynical reckoning that the Russians have caused many "Buchas" in Ukraine. His equating of the Dresden bombing victims in World War II with those of genocide makes clear that the reappraisal of history in Germany, at least in his case, has not been fruitful. The Dresden victims of several nights' bombing are the war dead, but not genocide victims, because unlike Nazi Germany, which committed genocide against Jews and the respective peoples in the invaded countries, the air raids on Dresden were part of the Allies' defense against the brutal German aggressor. The method of destroying cities across the board already led to fierce controversy among the Western allies during the war. The exact number of victims of the British and US bombings could never be precisely determined; experts assume up to 25,000 people. Does Thomas Geisel know that he is arguing like the neo-Nazis who instrumentalize the suffering of the Dresden victims for their own purposes every year? The Social Democrat from North Rhine-Westphalia doubts that Ukraine can win the war and worries not about Ukraine but about Russia, whether it is right to break off contact not only with Putin but with Russia as a whole, to isolate it. Because morally Putin has long since lost, continuing the war would be a tragedy. Because Geisel, who deleted his entry after massive public criticism, is not alone in this argument, it is worth listening to those who suffer most from this war: the Ukrainians.

Diana, a doctor from Kherson, is convinced that if Ukraine were to give in, it would encourage Russia to start an even bigger war. The Russian Army would invade again, just as it did in February 2022 after 2014, and might even have in their ranks forcibly recruited Ukrainians from areas occupied today, who would have to fight against their own compatriots. Diana fled west of the country because she was afraid that the occupiers would carry out a massacre like the one in Bucha in her hometown, which was conquered at the beginning of the war, and Putin had awarded medals to the soldiers who took part in it. Giving up is not an option for her, as it is for many Ukrainians, partly because they remember 1938 and 1939 better than some Germans when Hitler was not stopped immediately and invaded more and more countries. Winston Churchill, who led Britain through World War II as prime minister and was honored with the 1953 Nobel Prize for Literature, once described the advocates of the appeasement policy thus: "An appeaser is the one who feeds a crocodile, hoping it will eat him last."

Melnyk's persistent advocacy for arms deliveries to his country is also heard—and appreciated—in Kyiv. Because thanks to his persistence, something does move in Berlin in the end, even if it is usually much too slowly. Zelenskyy keeps a close eye on who is delivering results for the country in the field. Those who can neither provide weapons nor money, sanctions against Russia, or other support for the homeland's survival are removed, like the Ukrainian ambassador in Morocco and her colleague in Georgia. Zelenskyy, a political greenhorn until he took office in 2019, best exemplifies how it is done himself. The actor and comedian is proving to be a gifted communications professional rallying support for his country worldwide. With his international and national presence, the commander-in-chief is convincing and makes many a head of state or government not at war look old. When the US offered to help him and his family flee the country right at the start of the war, Zelenskyy declined with thanks: "The fight is here. I need ammunition, not a ride."

His speeches are tailored specifically to the addressees in foreign parliaments or committees; nothing is repeated. This is also the case during his appearance in the German Bundestag. As always, wearing an olive green shirt and speaking Ukrainian, he addresses the German members of parliament. On March 17, 2022, Zelenskyy is no less clear than his ambassador. Germany is only ever concerned with the economy, the economy, the economy. The "Never again!" routinely uttered in Germany sounds bitter for Ukrainians because "these words are worth nothing." Zelenskyy talks about Germany's refusal to admit his country to NATO and the EU and its reluctance to help with weapons while continuing to do business with Russia. All of this, he said, is building a new wall, complete with barbed wire, in Europe that is cutting off Ukraine. The members of the Bundestag applaud for a long time, standing up, although Zelenskyy has just publicly washed their heads. Then they all turn away from the large screen on which the speaker from Kyiv had been broadcasting and turn to the parliamentary routine. Not a single word to the president, who, in his despair day after day, begs one country after another for help. Chancellor Scholz seems paralyzed, motionless, and speechless. The Bundestag does not even manage a minute's silence for the war dead. What could have been a great parliamentary moment, with a broad, overdue debate on aid to Ukraine and the misguided policy toward Russia, ends in the minutiae of birthday wishes-without dignity.

On the same day, when Scholz still does not talk to the Ukrainian but about his country, it does not get much better. Scholz talks about the Ukrainian nation in general and the languages used in the country in particular:

"There is a Ukrainian nation, and it includes those who speak the Ukrainian language as their mother tongue. And also one or two of those who speak the Russian language." In fact, most Ukrainians speak Russian, and for more than a third, it is their native language. They live mostly, but not only, in the east or south of the country. Even on Kyiv's streets, one hears more Russian than Ukrainian. But people feel they belong to the Ukrainian nation regardless of whether they learned Ukrainian or Russian first. Paradoxically, the most important contribution to this nation-building has come from the Kremlin's longstanding anti-Ukrainian policy.

It is not until three days later that the deputies manage to rise from their seats in the plenary hall to pay tribute to 95-year-old Holocaust survivor Boris Romanchenko, who died in Kharkiv in a Russian bombing raid.

In April, the first rockets also hit Odesa. Roman Schwarzman, a good acquaintance of Boris Romantschenko, lives there. Schwarzman says on the phone that he has hardly slept a night since the war began. The 85-year-old longs to finally be able to go to bed in his pajamas again instead of sleeping dressed and rushing to the basement with a suitcase when the bomb alarm goes off, sometimes several times a night. Schwarzman was affected by the death of his brother in Kharkiv. He knows his story well and those of other survivors because he conducted 200 interviews for the Shoa Foundation, founded by Steven Spielberg. Schwarzman was a child in the ghetto of Berschad, 300 kilometers west of Odesa. At the time, he was too small to be afraid; today, by contrast, he is afraid, not so much for himself as for his children, grandchildren, and great-grandchildren. "Putin wants to free us from the Nazis? Which Nazis are they supposed to be with us? When Russia talks about the denazification of Ukraine, it sounds to me like the Final Solution of the Nazis. We Jews can judge this well. Today it is *Russian* fascism that wants to destroy the Ukrainian nation." And this is not just about Ukrainian nationality, he said. "We also have Russians, Poles, Hungarians, Armenians, Greeks, Jews, and many more. It is Putin who simply renames all our people, including us Jews, as Nazis!" The lively little man who wants to get the memorial for those murdered in the ammunition barracks in October 1941 off the ground in Odesa with Marieluise Beck is worried about the project. What if Putin throws a spanner in their works? His association of former Jewish prisoners in ghettos and concentration camps still has 275 members. Like many, he has had bad experiences with the Soviet Union's state anti-Semitism. "When I had to go to the party committee, it was unacceptable for me to mention my name: Schwarzman. My brothers preferred to take the Ukrainian surnames of their wives so as not to sound so Jewish. My daughter was not allowed to study medicine. Almost all my life, I encountered this kind of anti-Semitism, not anymore." Today, his grandchildren have university degrees in the subjects they were allowed to choose for themselves. Only in independent Ukraine, after the collapse of the USSR in 1991, did it become possible to talk about Jews and the Holocaust. In communist times, only Soviet victims were spoken of in general terms. Today, he said, he could go to the synagogue without being bothered; in Soviet times, there were none in Odesa. Neither were there Jewish schools, universities, kindergartens, organizations, or cultural centers.

The fact that Scholz consistently refers to the Russian invasion of Ukraine as "Putin's war" infuriates the sprightly man because the approval of the war was in the entire Russian people great. A bitter disappointment for Roman Schwarzman, who cannot imagine his grandchildren or great-grandchildren ever reaching out to their Russian neighbor again. "There is a different mentality in Russia, no one will ask us for forgiveness." In contrast, he said, many Germans have apologized to him personally, not only with words but even with admirable deeds that come from deep in their hearts.

Nevertheless, he is not sparing criticism in the direction of Berlin. He thinks that Germany and the West have allowed themselves to be intimidated by Putin. "Take an example from us, from Ukraine!" If there is one phrase he can no longer hear from German politicians, it is this: "We're worried." Born in 1936, Schwarzman is vital and wide awake, a temperamental man who knows that most of his life is behind him. For that very reason, he wonders impatiently why the war is taking so long. He blames Western diplomacy, which has failed to reform the World Security Council. The fact that the veto and not the majority rule still applies there is simply cynical, he says. "Do your homework!" he shouts down the phone while the sirens start sounding the air alarm again. Nevertheless, he is in no hurry to hang up because he still has something to get off his chest: He has often noticed that some people in Germany are susceptible to Russian propaganda, for example, the Russian warning about the fascists on the Maidan and the lie that Ukraine is not its own nation, not its own state. As the former occupiers or their descendants, the Germans should know better. But, unfortunately, the Germans know little about Ukraine; even about the dark chapter of the common history, there are big gaps in knowledge.

And in the future?

The suffering of war in Buchah, Irpin, Kharkiv, Mariupol, Severodonezk, and many other places makes them powerless and helpless. No means seems properly chosen if it is unsuitable for saving lives and stopping Putin's deadly troops. So what is to be done? Germany should give Ukraine what it needs for its defense. By their standards, politicians in this country were quick to rethink: the principle of not supplying weapons to war zones has not vanished into thin air, but it has been adapted to a new reality. For over 50 years, the doctrine adopted by the social-liberal government led by Willy Brandt in 1971 was valid. To continue to adhere to this principle would have been tantamount to failing to assist. Nevertheless, members of parliament—across all parties and even within the governing coalition—argued for months about which weapons could be supplied. The pivotal point was: do we supply what Ukraine needs and demands, or what does not put Germany in a difficult position?

Is it unfair to say that Chancellor Scholz comes across as a huckster who first sharpens his pencil and adds up how much it will cost before finally pushing the arms package over the counter? Yes, that is unfair because he is not concerned, as he used to be as finance minister, with keeping the Euros together and spending as low as possible. Military aid to Kyiv is not a question of money. Olaf Scholz does not argue with the monetary burden, although it will soon catch up with the country on an enormous scale. After all, the arms and financial aid for Ukraine, the retrofitting of the German armed forces, the special fund, which is, in reality, a loan, and the additional expenditures in the NATO alliance—all of this costs money. But the foreseeable budget deficit is not why Berlin hesitates to fulfill Kyiv's wishes and desires. It is the dilemma of acting in Germany's and Europe's interests on the one hand but not enforcing these interests at Ukraine's expense on the other.

The dispute over Berlin's arms deliveries has revealed major lapses in the public discussion of Germany's peace and security policy. Is it guided by values or determined by interests? The US is criticized more than almost any other country in this regard, often justifiably, not infrequently sweepingly, but no one has been bothered by the fact that Washington has provided and paid for Germany's and Europe's security all these years. The former Polish ambassador to Germany, Janusz Reiter, considers the Zeitenwende speech one of the most important speeches of the postwar period. The Germans had finally jumped over their shadows by taking responsibility for their own security and defense and that of their allies. The German government again felt responsible for an adequately equipped Bundeswehr, treated like a stepchild for decades. But then, according to the diplomat from Warsaw, people in Berlin suddenly seemed afraid of their own courage. Moreover, Reiter, who represented Poland in Germany from 1990 to 1995, states that the new federal government has not yet defined its role in European policy.

Olaf Scholz leaves both the German public and the partners in the EU member states, but above all Kyiv, in the dark about what he expects from the long-term EU membership.

The chancellor remains silent instead of going on the offensive and weighing up the risks and opportunities comprehensibly. That opens the door to speculation. Does he want to stand in Ukraine's way because this large country might shift the balance in the Union too far in the direction of Eastern Europe? Poland and Ukraine, where 80 million people live, could become too heavy for the Franco-German motor, which would no longer be the traction engine. Or does he not believe in the former Soviet republic's ability to reform? After all, even Zelenskyy has been previously mentioned in connection with corruption. Scholz shies away from the pathos of Ursula von der Leyen. The EU Commission president had already announced three days after the start of the war: "Over time, they [Ukrainians] are actually one of us. They are one of us, and we want them in."

The chancellor also lacks von der Leyen's Anglo-Saxon pragmatism: If the EU finances the reconstruction of the war-ravaged country, then it should be done according to Brussels rules. Moreover, the impression is created that Scholz talks more to Putin than Zelenskyy, which is not true. He speaks to the latter regularly on the phone. But the chancellor has been playing the silent game for too long now. The fact that he hesitated for two months to finally board a train to Kyiv, even though even German President Frank-Walter Steinmeier had long since settled the dispute with Kyiv, became increasingly incomprehensible. Every trip that Olaf Scholz took instead, whether to Africa, or the Balkans, was tainted by the fact that he was setting the wrong priorities. The guesswork about the German government's attitude did not end even when he finally got his act together in mid-June. At his side, he has brought French President Emmanuel Macron and Italy's Prime Minister Mario Draghi. In Kyiv, he is joined by Romania's President Klaus Johannis. Will the quartet appear before Zelenskyy together so that one does not have to deliver the bad news of a rejection of candidate status alone? Some in Kyiv, like presidential adviser Oleksiy Arestowych, fear that Zelenskyy will be persuaded to negotiate: "They will say that we must end the war, which is causing food problems and economic problems, that Russians and Ukrainians are dying, that we must save Mr. Putin's face, that Russians have made mistakes, that we must forgive them and give them a chance to return to world society." Ukraine wants to negotiate, and it made that clear in the very first days of the war. At that time, it was even willing to renounce its constitutionally enshrined goal of joining NATO. But it does not want a new edition of the Minsk Agreement, which grants Moscow even more land for the sake of peace than was the case in 2015. It lost Crimea and eastern Ukraine back then, and the war continued anyway.

    The fact that such speculations about the purpose of the chancellor's trip are being made is also due to his lack of language and positioning. Many people were relieved when he spoke out clearly in Kyiv in favor of an accession perspective and also promised President Zelenskyy to campaign for it until the vote among the 27 EU member states. But only one week is left between the Kyiv visit and the EU summit! And some countries are expressing reservations. Portugal fears that Ukraine will receive a lot of money for its reconstruction and become an important competitor for agricultural subsidies. Others see problems with the principle of unanimity with which the community has made its important decisions, especially in foreign policy.

A new agreement mechanism is even more urgent, but what will it look like? Will a constitutional convention have to be organized, and how quickly? These are scenarios that have been worrying all European colleagues for a while. Shouldn't Scholz have been mediating and convincing behind the scenes long ago? Like a spectator who arrives late at the theater, the Social Democrat has trouble finding his seat. He does not want to take the lead; he has been a second-tier politician for too long. But in the end, Scholz can report a success: "27 times yes!" he rejoices on Twitter. All EU states have unanimously expressed their support for Ukraine's accession prospects.

Many peace activists, including those in his party, believe they are against the war alone. They clap their hands over their heads and lament the victims as if the majority did not feel the same way. But those who proclaim their horror aloud are heard and feel good. And you are always on the right side. But it does not cost much either. When wishing still helped, wars often stopped by themselves. Unfortunately, they were ended militarily more often, even if negotiations often took place simultaneously. Not infrequently, these self-proclaimed pacifists show little interest in the reasons for the conflicts that led to war. They sometimes do not even know how to distinguish which party is the victim and the aggressor. The height of hypocrisy is that they label warmongers as those who offer aid and support to the distressed. Keeping one's hands in one's pockets, letting others do the work, and feeling morally superior as a bystander—that is fine.

The fact that Germany's head of government, Scholz, must never lose sight of the security of the Federal Republic, despite all the pressure, is his duty, which he took upon himself with the oath of office. He must constantly weigh up whether decisions could lead to an unintended escalation. There are fears triggered by Moscow that Russia could invade Lithuania via Kaliningrad or that it would like to "take back" the Estonian city of Narva on the Russian border, as Putin hinted at in an event with young entrepreneurs on the 350th anniversary of the birth of Tsar Peter the Great. Like his history essay on the alleged unity of the Russian and Ukrainian peoples, such a statement may be a hidden announcement. "One should take his words seriously," Angela Merkel advised. But can the German chancellor really prevent such plans by ruling out the delivery of certain weapons to Ukraine? Does it really depend on whether Putin considers NATO countries, individually or as an alliance, to be a war party? Massive military support has helped Ukrainian soldiers and volunteers impressively resist and drive Russian units out of the Kyiv countryside. A month after the war began, they withdrew from the area north of Kyiv. Putin's first wartime objective, to take the capital in a blitzkrieg and install a puppet government headed by Viktor Yanukovych, was thwarted. Allegedly, the ex-president, who fled in 2014, was already at heel in Belarus with his "shadow cabinet." He was to be reinstated as the legitimate president after the defection of President Zelenskyy and his team, although after Yanukovych's departure, two democratic and fair presidential elections have already taken place in Ukraine. The fact that Ukraine has been able to defeat this project is also thanks to military aid from abroad. If one takes Putin at his word, the *casus belli* has long since occurred.

As a reminder, in his speech on 24 February, the Russian president threatened, "Whoever tries to interfere with us, let alone endanger our country and our people, must know that Russia's response will be immediate and will lead to consequences the likes of which you have never experienced in your history."

It is pointless to define when the Russian aggressor considers the allies' assistance to Ukraine as interference. Is it howitzers or planes or tanks? Is it NATO soldiers on Ukrainian territory?

Poland and the Baltic states are unwilling to accept a gradation of when Moscow will take which measures because they have long since ceased to regard Putin as predictable. He is sacrificing tens of thousands of soldiers' lives, driving the elite out of the country, lying to his people, tearing down what his closest confidants and their corrupt network have built up, and risking that his budget's only strong financial source will soon dry up forever. Putin is the gravedigger of his country, which he is destroying as he megalomaniacally seeks to expand it by force. His game with fear does not impress the Ukrainians, but it does the Germans. The former KGB man with detailed knowledge of Germany is calibrated to exploit his opponents' weak points and knows that the fear of a nuclear war is particularly great in Germany. Has he threatened Scholz with this? The occupation of Europe's largest nuclear power plant in Zaporizhzhya and the ruined nuclear power plant in Chornobyl by Russian soldiers was intended primarily to scare foreign countries. The fact that the Germans are reluctant to continue using the existing nuclear power plants even in a possible energy crisis has probably confirmed Putin's assessment of the Germans. In this context, Russian energy sources are proving an effective weapon.

For his opponents, it is a choice between plague and cholera. If Germany were to favor a gas boycott after the oil boycott, the most important question would still not be answered: When and under what conditions will Putin end his war? He still has a large army and full weapons stockpiles to fall back on—or he can turn off the gas tap completely. He has as little compassion for his own people as the tsars, as little as Lenin or Stalin. The welfare or hardships of Russians have never guided Kremlin rulers in their actions, except for Mikhail Gorbachev. For Western democracies, however, their governments must decide today so that people will still be well off tomorrow. A gas freeze would presumably not slow Putin down, but Germany's economic strength would. What sounds like determination and unwavering solidarity with Ukraine could perhaps be a disservice. After all, with a significantly weakened economy, it would be harder to provide for the millions of people who have fled and for the supply of weapons. Ukraine must win this war so that Putin loses his appetite for more territory. Volodymyr Zelenskyy is right when he says: "Surely it's wiser for everyone in Europe to help us now so that you don't have to defend other nations later." Germany must be economically strong to support Ukraine with a kind of Marshall Plan. A concerted reconstruction program will prove to Russia and the world that Western democracies are standing up for each other and their freedom and well-being. Germany's and Europe's independence on Russian gas and oil is no longer just an economic and climate issue but now also a security issue, so Putin's rearmament will be made more difficult long after this war is over.

Currently, the federal government has to solve many tasks simultaneously, deciding life or death. That is why it must now explain itself in particular. The citizens are afraid. Most of them are informing themselves more than ever before, forming an opinion, and wanting to discuss it. Participation is the essence of democracy. Everyone is allowed to know and say almost everything, but politicians are not free to explain themselves; they have a duty to do so. Unfortunately, Germany currently presents itself as a developing country when it comes to communication—and is thus gambling away trust.

It is not a matter of discretion to answer how one of the worst crises in Europe since the Second World War could have come about. Nor is it an insult to majesty to demand them from those who have played a decisive role in shaping the policies of the past decades. Those who share responsibility for this must face the questions of the voters. They must explain why decisions were made the way they were and not differently. Respect for the citizens demands that forums be created now in which a reappraisal is possible. The discussion about this is still strangely restrained. Angela Merkel has begun to speak out sporadically since the end of her sabbatical from the chancellorship. First on Kyiv's denied NATO membership, then on the Baltic Sea gas pipeline.

In many cases, she still lacks distance. So far, there is little sign of her taking a self-critical look back. The main argument used to warn against energy dependence on Russia is that Putin could use gas as a weapon against Ukraine, Germany, and the European countries that are also supplied. To this day, the former chancellor does not accept this argument. In her first newspaper interview, she explains why she believes the warning that gas could become a weapon is not true: "The thesis at the time was that when Nord Stream 2 is operational, Putin will stop supplying gas through Ukraine or even attack it. But we made sure that gas was delivered through Ukraine anyway, thus ensuring that Ukraine would continue to receive fees for Russian gas deliveries to the West." Merkel alludes to the replacement arrangement for maintaining Ukraine's energy supply that she and US President Biden negotiated in Washington in July 2021. So far, however, this agreement has only existed on paper. Incidentally, no Ukrainian negotiator was involved in the drafting of this agreement. It has not yet been tested in practice because the gas transit through Ukraine has not yet been stopped at all, even after several months of the war. Merkel's argument does not hold water. Neither does her conclusion: "Putin then attacked Ukraine on February 24, even though not a single cubic meter of gas had flowed through Nord Stream 2. In that sense, gas was not a weapon." Again, she is not right because Moscow already uses this weapon. Unlike in the past, Gazprom has recently been throttling the supply volume for German customers at will, depending on whether the Kremlin wants to create security or uncertainty. Unlike her predecessor Helmut Kohl, the long-serving party chairwoman no longer wants to play a major role in the CDU. Despite her 30 years of membership, she did not want to become the honorary chair of the Union. She did not even agree to a farewell dinner with Friedrich Merz, who has finally arrived in the party and parliamentary group chair office he has sought for so long. The tablecloth between the two has long been cut. This makes it all the more surprising that the incumbent opposition leader is now reluctant to take stock of Angela Merkel's work in government precisely because she continues to justify her support for Nord Stream.

The connection between Moscow's export earnings and Russian rearmament need not be explained to her. The machinations of her predecessor in office, Schröder, together with the ex-Stasi collaborator Warnig, were by no means conducted only in dark back rooms. The successor project, Nord Stream 2, was not necessary for Germany's security of supply, but at most for those who profited from it. If one judges the damage from the end, as Helmut Kohl used to do, the interest in clarification is probably even greater today than in 1999 with the CDU party donations affair. Even if one should not equate criminal activity with political mistakes, it is unavoidable to deal with the Christian Democrats' policy toward the East. Former Secretary General Angela Merkel had an inkling of how vulnerable the party would be in the long run due to the donations affair if she did not try to clear it up herself. Her article in the *Frankfurter Allgemeine Zeitung* was a prelude that many saw as a betrayal of the CDU but made possible a new beginning after the Kohl era. But where is a newspaper article by Friedrich Merz similar to the one by Angela Merkel on December 22, 1999? He would only need to make minor changes to the text she wrote then.

Today, Friedrich Merz sits much more firmly in the saddle as CDU and parliamentary group chairman than Angela Merkel did back then. Former Chancellor Helmut Kohl had parked donations for the CDU in special accounts that were not disclosed in the party's statement of accounts but were used for party purposes. At least 1.5 to two million DM had been collected, but Kohl never disclosed the names of the donors. Compared to today's dimensions, the hidden donations of around two million DM seem like peanuts. Where is Friedrich Merz now, who has spent 16 years being convinced that he was the better party leader and chancellor? He has never forgiven Merkel for removing him as parliamentary group leader in 2002 because she felt that party and parliamentary group leadership belonged together.

As a leader of the opposition, Friedrich Merz could easily request a committee of inquiry in the Bundestag to review the grand coalition's Russia policy. In addition to the SPD, Bavarian Prime Minister Markus Söder of the CSU could explain why he did not oppose all attempts to soften Western sanctions after the Crimea annexation and why he did not put his then-party colleague Peter Gauweiler in his place when he tried to do just that. Gauweiler, who wanted to travel to the peninsula six months after the occupation but was prevented by Bundestag President Norbert Lammert, flew to Moscow instead, where he lashed out hard at the European Union. He said the sanctions policy was cowardly and went in the wrong direction. In addition, the CSU deputy chairman met the then parliamentary president Sergei Naryshkin, who eight years later would become world-famous for Putin's scolding of him like a schoolboy three days before the invasion of Ukraine.

In front of running cameras, the Russian president has the members of the Security Council in the Kremlin recite what they think of the current situation in Ukraine and the so-called Donezk and Luhansk People's Republics and what they intend to do about it. He deliberately did not consult them beforehand, Putin says at the beginning. Those present sit several meters away from his desk in a circle of chairs in front of him. Now it is up to the prime minister, the ministers of defense, foreign affairs, and the interior, the chairs of the two chambers of parliament, and the heads of the intelligence services to repeat what Putin has said in a sentence.

They are to propose that the independence of the two Donbas republics be recognized. On behalf of the Security Council, they are then to submit this proposal to the Duma, which in turn asks him, the president, to do the same. The president thus dictates what the Security Council and the Duma should do, demonstrating in public that the separation of powers in Russia is out of order. Sergei Naryshkin, whom Peter Gauweiler met in Moscow shortly after the start of the war in eastern Ukraine in 2014 when he was still Duma chairman, is now head of the foreign intelligence service SWR. He does not immediately understand his president's request in the live televised meeting. So he initially proposes to keep trying with negotiations and the Minsk peace process and is visibly unsettled. When Putin realizes that his SWR man is in danger of missing the mark, he examines Naryshkin—and the whole world can watch as Putin puts him on course. Putin not only watches carefully as each successive speaker and the loyal chairman of the Federation Council, Valentina Matviyenko, recite their little verses. He also ensures that the representatives of the Donbas turn to Moscow with a "call for help," after which he, as commander-in-chief, can set his troops in motion.

If Gauweiler had criticized the Moscow-backed war of the pro-Russian separatists back in 2014 and said that the sanctions were far too lax a reaction given the breach of international law by the occupation of Crimea, he would be on the right side of history today. What was his motive for going easy on Russia? Why did Söder not call his deputy back then?

Even though Söder and Armin Laschet fought each other in the 2021 Bundestag election campaign—they were often not far apart on Russia policy. Laschet called only a few days after the annexation of Crimea in the *Frankfurter Allgemeine Zeitung* not to demonize Putin. He warned against "anti-Putin populism" and pleaded for empathy with the interlocutor, even if the referendum in Crimea, by which the Kremlin annexed the peninsula, was "clearly contrary to international law." The man from Aachen demanded more empathy for a president who has just revealed himself as an aggressor by shifting Europe's borders for the first time since the end of World War II. Like most German politicians, for whom the sanctions already went too far, Laschet was thinking first and foremost of the economy and the more than 1,000 companies in North Rhine-Westphalia that maintained trade relations with Russia. He was just as unsettled as when Crimea was annexed after the attack on Sergei Skripal and his daughter in Great Britain, in which Russian contract killers used the chemical agent Novichok. Laschet questioned the simultaneous expulsion of Russian diplomats from Britain, France, the United States, and Germany, on Twitter. "If you force almost all NATO countries to show solidarity, shouldn't you have secure evidence? You can stand by Russia as you like, but I learned a different way of dealing with states in my studies of international law."

Laschet gave an even more embarrassing performance as minister-president of North Rhine-Westphalia at the Petersburg Dialogue 2019 in Königswinter near Bonn. Softly the host reminded the audience that the ties between Germany and Russia must be strengthened.

The Russian delegates were convinced they had to "forge stronger ties and intensify understanding," even if the divisions had to be addressed openly. Throwing cotton balls would have attracted more attention than this half-hearted attempt to talk the Russian delegates into their conscience. Laschet did not notice that he was stabbing German Foreign Minister Heiko Maass in the back with so much appeasement on the open stage. Maaß, who was initially firm on Russia, had just called on his colleague Lavrov to take the outstretched hand of the then-new Ukrainian President Volodymyr Zelenskyy and get closer to him on the issue of eastern Ukraine. Laschet did not oppose Lavrov when he told the audience in Königswinter the well-known lie that Russia had protected the Donbas from neo-Nazis. The Russian side was allowed to lament at length how tired it was of the sanctions, how unfortunate it was that the EU was withholding loans for investments from Russian companies, how much the Russian population was suffering from the counter-sanctions imposed by Moscow because foodstuffs such as cheese, dairy products, fruit, and vegetables could no longer be imported from the EU. Not a word about the thousands of Ukrainian (!) dead, who have already been killed in the five-year-long war in the Donbas. The organizers of the Petersburg Dialogue did not manage to put the real problem, the Russian policy of intervention and expansion against Ukraine, on the agenda. The meeting was a mere token event, useful above all for the Kremlin, which showed that it is by no means isolated internationally.

Even during the interviews for the election of the CDU chairmanship in 2020, Laschet advocated completing the Nord Stream 2 project, while his competitors were much more sure-footed in Russia policy. Norbert Röttgen called for a halt to construction, Merz for a two-year moratorium, and sanction the poisoning of opposition member Alexei Navalny on August 20, 2020.

It does not look like the CDU/CSU will get together to come to terms with the past 16 years. Secretary General Mario Czaja says that Angela Merkel's policy on Russia is burdening the party's new beginning with Friedrich Merz at the top. When incumbent politicians today evaluate their past actions differently and take responsibility for them, he says that demands great respect from him, referring to German President Frank-Walter Steinmeier. And about the retired chancellor: she is retired, he says and has clearly positioned herself against the Russian war, thus making it clear what she stands for. "That is sufficient."

The CDU state association of North Rhine-Westphalia needs more clarification from the SPD: its top candidate receives a catalog of questions about his party's "Russia connection" in April 2022 – shortly before the state elections. Thomas Kutschaty, who was approached, takes the questions as accusations and rejects them all. For 160 years, as long as the SPD has existed, there have always been the same slanders against his party. He dismisses them as the usual election campaign bluster, especially since the federal CDU is conspicuously lenient. Mario Czaja admits that President Steinmeier has already taken responsibility. But in what way? What are the consequences for the former foreign minister, parliamentary group leader, and head of the chancellor's office, who played a decisive role in shaping the questionable and dangerous Russia policy for years? What consequences does he draw from the fact that there is unprecedented energy insecurity in the Federal Republic of Germany, which even dwarfs the 1973 oil crisis?

The Schwerin Climate and Environment Foundation is also likely to become a yardstick for the SPD's handling of its past. The refusal of the state chancellery to release records about the foundation, the reference to files that have suddenly disappeared from the face of the earth, and the blame game played by Minister President Manuela Schwesig does not bode well. As former vice-chancellors, Angela Merkel and Olaf Scholz knew the foundation's plans, including the sums with which Russia's Gazprom provided it. Why did they allow a Russian company to hijack German politics? To what extent Schwerin's state politicians will be criminally prosecuted remains to be seen. Finance officials and lawyers are already investigating whether the foundation should have paid gift taxes on the 20 million Euros in start-up capital from Russia. In Schwerin, the political aftermath has long since begun. The Greens in the state parliament, who did not vote for the foundation, agree with the federal party that the entanglement between the Schwerin state government and the Russian state corporation Gazprom must be called "disastrous". They demand that this complex finally be dealt with.

Whether there will actually be a clarification and whether Manuela Schwesig will survive it politically depends by no means only on herself but just as much on her party, for which she has been seen as a beacon of hope for years. For the first time, the brilliant election winner from September 2021 sees her hopes dashed. To not sink, she is clinging to her former energy minister Christian Pegel, figuratively pushing him underwater. The initiative for the foundation came from him. If you have comrades like that, you do not need any more enemies.

Another problem could be Schwesig's foster father Erwin Sellering, who would prefer not to disclose any information about what he considers to be a private foundation, regardless of whether the district court insists on it. The former administrative judge is also against handing over the foundation's million-euro capital as reconstruction aid for Ukraine. The foundation's dual purpose also requires closer examination. Officially launched as a climate and environmental protection organization, it is now difficult to understand why this working objective has been abandoned, and the foundation is to be wound up in a flash.

That Schwesig would like to bury it sooner rather than later is understandable from her point of view; after all, she could stumble over the Gazprom Foundation and fall.

The past teaches that a committee of inquiry is not necessarily the forum in which one really learns about past mistakes in politics to learn from them. Unfortunately, such control committees tend to put on plays with roles distributed according to party books. Helmut Kohl never disclosed the names of the donors, and Steinmeier's Murat-Kurnaz committee of inquiry in 2008 showed how it is feasible to clarify as little as possible. In any case, Steinmeier concluded that he had behaved completely correctly and drew the conclusion: regret, yes — apologize, no.

An Enquete Commission may be much more thorough, so it is being considered in the CDU. But who knows, for example, the results of the most recent one, which dealt with "vocational education in the digital world of work"? Who is aware of the Enquete Commission's study on artificial intelligence? Probably only those who are particularly interested. While coming to terms with the SED dictatorship, experts, politicians, and contemporary witnesses dealt with the dark history of the GDR in no less than two commissions. The two final reports were each around 300 pages long. But presumably, not many citizens read them. That leaves the party's internal history commissions. Perhaps a start would be made if the SPD first removed its ex-chancellor as a legacy. Apparently, this is easier said than done, even if most members regard Schröder's behavior as damaging to the party. Since mea culpa is not his thing, as he declared on April 23, 2022, party co-chair Saskia Esken has taken the Mikado game in their party leadership ended, and Gerhard Schröder was asked to resign.

SPD co-leader Lars Klingbeil, who used to be employed in Schröder's constituency office, could not bring himself to do so. Secretary-General Kevin Kühnert was also against expulsion proceedings, allegedly because Schröder could abuse the process as a stage. Stefan Weil, minister-president of Lower Saxony, did not even ask him back the state medal since Federal President Steinmeier had not revoked his Federal Cross of Merit. For Esken, however, the barrel had overflowed when Schröder defended his friend Putin against accusations of war crimes. In the Hanover Arbitration Commission, the applications of several local and state associations for party expulsion proceedings, i.e., Schröder's expulsion, are piling up. The former chancellor can no longer be seen anywhere because he has ruined his reputation and his country, whose well-being he supposedly cares about. In the meantime, he is probably only welcomed with open arms in Russia.

Gerhard Schröder's expulsion from the SPD, which currently leads the government, would not be a liberating blow. But it could be a sign of coming to terms with a policy that caused Germany an immense loss of prestige and proved disastrous for Ukraine. Russia's war against Ukraine goes hand in hand with a separation for the SPD. It has to leave behind its previous Ostpolitik, which is difficult for it; after all, it was a kind of unique selling point for the party for a long time. For decades, the comrades have credited themselves with understanding Russia and, before that, the Soviet Union, far better than the other German parties in the center. The CDU-led federal governments have continued this course for a long time with the SPD. The fact that Russian policy, of all things, is now turning out to be the greatest weakness of German foreign and security policy is difficult for the parties in charge to cope with. The alleged mutual dependency — Russia on energy revenues, Germany on natural gas, oil, and coal — was a false assumption because it has always presupposed that Moscow's business interests are just as great as Berlin's. The invasion of Ukraine has taught Germany otherwise: Russia's economy must take a back seat to Putin's imperialism. The Social Democrats still resist a fundamental reassessment of their tried-and-tested Russia strategy. The pain of parting is omnipresent. It is obvious that the older generation feels it more strongly than the younger generation, but for the sake of its future, the party should urgently address this chapter. Otherwise, it risks losing the young party members who expect German Ostpolitik to become a European policy that includes Eastern Europe and Ukraine.

The European Union and the transatlantic alliance develop their strength and persuasiveness when countries stand up for each other. This great democratic power has the potential to help Ukraine win the war, to survive. It has the economic capacity to supply weapons over a long time, even without Russia's fossil fuels, and to back Kyiv in peace negotiations. When and about which areas negotiators will talk to Russia will be decided by politicians and policymakers in Kyiv. The EU will help Ukraine to become part of the European family in the common European house that Soviet President Gorbachev would have liked to live in but in which Putin's Russia does not want to settle.

Sources

The author draws on interviews and research she conducted as part of her work as an Eastern European correspondent for Deutschlandfunk. She translated quotations and wordings from Russian herself. The sources are cited chapter by chapter and in the order in which they appear in the text.

The tragedy

Robert Habeck im Gespräch mit Philipp May, Deutschlandfunk, 26. 5. 2021, online abrufbar: https://www.deutschlandfunk.de/ habeck-gr uene-zu-waffenlieferungen-an-ukraine-die-ukraine-100. Html SPD-Fraktion: Waffenlieferungen dürfen Konflikte nicht anheizen, dpa, 26. 5. 2021

Nina Breher: »Kälte, Unkenntnis und Verzerrung der Fakten«: FDP-Frau Strack-Zimmermann weist Michael Müllers Vor würfe nach Ukraine-Reise zurück, Tagesspiegel, 22. 4. 2022, online abrufbar: https://chec kpoint.tagesspiegel.de/langmeldung/4JvR25Hq4XqBgh7VWm96j8 ?utm_medium=social-button-nl-web

Sevim Dagdelen, Deutscher Bundestag, Auswärtiger Ausschuss, 26. 5. 2021, online abrufbar: https://www.sevimdagdelen.de/habecks-kri egsapologetik-ist-eine-gefahr-fuer-die-sicherheit-in-europa

Daria Kaleniuk, Twitter, 24. 1. 2022 [nicht mehr verfügbar] 230-231

Ukrainer sauer auf Deutschland. Klitschko: »5.000 Helme sind ein absoluter Witz«, t-online, 26. 1. 2022, online abrufbar: https://www.t-online.de/nachrichten/ausland/id_91551430/vitali-klitschko-deut sche-helmlieferung-an-ukraine-ist-ein-absoluter-witz-.html

Chechnya as a blueprint for Ukraine

Jens Høvsgaard: Gier, Gas und Geld. Wie Deutschland mit Nord Stream Europas Zukunft riskiert, München 2019

Maria Scholobowa / Roman Badanin: Chechen Leader Ramzan Kadyrov Has a Second Wife—And Her Properties Are Worth Millions, Recherchegruppe »Projekt«, 7. 4. 2021, online abrufbar: https://maski-proekt. media/ramzan-kadyrov-family

Putin, Schröder, Warnig — pretty smart friends

Jens Høvsgaard: Gier, Gas und Geld. Wie Deutschland mit Nord Stream Europas Zukunft riskiert, München 2019

Oliver Stock: Russische Seele, Handelsblatt, 12. 1. 2007, online abrufbar: https://www.handelsblatt.com/unternehmen/management/matthias-warnig-russische-seele/2755000.html

Andreas Nölting / Arne Stuhr: »Sollten wir uns als Oberrichter aufspielen?«, manager magazin, 23. 2. 2005, online abrufbar: https://www.manager-magazin.de/unternehmen/artikel/a-343372.html

Katrin Bennhold: The Former Chancellor Who Became Putin's Man in Germany, The New York Times, 23. 4. 2022, online abrufbar: https://www.nytimes.com/2022/04/23/world/europe/schrodergermany-russia-gas-ukraine-war-energy.html

Hans Michael Kloth: Indirekter Hitler-Vergleich. Polnischer Minister poltert gegen Schröder und Merkel, Spiegel Online, 30. 4. 2006, online abrufbar: https://www.spiegel.de/wirtschaft/indirekter-hitler-vergleich-polnischer-minister-poltert-gegen-schroeder-und-merkel-a-413931.html

Tagesschau: Es begann mit Schröder, 23. 2. 2022, online abrufbar: https://www.tagesschau.de/inland/innenpolitik/nordstream2-chronologie-101.html

Merkel's no to Kyiv's NATO membership

Wiktoria Bieliaszy: Einblicke in das System Putin. Interview mit Igor Wolobujew, Die Welt / Gazeta Wyborcza, 20. 5. 2022, übersetzt aus dem Polnischen von Klaus Geiger, online abrufbar: https://www.welt.de/politik/ausland/plus238863433/Krieg-in-der-Ukraine-BeiGazprom-sprachen-wir-gern-von-der-Schroederisierung-Europas.html?

Hannes Adomeit: Russische Militär- und Sicherheitspolitik. In:

Heiko Pleines / Hans-Henning Schröder (Hrsg.): Länderbericht

Russland. Bundeszentrale für politische Bildung, Bonn 2010, S. 268 f.

Jens Høvsgaard: Gier, Gas und Geld. Wie Deutschland mit Nord Stream

Europas Zukunft riskiert, München 2019

Sven Felix Kellerhoff: Was diese Notiz über die Nato-Osterweiterung tatsächlich bedeutet, Die Welt, 18. 2. 2022, online abrufbar: https://www.welt.de/geschichte/article237005361/Archivfund-Was-die-Notiz-ueber-die-Nato-Osterweiterung-bedeutet.html

Andreas von Westphal: Die Wurzeln des Misstrauens. Russland und die Deutsche Einheit 1990, Feature, Deutschlandfunk, 10. 12. 2019, online abrufbar: https://www.hoerspielundfeature.de/russlandund-die-d eutsche-einheit-1990-die-wurzeln-des-100.html; https://assets.deutschl andfunk.de/c6595e5c-a1e6-4f16-85ef-47fed691e430/original.txt

Ralf Fücks / Christoph Becker: Faktencheck: Kreist die NATO Russland ein?, Russland verstehen. Ein Projekt von Zentrum Liberale Moderne, 15. 1. 2019, online abrufbar: https://russlandverstehen.eu/fu ecks-becker-faktencheck-einkreisung-russland-nato

Petro Poroschenko im Interview mit Udo Lielischkies, ARD / WDR, 30. 11. 2014, online abrufbar: https://www1.wdr.de/unternehmen/ der-w dr/unternehmen/interviewporoschenko100.html

Paul Flückiger: Ukraine gibt Blockfreiheit auf und will in die Nato, Tagblatt, 24. 12. 2014, online abrufbar: https://www.tagblatt.ch/inte rnational/ukraine-gibt-blockfreiheit-auf-und-will-in-die-nato-ld.696340

»Ich lade Frau Merkel ein, Butscha zu besuchen.«, Wolodymyr Selenskyj, Videobotschaft, tageschau, 4. 4. 2022, online abrufbar: https://www. tagesschau.de/ausland/ukraine-selenkyj-merkel- sarkozy-101. html

Angela Merkel im Gespräch mit Alexander Osang, Berliner Ensemble, 7. 6. 2022, online abrufbar: https://www.ardmediathek.de/video/phoe nix-vor-ort/angela-merkel-im-gespraech/phoenix/Y3JpZDovL2322 333Bob2VuaXguZGUvMjgyMDAxOQ

Ukraine
— a jewel in Putin's tsarist crown

Sabine Adler: EU-Gipfel. Europa steckt in einem kalten Krieg, Deutschlandfunk Kultur, 29. 11. 2013, online abrufbar: https://www.deutsch landfunkkultur.de/eu-gipfel-europa-steckt-in-einem-kaltenkrieg-10 0.html

Sabine Adler: Wie stark sind die Rechtsradikalen in der Ukraine?, Deutschlandradio Berlin, 5. 3. 2014

Euromaidan: Keine extremistische, sondern freiheitliche Massenbewegung, Heinrich Böll Stiftung, 20. 2. 2014, online abrufbar: htt ps://www.boell.de/de/2014/02/20/euromaidan-freiheitliche-mas senbewegung-zivilen-ungehorsams

Ex-Präsident der Ukraine Viktor Janukowitsch in Abwesenheit zu 13 Jahren Gefängnis verurteilt, hromadske, 24. 1. 2019, online abrufbar: http s://hromadske.ua/ru/posts/eks-prezydenta-ukrayny-yanukovych a-pryhovoryly-k-13-hodam-tiurmy

Nils Casjens / Polina Davidenko / Johannes Edelhoff / John Goetz / Johannes Jolmes: Putsch in Kiew: Welche Rolle spielen die Faschisten?, ARD / Panorama, 6. 3. 2014, online abrufbar: https://daserste.ndr.de /panorama/archiv/2014/Putsch-in-Kiew-Welche-Rolle-s pielendie-Faschisten,ukraine357.html

Sabine Adler: Die Krim schließt sich Russland an, Deutschlandfunk, 6. 3. 2014

Sabine Adler: Vom Maidan auf die Krim, Deutschlandradio Kultur, 10. 3. 2014

Sabine Adler: Diplomatische Beziehungen um die Krim zeigen keine Wirkung, Deutschlandfunk, 9. 3. 2014

The Crimean "referendum" — a vote under Russian occupation

Jochen Gaugele: Michael Kretschmer:»Die DDR war ein Unrechtsstaat«, Berliner Morgenpost, 8. 10. 2019

Thesen zum 50. Jahrestag der Berliner Mauer. Ein Positionspapier der

Genossinnen und Genossen Arnold Schoenenburg, Wolfgang

Dietrich, Torsten Koplin, Birgit Schwebs, Carsten Hanke, Birgit

Krause, Waltraut Tegge, Ingrid Memmrich, Wolfhard Goldbach,

Nico Burmeister, Ralf Malachowski, Gerd Walther, Barbara

Borchardt, Christoph Küsters und Michael Knischka, 13. 8. 2011,online abrufbar: http://www.originalsozial.de/fileadmin/lv/Dokumente /LPT08_2011/NEU_Thesen_zum_50._Jahrestag_der_Berliner_Mau er_13072011.pdf

Sabine Adler: Krim-Referendum unter Kriegsgefahr, Deutschlandfunk, 14. 3. 2014, online abrufbar: https://www.deutschlandfunkkultur.de/k rim-referendum-unter-kriegsgefahr-102.html

Sanctions as threatening as cotton balls

Verordnung (EU) Nr. 208/2014 des Rates vom 5. März 2014 über restriktive Maßnahmen gegen bestimmte Personen, Organisationen und Einrichtungen angesichts der Lage in der Ukraine, Amtsblatt der Europäischen Union, online abrufbar: https://eur-lex.europa. eu/legal -content/DE/TXT/?uri=CELEX%3A32014R0208

Verordnung (EU) Nr. 269/2014 des Rates vom 17. März 2014 über restriktive Maßnahmen angesichts von Handlungen, die die territoriale Unversehrtheit, Souveränität und Unabhängigkeit der Ukraine untergraben oder bedrohen, Amtsblatt der Europäischen Union, online abrufbar: https://eur-lex.europa.eu/legal-content/DE/TXT/?uri= CELEX:32014R0269

Josef Joffe: Die bizarre Russland-Apologetik der Linken, Zeit Online, 19. 3. 2014, online abrufbar: https://www.zeit.de/politik/ deutschland/2 014-03/sahra-wagenknecht-krim-russland

Sabine Adler: Referendum unter Kriegsgefahr, Deutschlandfunk, 14. 3. 2014

Ann-Dorit Boy / Friedrich Schmidt / Andreas Ross / Majid Sattar / Nikolas Busse: Ukrainischer Marine-Kommandeur läuft über, Frankfurter Allgemeine Zeitung, 2. 3. 2014, online abrufbar: https://www.faz.net /aktuell/politik/ausland/europa/krim-krise-ukrainischer-marine-kommandeur-laeuft-ueber-12828574.html

Daniel Romein: MH17–Potential Suspects and Witnesses from the 53rd Anti-Aircraft Missile Brigade, Bellingcat, 23. 2. 2016, online abrufbar: https://www.bellingcat.com/news/uk-and-europe/2016/02/23/5 3rd-report-en/ 234 235

Daniel Wechlin: Die Spur nach Russland wird deutlicher, Neue Zürcher Zeitung, 24. 2. 2016, online abrufbar: https://www.nzz. ch/ internati onal/europa/die-spur-nach-russland-wird-deutlicherld.100990

Oliver Kühn: »Die russische Führung ist schuld«, Frankfurter Allgemeine Zeitung, 24. 2. 2016, online abrufbar: https://www.faz.net/ aktuell/ politik/abschuss-von-mh17-die-russische-fuehrung-istschuld-14087 907.html

Julian Hans: Absturz von MH 17: Immer weniger Verdächtige, Süddeutsche Zeitung, 25. 2. 2016, online abrufbar: https://www. sue ddeutsche.de/politik/ukraine-konflikt-neuer- bericht-zumh-17-1.28 78462

François Hollande: Les leçons du pouvoir, Paris 2018

Fascists, patriots, and pacifists

Sabine Adler: Wie stark sind die Rechtsradikalen in der Ukraine?,

Deutschlandradio Berlin, 5. 3. 2014

Sabine Adler: Das Freiwilligen-Bataillon Rechter Sektor, Deutschlandfunk, 10. 9. 2014

Viktoria Kolomiets: Der ehemalige Führer des Rechten Sektors Dmytro Jarosch sagt, dass er Berater des Oberbefehlshabers der S treitkräfte wurde, hromadske, 2. 11. 2021, online abrufbar: https://hromadske. ua/ru/posts/eks-lider-pravogo-sektora-dmitrij-yarosh-govorit-chto stal-sovetnikom-glavnokomanduyushego-vooruzhennyh-sil

Was erwartet die ukrainischen »Asow«-Kämpfer–der Austausch oder die russische Haft?, BBC News, 19. 5. 2022, online abrufbar: https:// ww w.bbc.com/russian/features-61508642

Quo Vadis, Ukraine? Ein Jahr nach den Euromaidan-Protesten, Ukraine-Analysen, Nr. 142, 26. 11. 2014, online abrufbar: https:// www.laender-analysen.de/ukraine/pdf/UkraineAnalysen142.pdf

Sabine Adler: Kremlkritikerin lässt sich nicht den Mund verbieten, Deutschlandfunk, 10. 10. 2014, online abrufbar: https://www.deutschlandfunk.de/reaktion-auf-russische-zensur-kremlkritikerin-laesst-sich-100.html

Aufruf für eine andere Russland-Politik: »Nicht in unserem Namen«, Der Tagesspiegel, 5. 12. 2014, online abrufbar: https://www. tagesspiegel.de/politik/aufruf-fuer-eine-andere-russland-politik-nicht-in-unserem-namen/11080534.html

Internationales Konservatives Forum in St. Petersburg, Coba, 1. 4. 2015, online abrufbar: https://www.sova-center.ru/racism-xenophobia/publications/2015/04/d31627/

Sabine Adler: Europas Ultra-Rechte treffen sich in Sank Petersburg, Deutschlandfunk Kultur, 21. 4. 2015, online abrufbar: https://www.deutschlandfunkkultur.de/russland-europas-ultra-rechte-treffensich-in-sankt-100.html

Klaus Rimpel: »Enormer Sprengstoff für die westliche Welt«–Le Pen hat noch massive Schulden in Russland, Merkur, 24. 4. 2022, online abrufbar: https://www.merkur.de/politik/frankreichwahl-le-pen-macron-praesident-russland-europa-kreml-putin-russland-91496277.html

Bahr, Eppler, Schmidt, and Schröder — the quartet of vain old men

Ian Kershaw: Hitler 1889–1945, München 2009

Christoph von Marschall: Putin gibt Polen Mitschuld am Zweiten Weltkrieg, Der Tagesspiegel, 7. 1. 2020, online abrufbar: https://www.tagesspiegel.de/politik/geschichtsstreit-putin-gibt-polen-mitschuldam-zweiten-weltkrieg/25397584.html

Erhard Eppler: »Waffenruhe nutzen«, resonanzboden. Der Blog der Ullstein Buchverlage, 23. 10. 2014, online abrufbar: https://www.resonanzboden.com/echtzeit/erhard-eppler-waffenruhe-nutzen/

Dietmar Neuerer: Die Rechtsverdreher. Völkerrecht und die Krim-Krise, Handelsblatt, 13. 3. 2014, online abrufbar: https://www.handelsblatt.com/politik/international/voelkerrecht-und-die-krim-krise-dierechtsverdreher/9605122.html

Auszüge aus der Joschka Fischer-Rede, Der Spiegel, 13. 5. 1999, online abrufbar: https://www.spiegel.de/politik/deutschland/wortlauta uszuege-aus-der-fischer-rede-a-22143.html

»Davon wird Putin nicht zittern«, Egon Bahr im Gespräch mit Jürgen Zurheide, Deutschlandfunk, 26. 7. 2014, online abrufbar: https://www.d eutschlandfunk.de/eu-sanktionen-davon-wird-putin-nichtzittern-1 00.html

Der Streit der Ideologien und die gemeinsame Sicherheit, Politikinformationsdienst der SPD, NR. 3, 3. 8. 1987, online abrufbar: http://library.fes.de/library/netzquelle/ddr/politik/pdf/verfemte_4.pdf23 6237

Daniel Friedrich Sturm: Die SPD und der »Wandel durch Anbiederung«, Die Welt, 20. 5. 2018, online abrufbar: https://www.welt.de/politik/ deutschland/article176522859/Russland-Politik-SPD-undder-Wand el-durch-Anbiederung.html

Johano Strasser: Rolf Reißig: Dialogue durch die Mauer. Die umstrittene Annäherung von SPD und SED, Buchbesprechung, Deutschlandfunk, 23. 9. 2002, online abrufbar: https://www.deutschlandfunk.de /rolf-reissig-dialogue-durch-die-mauer-die-umstrittene-100.html

Franz Walter: Wie SPD und SED die DDR destabilisierten, Der Spiegel, 26. 8. 2007, online abrufbar: https://www.spiegel.de/politik/deutschla nd/20-jahre-dialogpapier-wie-spd-und-sed-die-ddr-destabilisierten -a-502059.html

Daniel Friedrich Sturm: Die eitlen Alten der SPD nerven, Die Welt, 20. 5. 2014, online abrufbar: https://www.welt.de/debatte/kommentare/ article128229260/Die-eitlen-Alten- der-SPD-nerven.html

Harald Wiederschein: Helmut Schmidt sagt: Die Ukraine ist keine Nation! Stimmt das überhaupt?, Focus Online, 21. 5. 2014, online abrufbar: ht tps://www.focus.de/wissen/mensch/umstrittene-these-des-altbunde skanzlers-ist-die-ukraine-ueberhaupt-einenation_id_3859492.html

German business in the interests of the Kremlin

Julia Smirnova: Gabriel spielt in Moskau den Gerhard Schröder, Die Welt, 29.10.2015, available online: https://www.welt.de/politik/ausland /article148156440/Gabriel-spielt-in-Moskau-den-Gerhard- Schroede r.html

Katrin Bennhold: The Former Chancellor Who Became Putin's Man in Germany, The New York Times, 4/23/2022, available online: https://www.nytimes.com/2022/04/23/world/europe/schroder-germany-russia-gas-ukraine-war-energy.html. abgeordnetenwatch.de, Twitter, 4/23/2022, available online: https:// twitter.com/a_watch/status/1517967584032956418

Platzeck: Legalize Crimea annexation retroactively, Frankfurter Allgemeine Zeitung, Nov. 18, 2014, available online: https://www.faz.net/aktuell/politik/affront-against-merkel-platzeckkrim-annexion-nachtraeglich-legalisieren-13273424.html

SPD politician Platzeck retracts statements on Crimea, Der Spiegel, Nov. 19, 2014, available online: https://www.spiegel.de/politik/deutschland/matthias-platzeck-ruder-in-debate-about-crime

Deutschlandfunk, 30.9.2014, available online: https://www.deutschlandfunk.de/wirtschaft-kritik-am-rostocker-russlandtag-100.html

Ukraine-Eklat: Diese Aussagen von Marinechef Kay-Achim Schönbach sorgen für Empörung, YouTube, 21.1.2022, available online: https://www.youtube.com/watch?v=MhpA3D7nZcc

Claudia Kade: Armaments for Ukraine? "Germany should abandon strict anti-attitude", Die Welt, 23.1.2022, available online: https://www.welt.de/politik/deutschland/article236419637/Traffic-lights-restoration-for-Ukraine-Germany-should-abandon-antiattention.html

Harald Kujat in an interview with Judith Rakers, Tageschau24, 23.1.2022

Rüdiger Lucassen/Joachim Wundrak: Fall Schönbach zeigt den Irrweg einer wertebasierten Außenpolitik, Alternative für Deutschland, Kreisverband Hochtaunus, 23.1.2022, available online: https://www.afdhochtaunus.de/blog/2022/01/23/ruediger-lucassen- joachimwundrak-fall-schoenbach-shows-the-errant-path-of-a-valuebased-foreign-policy

Steinmeier warns of tougher Russia sanctions, Der Spiegel, Dec. 19, 2014, available online: https://www.spiegel.de/politik/deutschland/russia-steinmeier-warns-vor-schaerferen-sanktionen-a-1009491.html

Russia Day and Climate Foundation

Claudia von Salzen: Mit freundlicher Unterstützung aus Moskau, Der Tagesspiegel, 20. 9. 2018, online abrufbar: https://www.tagesspiegel.de/themen/agenda/russlandtag-in-rostock-mit-freundlicher-unterstuetzung-aus-moskau/23077798.html

Russland-Tag Mecklenburg-Vorpommern. Plattform für den wirtschaftlichen Austausch zwischen Mecklenburg-Vorpommern und dem Leningrader Gebiet, Ostinstitut Wismar, 17. 10. 2018, online abrufbar: https://www.ostinstitut.de/russlandtag

Programm 3. Unternehmertag Russland in Mecklenburg-Vorpommern, 17. 10. 2018, online abrufbar: https://www.russlandtag-mv.de/static/RLT/Dateien/pdf-Dokumente/STK_Konferenzunterlage_181011_DR.pdf, 238239

Almuth Knigge: Kritik am Rostocker Russlandtag, Deutschlandfunk, 30. 9. 2014, online abrufbar: https://www.deutschlandfunk.de/wirtschaft-kritik-am-rostocker-russlandtag-100.html

Wladimir Putin, Rossija 24, 26. 11. 2010, online abrufbar: https://www.youtube.com/watch?v=hrYTboeCpPQ

Wolfgang Kubicki im Gespräch mit Dirk-Oliver Heckmann, Deutschlandfunk, 22. 3. 2018, online abrufbar: https://www.deutschlandfunk.de/skripal-affaere-kubicki-kritisiert-den-westenwer-weiss-wer-100.html

Timo Lange: FDP: Wie weit reicht der Einfluss der russischen Gaslobby?, LobbyCONTROL, 24. 11. 2017, online abrufbar: https://www.lobbycontrol.de/2017/11/fdp-wie-weit-reicht-der-einfluss-der-russischen-gaslobby

Ist die neue Umweltstiftung von MV eine Mogelpackung, Herr Sellering?, Ostsee-Zeitung, 17. 2. 2021, online abrufbar: https://www.ostsee-zeitung.de/mecklenburg-vorpommern/ist-dieneue-umweltstiftung-von-mv-eine-mogelpackung-herr-sellering-2GX5ABVGB5K63MDMAFY4JZQBDM.html

Dangerous amateur historian — Putin declares the unity of Russians and Ukrainians

Wladimir Putin: »Über die historische Einheit von Russen und Ukrainern«, 12. 7. 2021, online abrufbar: http://kremlin.ru/events/president/news/66181

Wolodymyr Selenskyj, Ansprache anlässlich des 1033. Jahrestages der Taufe der Kiewer Rus, 28. 7. 2021, online abrufbar: https://www.president.gov.ua/ru/news/ukrayina-kiyivska-rus-1033-zvernennyaprezidenta-volodimira-69757

Oleksandr Tkachenko über Wladimir Putins Artikel »Über die historische Einheit von Russen und Ukrainern«, Ukrinform. Multimedia-Plattform des ausländischen Rundfunks der Ukraine, 12. 7. 2021, online abrufbar: https://www.ukrinform.ru/rubric-polytics/3279437-traktovka-istorii-v-state-putina-ne-originalnatkacenko.html

Shoigu befahl dem Militär, Putins Artikel über die Ukraine zu studieren, RosBusinessConsulting, 15. 7. 2021, online abrufbar: https://www.rbc.ru/politics/15/07/2021/60f0475d9a7947b61f09f4be

Sabine Adler: Putins Geschichtsverständnis über die Ukraine, Deutschlandfunk, 26. 7. 2021

Wolodymyr Fesenko im Interview mit Michail Friedman, Doshd, 25. 7. 2021

Blank spaces
— Stalin's Terror and the Unknown Holocaust

Anne Applebaum: Roter Hunger. Stalins Krieg gegen die Ukraine, München 2019

Corinna Kuhr-Korolev / Ulrike Schmiegelt-Rietig / Elena Zubkova / Wolfgang Eichwede: Raub und Rettung. Russische Museen im Zweiten Weltkrieg, hrsg. Kulturstiftung der Länder und Stiftung Preußischer Kulturbesitz, Köln 2019

Serhij Bilokin: Polina Kulschenko, Website Serhij Bilokin, online abrufbar: https://www.s-bilokin.name/Bio/Memoirs/Kulzhenko.html

Margaret Siriol Colley: More Than a Grain of Truth: The Biography of Gareth Richard Vaughan Jones, Newark 2005

В Украине умерло от голода 140 тысяч немцев, Дело, Львов 14 февраля 1934

Patrick Desbois: Der vergessene Holocaust. Die Ermordung der ukrainischen Juden. Eine Spurensuche, übers. Hainer Kober, Berlin, 2009

Sabine Adler: Massengräber werden Holocaust-Gedenkstätten, Deutschlandfunk, 29. 6. 2015, online abrufbar: https://www.deutschlandfunk.de/ukraine-massengraeber-werden-holocaust-gedenkstaetten-100.html

Zur Zwangsauflösung der Menschenrechtsorganisation Memorial, Pressemitteilung, Zentrum Liberale Moderne, 28. 12. 2021, online abrufbar: https://libmod.de/pressemitteilung-menschenrechterussland-memorial-aufloesung/

Gabriel Berger: Umgeben von Hass und Mitgefühl. Jüdische Autonomie in Polen nach der Schoah 1945–1949 und die Hintergründe ihres Scheiterns, Berlin 2016

One-sided consideration due to selective memory

Steinmeier kritisiert »Säbelrasseln« gegenüber Russland, Süddeutsche Zeitung, 18. 6. 2016, online abrufbar: https://www.sueddeutsche.de/politik/nato-in-osteuropa-steinmeier-kritisiert-saebelrasseln-gegenueber-russland-1.3040243

Rede von Außenminister Frank-Walter Steinmeier an der Universität Jekaterinburg, Auswärtiges Amt, 15. 8. 2016, online abrufbar: https://www.auswaertiges-amt.de/de/newsroom/160815-bm-jekaterinburg/282744

Rede von Bundespräsident Dr. Frank-Walter Steinmeier zum 75. Jahrestag der Befreiung vom Nationalsozialismus und des Endes des Zweiten Weltkrieges in Europa, Die Bundesregierung, 8. 5. 2020, online abrufbar: https://www.bundesregierung.de/breg-de/service/bulletin/rede-von-bundespraesident-dr-frank-walter-steinmeier-1752232

Gedenkveranstaltung zum 80. Jahrestag der Massenmorde von Babyn Jar, Frank-Walter Steinmeier, Der Bundespräsident, 6. 10. 2021, online abrufbar: https://www.bundespraesident.de/SharedDocs/Reden/DE/Frank-Walter-Steinmeier/Reden/2021/10/211006-Ukraine-Babyn-Jar.html

Bettina Klein: Gezielter Putin-Hitler-Vergleich ist möglich, Deutschlandfunk, 11. 6. 2022, online abrufbar: https://www.deutschlandfunk.de/ukraine-historische-vergleiche-erlaubt-int-martin-schulzewessel-historiker-dlf-c6715c55-100.html

Sabine Adler: »Ich war lebendig begraben«, Deutschlandfunk Kultur, 29. 9. 2016, online abrufbar: https://www.deutschlandfunkkultur.de/75-jahrestag-von-babi-jar-ich-war-lebendig-begraben-100.html

Timothy Snyder: Bloodlands. Europa zwischen Hitler und Stalin, München 2011

More than just art theft — the Nazi foray through Ukraine

Sabine Adler: Verschleppt und versteckt. Nazi-Beutekunst aus der Ukraine, Deutschlandfunk Kultur, 8. 12. 2021, online abrufbar: https://www.deutschlandfunkkultur.de/verschleppt-und-versteckt-nazi-beutekunst-aus-der-ukraine-100.html

Nazarii Gutsul: Der Einsatzstab Reichsleiter Rosenberg und seine Tätigkeit in der Ukraine (1941–1944), Dissertation, Justus-Liebig-Universität Gießen, 2013, S. 159, online abrufbar: https://d-nb.info/1068591870/34

Alfred Rosenberg: Die Tagebücher von 1934 bis 1944, hrsg. v. Jürgen-Matthäus und Frank Bajohr, Frankfurt am Main 2018

Hanns Christian Löhr: Kunst als Waffe. Der Einsatzstab Reichsleiter Rosenberg. Ideologie und Kunstraub im »Dritten Reich«, Berlin, 2018 Wolfgang Eichwede / Ulrike Hartung (Hrsg.): »Betr.: Sicherstellung«. NS-Kunstraub in der Sowjetunion, Bremen 1998, S. 34

Merkel's cold farewell, Chancellor Scholz's tough start and a scuttled joker

Werner Schulz, Dankesrede zur Verleihung des Deutschen Nationalpreises, 14. 6. 2022

Pressekonferenz von Bundeskanzler Scholz und dem Präsidenten der Vereinigten Staaten von Amerika Biden am 7. Februar 2022 in Washington, Die Bundesregierung, online abrufbar: https://www.bundesregierung.de/breg-de/suche/pressekonferenz-von-bundeskanzler-scholz-und-dem-praesidenten-der-vereinigtenstaaten-von-amerika-biden-am-7-februar-2022-in-washington-2003648

Kriegserklärung. Die Ansprache des russischen Präsidenten am Morgen des 24. 2. 2022, online abrufbar: https://zeitschrift-o steuropa.de/blog/vladimir-putin-ansprache-am-fruehen- morgen-des-24.2.2022/

Polen kritisiert deutschen »Egoismus«, Tagesschau, 26. 2. 2022, online abrufbar: https://www.tagesschau.de/ausland/europa/ukraine-waffen-unterstuetzung-103.html

Scholz erklärt sich nach Kurswechsel in der Ukraine-Krise, Die Zeit, 26. 2. 2022, online abrufbar: https://www.zeit.de/politik/deutschland/2022-02/bundeskanzler-olaf-scholz-regierungserklaerung-ukraine-russland

Anna-Nicole Heinrich im Gespräch mit Benedikt Schulz, Deutschlandfunk, 17. 4. 2022, online abrufbar: https://www.deutschlandfunk.de/anna-nicole-heinrich-praeses-evangelische-kirche-deutschland-100.html

The *Zeitenwende* (turn of the times) speech

Regierungserklärung von Bundeskanzler Olaf Scholz, 27. 2. 2022, online abrufbar: https://www.bundesregierung.de/breg-de/aktuelles/regierungserklaerung-von-bundeskanzler-olaf-scholzam-27-februar-2022-2008356

Plenarprotokoll 20/19, Deutscher Bundestag, stenografischer Bericht, 19. Sitzung, 27. 2. 2022, online abrufbar: https://dserver. bundestag.de/btp/20/20019.pdf#P.1360

So haben sich die Spritpreis seit 1950 entwickelt, ADAC, 1. 6. 2022, online abrufbar: https://www.adac.de/verkehr/tanken-kraftstoff-antrieb/deutschland/kraftstoffpreisentwicklung/

Olaf Scholz im Interview mit Angela Ullrich, RBB, 13. 3. 2022, online abrufbar: https://www.youtube.com/watch?v=f1tbfhI1428 Sérgio Ferreira de Almeida: Von der Leyen verspricht Ukraine in Kiew raschen EU-Beitritt, euronews, 8. 4. 2022, online abrufbar: https://de.euronews.com/2022/04/08/kriegstag-44-von-der-leyen-verspricht-ukraine-in-kiew-raschen-eu-beitritt

Viktor Pintschuk: Warum Deutschland mehr tun muss, Frankfurter Allgemeine Zeitung, 15. 4. 2022, online abrufbar: https://www.faz.net/aktuell/politik/ausland/ukraine-krieg-warum-deutschlandmehr-tun-muss-17954907.html?premium

Claudia von Salzen / Georg Ismar: Melnyk macht den Ampel- Ministern schwere Vorwürfe, Der Tagesspiegel, 3. 4. 2022, online abrufbar: https://plus.tagesspiegel.de/politik/melnykmacht-ampel-ministern-schwere-vorwurfe-habeck-ist-der-einzige-in-der-regierung-der-auf-meine-sms-antwortet-444910.html

Georg Ismar / Claudia von Salzen: Ukraine-Botschafter rechnet mit Steinmeier ab–und fordert mehr schwere Waffen, Der Tagesspiegel, 2. 4. 2022, online abrufbar: https://www.tagesspiegel.de/politik/andrij-melnyk-im-interview-ukraine-botschafter-rechnetmit-steinmeier-ab-und-fordert-mehr-schwere-waffen/28222954.html

Anna Sauerbrey: Der Diplomat im Kampfeinsatz, Die Zeit, 7. 4. 2022, online abrufbar: https://www.zeit.de/2022/15/andrij-melnyk-botschafter-ukraine-krieg

Düsseldorfs Ex-Bürgermeister irritiert mit Aussagen zu Butscha, Der Tagesspiegel, 24. 2. 2022, online abrufbar: https://www.tagesspiegel.de/politik/es-reicht-herr-melnyk-duesseldorfs-ex-buergermeister-irritiert-mit-aussagen-zu-butscha/28275330.html

Patrick Reilly: »I need ammunition, not a ride«: Zelensky declines US evacuation offer, New York Post, 26. 2. 2022, online abrufbar: https://nypost.com/2022/02/26/ukraine-president-volodymyrzelensky-declines-us-evacuation-offer/

Wolodymyr Selenskyj, Rede im deutschen Bundestag, 17. 3. 2022, online abrufbar: https://www.bundestag.de/dokumente/textarchiv/2022/kw11-de-selenskyj-883826

Markus Wehner: Scholz' missverständlicher Satz zur ukrainischen Nation, Frankfurter Allgemeine Zeitung, 18. 3. 2022, online abrufbar: https://www.faz.net/aktuell/ukraine-konflikt/olaf-scholz-missverstaendlicher-satz-zur-ukrainischen-nation-17888992.html?premium

And in the future?

Jan Puhl: »Das war eine völlige Selbstüberschätzung«, Interview mit Janusz Reiter, Der Spiegel, 5. 6. 2022, online abrufbar: https://www.spiegel.de/ausland/polen-ex-botschafter-janusz-reiter-ueber-die-deutsche-russland-politik-a-e3ec3f00-fa5b-420e-8e42-8e3549462ce3?sara_ecid=soci_upd_KsBF0AFjflf0DZCxpPYDCQ gO1dEMph

Damir Fras: Selenskyj will in die EU–doch das wird dauern, Redaktions Netzwerk Deutschland, 28. 2. 2022, online abrufbar: https://www.rnd.de/politik/ukraine-in-der-eu-geht-das-und-wenn-ja-wann-X6LT7MTZ6FBRLJ46Q5TI2LMSM4.html

Ukraine gegen neues Minsker Abkommen, Forderung nach Raketenabwehr, Zeit Online, 15. 6. 2022, online abrufbar: https://www.zeit.de/politik/ausland/2022-06/ukraine-uebersicht-friedensvertragselenskyj-eu-gas-israel

Wladimir Putin, Rede am Vorabend des Internationalen Wirtschaftsforums in St. Petersburg, 9. 6. 2022, online abrufbar: http://kremlin. ru/events/president/news/68606

Kristina Dunz / Eva Quadbeck: »Jetzt bin ich frei«, RedaktionsNetzwerk Deutschland, 17. 6. 2022, online abrufbar: https://www. rnd.de/politik/interview-mit-angela-merkel-jetzt-bin-ich-frei-3XQDWM4EBFFLJG76ZSL47KWNAA.html

Michail Samus im Interview mit dem Nachrichtenportal M eduza, 3. 6. 2022, online abrufbar: https://meduza.io/feature/2022/06/244245, 03/s-nachala-voyny-proshlo-100-dney-chego-za-eto-vremya-dobilas rossiya-a-ukraina-k-chemu-idut-otnosheniya-kieva-s-zapadom-ikog da-mogut-vozobnovitsya-peregovory

Cathrin Gilbert: »Am 24. Februar begann der totale Krieg«, Interview mit Wolodymyr Selenskyj, Zeit Online, 14. 6. 2022, online abrufbar: https://www.zeit.de/2022/25/wolodymyr-selenskyj-ukraine-kriegeuropa

Wladimir Putin, Sitzung des Sicherheitsrates im Kreml, 21. / 22. 2. 2022, online abrufbar: https://www.youtube.com/watch?v=_YRUlb_7T9o

CDU-Führung unzufrieden. Hinter der vordergründigen Verteidigung der früheren Kanzlerin durch CDU-Generalsekretär Czaja verbirgt sich Kritik, Frankfurter Allgemeine Zeitung, 11. 4. 2022, online abrufbar: https://zeitung.faz.net/faz/seite-eins/2022-04-11/91019b2c2b4fa0a e13fe39cedb932b5b/?GEPC=s9

Acknowledgements

Writing a book about Germany's relationship with Ukraine was not my idea. Nevertheless, when Maike Nedo from Ch. Links Verlag approached me with this proposal, and I was ready to do it immediately because the war had raised many questions.

For this, a book project I had started with my Ukrainian friend Valeriya Golovina had to be postponed. She stayed close by my side, for which I greatly thank her. We will continue our original project as soon as the war is over.

I would like to express my gratitude to my interlocutors in Ukraine, who were available almost anytime, even during the war. Serhij Kot, unfortunately, no longer; he died in the first days of the war. Professor Wolfgang Eichwede brought us both together and provided me with valuable advice.

Writing a book during an ongoing war initially allows us to take a snapshot. Much cannot be conclusively portrayed or evaluated, but this need not prevent us from taking a critical look back.

The fact that *Ukraine and its Western Allies* came into being so quickly is, first and foremost, thanks to my husband, Friedrich Schmidt. He is always the first reader—turned toward me, but no less critical, always very close, and above all, inspiring. I learned to appreciate my editor Maike Nedo for her open-mindedness, curiosity, meticulousness, and patience. Working together was a pleasure. Stephan Pauli thankfully let his scrutinizing eye roam over the pages, as did best friends. I would also like to thank Deutschlandfunk, which supported the project so benevolently.

ibidem.eu